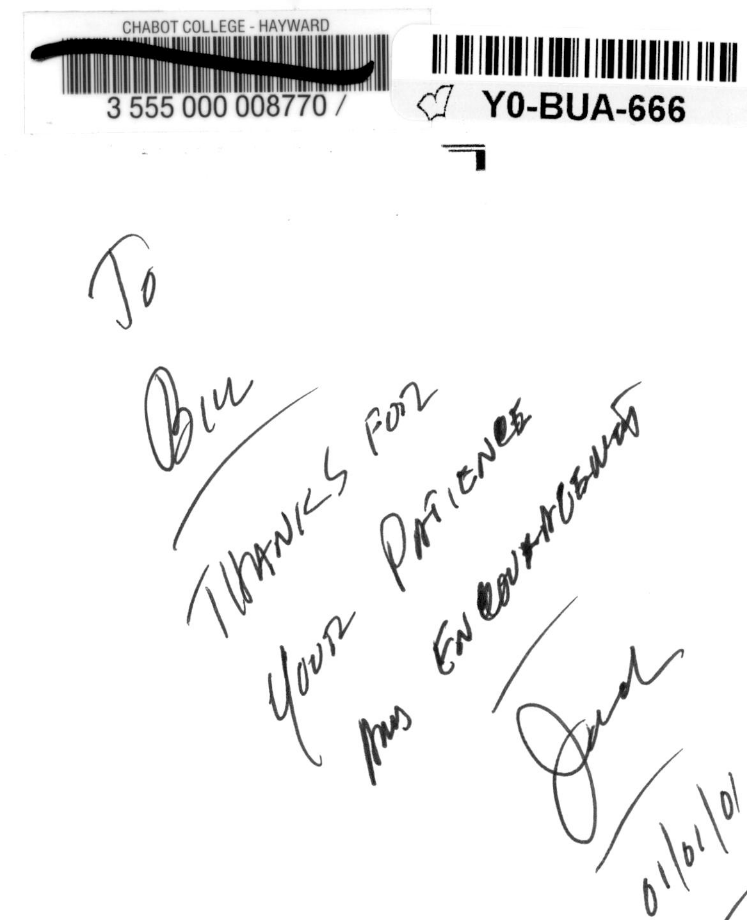
To
Bill
Thanks for
your Patience
and encouragement
01/01/01

HRD
TRENDS
WORLDWIDE

Jack J. Phillips, Ph.D.

HRD TRENDS WORLDWIDE

Shared Solutions to Compete in a Global Economy

Gulf Publishing Company
Houston, Texas

HRD Trends Worldwide

Shared Solutions to Compete in a Global Economy

Gulf Publishing Company
Book Division
P.O. Box 2608 • Houston, Texas 77252-2608

10 9 8 7 6 5 4 3 2 1

Library of Congress Cataloging-in-Publication Data

Phillips, Jack J., 1945–
HRD trends worldwide : shared solutions to compete in a global economy / Jack J. Phillips.
p. cm. — (Improving human performance series)
Includes bibliographical references and index.
ISBN 088415-356-8 (alk. paper)
1. Occupational training—Case studies. I. Title. II. Series.
HD5715.P49 1999
658.3′124—dc21 98-51367
CIP

Printed on acid-free paper (∞).

CONTENTS

PREFACE

Origins of the Book

Today, we are operating in a global economy that influences all of us. Our firm's experience with globalization underscores this important trend. In 1993, as the members of our human resources firm began conducting consulting assignments with organizations around the globe, we realized that learning, human resource development (HRD), and performance improvement departments experience some of the same issues regardless of where they are located. As we assisted more organizations, we identified emerging trends that were actually occurring all across the globe. To verify our assumptions, we conducted research with training and development organizations in thirty-five countries, and that research helped us explain emerging issues and trends in each country. Additional research confirmed our assumptions that most of the issues and trends are similar throughout the world. The results are sixteen critical trends that every training and performance-improvement professional must understand and prepare to cope with in a productive way.

Change, Change, Change

It has often been said that the only constant in dynamic organizations in the 1990s is change. Nowhere is change more visible and significant than in the training and performance improvement field. The individuals with training and development responsibilities differ vastly in terms of background, experience, approach, and expectations. Clients are placing unusual and taxing demands on the training staff. The learning environment is rapidly changing. Participants in training, learning, and performance improvement programs have new expectations and requirements. Consequently, it is important for all stakeholders to be aware of the indicators of change and be prepared to adjust to these changes.

Importance of Trends

Monitoring and reacting to trends are an important part of developing an effective training and HRD function. The first step in this process is to be aware of distinct trends that will have an impact on the function. This book clearly identifies those significant trends and provides appropriate evidence and examples to substantiate not only the existence of each trend, but also its importance.

The next three steps in the process are to examine the drivers for the trend, understand the issues, and explore the potential impact of the trend within the organization. Some trends have or will have a significant impact on the organization. For others, the short-term effect may be minimal.

The fifth step is to make adjustments based on the potential impact of the trend. In most situations, the trend is positive, and planned actions may be necessary to continue to adjust and react to the trend. For others, the trend can be negative, and efforts to counter or minimize the effects will be needed.

A final step is to continue to monitor the trend, reassessing its impact and the need for further adjustments.

In short, the major purpose of this book is to help individuals examine each trend, explore its impact on the organization, and make adjustments and refinements to make the trend work internally for the success of the training and development function and the organization.

Research Base

Although the research for this book is comprehensive, it is also grounded in actual practice from those who are leading the training and development functions in organizations. The research involves these major inputs, including a comprehensive survey of training and development organizations in industrialized and emerging nations. This survey provided some initial insight into the major issues and trends facing training and development functions in these countries. An exhaustive literature search covering major international and domestic publications revealed key issues, challenges, and trends facing training and development organizations in different countries. A second survey, listing the results of the initial survey, was administered to training and development managers to determine the existence of each trend and its importance.

Although these major inputs provide the overall research basis, the trends also have been discussed in several workshops conducted outside the United States.

Initially, fifty trends were identified, and we gradually pared them to the sixteen in this book. These trends occur from organization to organization, from country to country, from culture to culture. We have purposefully made no attempt to address the various cultural differences and cultural issues that are unique to a particular organization or country. Instead, the book focuses on those trends that should be common to every major organization and important to the success of the training and development function.

Target Audience

This book is intended to serve several audiences. The primary audience is those individuals who hold leadership roles in the learning, education, and performance improvement fields. These individuals must be aware of trends and help guide the organization to react to them in an appropriate and productive way.

The second audience is those professionals and specialists actively involved in all aspects of training, education, development, learning, and performance improvement. Whatever the specific title and responsibility, this book should provide insight into the important issues that will influence their work in the future.

The third audience is those individuals who support the training and education process in a variety of ways. This group includes executives who fund training and development and provide support and commitment to the process. It also includes key managers who are becoming more actively involved in the process and who are demanding and expecting impressive results and performance from the learning and training process.

A fourth audience is those individuals who are observing important trends in organizations. Because people are an organization's greatest asset, the trends that affect training, learning, and development represent critical issues in an organization. Consultants, advisors, and futurists should find this information helpful when planning and adjusting to future events.

The Uniqueness of This Book

No other publication presents important education and training trends that cut across a variety of organizations and cultures. We are operating in a global environment moving toward a unified and interlocking economy. Most published trends narrowly focus on one or more specific issues, such as technology, or specifically on one country. No other book has captured global HRD trends and presented them in a way that is meaningful to an organization while showing precisely how to utilize each trend. Because of this unique approach, this book should represent a valuable contribution, reflecting significant research, while providing practical insight and advice.

Acknowledgments

No book is the work of the authors alone. Several individuals have helped make this a reality. First we would like to thank the many clients that have allowed us to assist them in recent years, particularly the multinational organizations with operations all across the world. They have shared with us their concerns, desires, problems, and opportunities, which we have captured in this book. Some clients are listed in the first chapter, others are noted throughout the material, and still others are not named directly but have provided thoughts, comments, or input along the way. Without this valuable group of professional colleagues, it would have been difficult to develop this book.

Several individuals have helped conduct the research associated with this book. Special thanks go to Karen Fite, who conducted much of the research as she served as a graduate assistant at Middle Tennessee State University. Karen was thorough with her work and eager to track down specific information that turned out to be quite useful in developing the manuscript.

Patti Pulliam was instrumental in bringing this book to publication. Patti directed the project during most of its phases and contributed three chapters (13, 15, and 17). Without her untiring support and dedication, the book would not have been completed.

A special thanks goes to the staff members of Gulf Publishing for their patience with my hectic schedule. Kelly Perkins, editor, has provided extraordinary support and assistance throughout this project.

Vicki Wear has done an excellent job of helping to prepare the manuscript for publication. Terry Cantrell assisted in the final coordination of the manuscript. Terry inherited a tough challenge and has delivered the product in an excellent presentation.

Jack J. Phillips
Performance Resources Organization
P.O. Box 380637
Birmingham, AL 35238-0637

1

THE IMPORTANCE OF TRENDS

This book describes important trends that will have a significant impact on learning, training, and performance improvement. The information about these trends comes from thousands of organizations located all across the world. Most of the organizations are medium to large in size and are engaged in international commerce, which means that their products and services are sold outside the borders of their countries. In addition, many have facilities or operations in other countries and function as global firms or multinational corporations. As with most organizations, they participate in the international economy.

The important point of this book is not that the work of the organizations occurs across borders, but that the training and development function is undergoing tremendous change, regardless of the location of headquarters or operations. Training and development functions in medium to large organizations are more alike than dissimilar from one country to another. They face common issues and are being influenced, significantly, by the vast number of changes taking place in organizations and the workplace. This book attempts to capture these changes and present them as sixteen critical trends in learning, HRD, and performance improvement.

In this book, training and development trends are distinguished from general trends affecting workplace issues. The trends presented involve training and development directly and significantly impact the training and development function in an organization. Other workplace issues may influence specific programs and delivery mechanisms but do not directly involve changes in training and development. For example, information about the development and implementation of work teams throughout the world continues to make the news. Although work teams may influence the training program design and delivery, they are not a training and development trend. Thus, these sixteen trends focus directly on the training process, including the aspects of needs assessment, design and development, delivery, evaluation, and follow-up. In addition, the leadership and management of the function are represented in these trends.

Observing and Reacting to Trends

Monitoring and reacting to trends is an essential part of developing an effective training and development policy and practice. Trends are not solutions in search of a problem or tools and techniques in search of a prescription. Trends represent important changes that must be followed and addressed. Figure 1-1 shows the major steps needed to use trend data effectively. The first step in this process is to be aware of specific trends that will influence the training and development function. Building on a significant research base, this book identifies the most critical trends and provides appropriate evidence and examples to substantiate the existence and importance of the trends.

The second step is to examine the drivers, the major influences that cause the trend. The presence or absence of these influences can reveal much insight about the progress of the trend and how it can be managed. Understanding the drivers can help predict the magnitude and scope of the trend or similar trends in the future.

The third step is to thoroughly understand the trend in terms of key issues, concepts, models, principles, and theories. A complete understanding provides the necessary information and framework to explain the trend and address it in an appropriate and effective way.

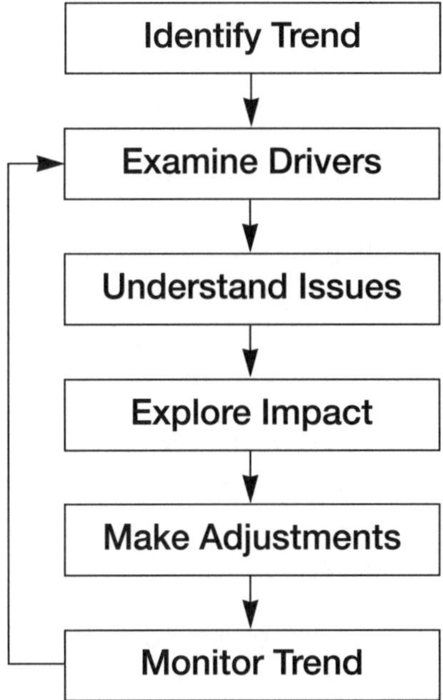

Figure 1-1. *Using Trend Data.*

The fourth step is to examine the potential impact of the trend within the current training and development function. Some trends have had (or will have) a significant impact on the training and development department, while others will have a minimal, short-term effect. A few trends will impact the entire organization. This important analysis is a key step in taking decisive action.

The fifth step is to make adjustments in training and development based on the potential impact of the trend. In most situations the trend is positive, and planned actions may be necessary to continue to react to the trend and enhance its effects. In others, the trend can be negative, and efforts to inhibit or minimize the effects will be needed.

The sixth step is to continue to monitor the trend, reassessing its impact and exploring the need for further adjustments. Because of the rapid change of some of these trends, constant monitoring may be necessary. Also, constant monitoring may reveal new or emerging trends.

This book provides the information required to examine each trend, explore its impact on the training and development organization, and make adjustments to effectively address the trend internally. A chapter is devoted to each trend, and the final chapter provides more information about how to make additional progress with the trends.

Research Base

Although the research base for this book is comprehensive, it is also grounded in actual practice by those individuals who are leading the training and development functions in major organizations. As depicted in Figure 1-2, the research involves several major elements:

1. An initial listing of the trends was developed from direct observation in organizations through the work of Performance Resources Organization (PRO), an international consulting firm that primarily focuses on developing a results-based training and development process. In these contacts with clients all across the globe, several trends common among organizations were identified and initially published as an internal document within PRO.
2. The initial list prompted a review of the literature to determine the extent to which the trends appeared common from one country to another. This review added a few trends and prompted adjustments to the initial list.
3. A survey was conducted among thirty-five training and development organizations that are members of the International Federation of Training and Development Organizations (IFTDO). All industrialized and emerging nations were represented in the survey. This initial survey provided additional insight into the major issues facing training and development functions in these countries.
4. An exhaustive literature search was conducted throughout major international and domestic publications. This research revealed additional issues, challenges, and trends facing training and development organizations.
5. A survey was administered to training and development managers to determine the existence and the importance of each trend. This survey, along with the results, is reproduced as Appendix 1. The survey has been administered in twenty coun-

tries to groups of people whose typical job titles are manager of training and development, manager of education and training, manager of learning, and manager of performance improvement.

6. Although these major research elements provide the overall basis for trend development, these trends also have been discussed in several programs including a workshop for chief training officers conducted outside the United States by the author.
7. This list of trends was also validated through associates of PRO as the company continued to work with clients in all the industrialized nations and several of the emerging countries. It is one thing to identify trends from the literature, but it is another to observe the trends in action within an organization or have them described by the internal training and development staff.

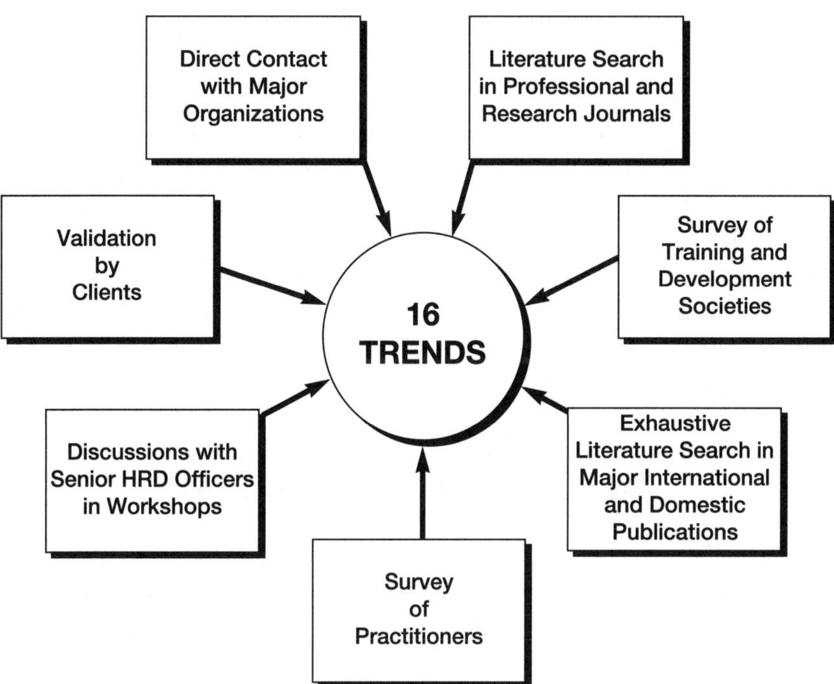

Figure 1-2. *Research Base for Trends.*

In all, fifty trends were identified and gradually pared to the most important sixteen, which this book reports. These trends occur from organization to organization, from country to country, from one culture to another culture. We have purposefully made no attempt to address the various cultural differences and cultural issues that are unique to a particular organization or country. Instead, the book focuses on those trends that should be common, important, and critical in every major organization.

A list of organizations examined for this book is quite exhaustive, and Figure 1-3 attempts to present a partial list of private-sector organizations examined. Many of these are identified in the book. Others, not identified, provided information about the issues and content. This is not meant to imply that this study, in any way, was limited to this group. However, this particular group of organizations either provided access to information or provided information in the literature about a particular issue.

Most of the organizations are truly global in scope, with operations on virtually every continent. In a truly global enterprise, it is difficult to determine the headquarters location, and knowing the location is not as important as it used to be. Still, North America, Europe, and Asia dominate the list of organizations studied. Firms in other countries are also included and were studied to provide information for the book; some of these organizations are well known, such as McDonald's, while others, such as Izhorsky Zavod in Russia, may not be so familiar. Collectively, these organizations provide a rich source of data, some through their individual training managers, some through published information about the organization, and others through contacts with various individuals.

Training, Learning, Education, Performance Improvement, Development, Etc.

As the trends presented in the book reveal, many changes are rapidly developing in this important field of training and develop-

AIB Group (Ireland)
Alaska Petroleum Contractors Inc.
Allstate Insurance Company
American Express
Amoco
Andersen Consulting
Apple Computer
Arthur Andersen & Company
Asia Pacific Breweries
Bank of America
Bank Central Asia (Indonesia)
Bell Atlantic
Blue Cross/Blue Shield
Bristol-Myers Squibb
Burger King
Caltex–Pacific
Canadian Imperial Bank of Commerce
Chevron
CN Rail (Canada)
Commonwealth Edison
Compaq Computers
Corestates Financial
Deloitte & Touche
DHL Worldwide Express (Belgium)
Digital Equipment
DuPont
Entergy Corporation
Eskom (South Africa)
Exxon
Federal Express
FINA (Belgium)
First Union National Bank
Ford Motor Company
General Motors
Harley-Davidson Motor Company
Honda Motor Company
Hong Kong Bank
IBM
Illinois Power
Intel Corporation
Izhorsky Zavod (Russia)
Johnson Controls
Land O'Lakes
Lockheed Martin
M&M Mars
McDonald's
MCI
Mead
Microsoft
Motorola
NCR
Nestlé (Switzerland)
Nortel (Canada)
Nova Corporation (Canada)
Novus Services
NYNEX
Overseas–Chinese Banking Corp.
Pacific Gas & Electric
Pertamina (Indonesia)
Polaroid Corporation
PricewaterhouseCoopers
Public Bank (Malaysia)
Rhone–Poulenc Rorer (France)
Rohm and Haas
Rover Group (England)
Saturn Corporation
Saudi Arabian Airlines
SGS (Geneva)
Shell
Singapore Airlines
Singapore Technologies
Sprint
Standard Bank of South Africa
Standard Products (Canada)
State Street Bank
Telkom Indonesia
Texaco
Toronto Dominion Bank
United Parcel Service
Unocal
Volvo
Walt Disney Company
Westpac
Whirlpool
Xerox

Figure 1-3. *Partial List of Private-Sector Organizations Studied.*

ment. These include changes in the focus of the traditional training function and in the use of different terminology to label the function. Although many global organizations still prefer to use the words *education and training* to represent the process of improving job-related skills and preparing individuals for future jobs, others prefer the terms *learning* and *learning solutions* as they become an important part of developing a learning organization. Still others find *learning* restrictive and prefer to focus on *performance* or *performance improvement,* where the overall scope of training has been broadened to become the performance improvement function. And even others emphasize the development aspect of employees and prefer to use *development* in the title of the term.

Although these distinctions are important, to remain consistent throughout the book, the terms *training and development, education and training, learning,* and *performance improvement* will be used interchangeably to reflect the overall function. For a particular sentence or paragraph, this terminology is not meant to be limiting or reflect different emphasis. A mixture will be used because, in reality, a mixture exists in organizations and sometimes within the same organization.

Structure of the Book

This book examines each trend carefully in a helpful and useful way to provide a basis for action. Each trend is presented in a separate chapter, and within each chapter, three major sections are presented for each trend:

Trend Definition and Validation

This section answers four basic questions:

- What is the trend? (a brief definition)
- Who is experiencing the trend? (one or two cases illustrating the trend)
- How do we know that the trend exists? (relevant research and evidence of the trend)
- What are the drivers for the trend? (influences that have caused the trend)

Trend Description

In describing the details of the trends, six important questions are answered:

- What does the trend actually mean? (basic concepts)
- How does it work? (basic principles)
- What are the key issues and concerns? (major points and obstacles)
- What are the processes and steps? (the mechanics of the trend)
- What is a typical model of the trend? (a commonly accepted model, if available)
- How is it implemented? (steps to implement, utilize, or expand the trend)

Trend Consequences

As a final section, the trend consequences cover six important questions:

- How will the trend affect my organization and me? (impact of the trend in the training function and organization)
- What problems/barriers exist? (obstacles that will get in the way)
- What should I do about the trend? (a review of current status)
- How can I make the trend enhance my organization? (planning the implementation)
- Will the trend continue in the future? (the outlook of continued movement in the trend)
- Where can I find more information? (references)

Collectively, this three-pronged structure provides a helpful guide to address these important trends so that the adverse impact of trends can be utilized in a positive way.

Trends

The sixteen trends presented in this book are as follows.

Importance Ranking	Trend	Chapter
1	Training and development costs are monitored more accurately to manage resources and demonstrate accountability.	10
2	Measuring the return on investment in training and development is growing in use.	9
3	Systematic evaluation processes measure the success of training and development.	8
4	Needs assessment and analysis are receiving increased emphasis.	3
5	Training and development staff and line management are forming partnerships to achieve common goals.	14
6	Training and development is linked to the strategic direction of the organization.	2
7	The learning organization concept is being adopted.	13
8	The delivery of training and development is changing rapidly.	6
9	Training is shifting to a performance improvement role.	4
10	The technology of training and development is developing rapidly.	15
11	The responsibility of training and development is shared among several groups.	7
12	More training and development is outsourced to contractors.	17
13	More training and development is designed for global use.	16
14	Training and development functions are converting to a profit center concept.	11
15	Training and development budgets are increasing.	12
16	Corporate universities continue to gain acceptance.	5

Each trend listed has been given a numerical importance ranking to show its relationship to the importance of the other trends in this book. However, the previously discussed survey of practitioners rendered all sixteen of these trends significant. This book reports only the trends that received an importance ranking of 4 or higher, out of a scale of 5, in the survey. The next sixteen trends received importance rankings of less than 4 and are presented in Appendix 2.

The trends in this book are presented in the same order that the issues are usually addressed in the training and development cycle. For example, the first trend (presented in Chapter 2) concerns the initial step of connecting training to strategy. The last trend (Chapter 17) focuses on outsourcing, which is often the last step in the training cycle.

2

STRATEGY AND TRAINING

Trend Definition and Validation

Brief Definition of Trend

Training and development is closely linked to the strategic direction of the organization. Programs and services provided by the training and development function are more customer-focused and proactive as they support strategic goals. Program successes are measured in outcomes linked to strategic initiatives. The objectives for new programs represent measures that support strategic objectives directly or indirectly.

Case Studies: Singapore Airlines and Rhone-Poulenc Rorer

Singapore Airlines. One of the most profitable airlines with an impeccable record for customer service, Singapore Airlines, has been operating for fifty years and now serves a network of seventy-four cities in forty-one countries. In *Travel* magazine, Singapore Airlines has been consistently rated the world's best airline. In addition, it has the most modern fleet of any major airline in the world. Its reliability and safety records are beyond reproach, and the on-time departure record is at the top.

Singapore Airlines spends an average of $5,600 per employee per year on training, representing 12 percent of payroll—one of the largest budgetary commitments to training of any company in the world.[1] With 28,000 employees, this investment represents a tremendous commitment to training and development. According to the managing director of Singapore Airlines, the training and development function has been an important link in meeting the company's key strategic goals. Those goals include customer service, profitability, reliability, and safety. Cabin crew training, flight operations training, management development, commercial training, and computer training are all major influences on these important strategic goals.[2] Not only has training driven the key strategic initiatives, but it has also helped build the reputation of this successful airline. Singapore Airlines has ranked either first or second in Asia's most-admired companies since the list has been published. The managing director attributes this impressive record to the employees and management of the airline, and training and development has played an important part in the developing and shaping of competencies to achieve this success.

Rhone-Poulenc Rorer. Within the past twenty years, Rhone-Poulenc Rorer (RPR) has transformed itself from a struggling French company to a highly successful global corporation with more than 90,000 employees in more than 140 countries. A key element in this remarkable transition was RPR's global human resource development (HRD) strategy.[3] The company places strong emphasis on the need to recruit managers on a global scale and move these managers around the world. These international assignments provide several benefits for the managers, as well as economic payoffs for RPR. For example:

- Managers become more aware of the geographic, industrial, and cultural aspects of the company.
- There is a greater integration of businesses, as well as a building of appropriate relationships.
- The flow of technical and marketing information increases.

An important part of the HRD strategy is the mentoring of new expatriate managers. A mentor at RPR is generally a senior manager at headquarters who has an excellent reputation for technical expertise, is a good communicator, and is willing to take on the mentoring assignment. The new expatriate manager maintains regular contact with the mentor and consults with him or her about career moves and career issues. The mentor actually negotiates assignments with other executives on behalf of the manager. Essentially, the mentor guides the manager's career through the company.

Essential to RPR is the development of truly global managers as RPR recruits more non-French employees and managers to achieve the ultimate aim of developing "citizens of the world"—people who think of the world as a corporate center.

Evidence of Trend

In the practitioner survey about global trends, this trend received a high level of agreement, with its existence achieving a score of 3.96 out of 5 (see Appendix 1). Practitioners rated the importance of the trend as 4.48 out of 5, one of the highest of the importance ratings. Clearly, training and development practitioners view the trend as significant, with much progress made toward linking training to corporate strategy. It has become a standard way of operating for many organizations.

One major publication identified five changing mind-sets with training and development professionals, one of which focused directly on the linkage with strategy. In this new corporate reality, strategic HRD actions are being aligned with business strategies.[4] A British study, identifying the changing world of training, revealed that training is now directly linked to, and is a part of, the strategic plan. This underscores the progress made by European training organizations to connect training and performance improvement initiatives directly to the strategic objectives of firms.[5]

Connecting HRD to strategy has been developing for some years. One major review of global human resource development suggested that HRD managers have been participating increasingly in the strategic planning process and that evidence suggests that the strategic planner is an emerging role in human resource development. This role will be increasingly important in the coming years.[6] This conclusion is based on the role of training and development in helping to answer three basic questions that surround the strategic planning process:

- What is our business?
- What will our business be?
- What should our business be?

Training and development is an important part of framing the appropriate responses to these questions. The training and development manager, as part of the top-management strategic planning effort, can assist with the knowledge and vision necessary to make decisions and take action that will provide developed employees the opportunity to achieve success.

Many organizations today are making efforts to completely redesign or transform the training and development function. The result is a creation of strategic, value-added critical business processes within the organization.[7] To achieve this truly strategic value, the training and development function is creating strategic results, assisting in strategy implementation, and helping in strategy formulation.

Implementing HRD strategy is a difficult issue to identify when organizations have succeeded in achieving the appropriate connection between organizational strategy and HRD programs. In a recent casebook, one researcher concluded that more evidence of success exists than organizations will admit or divulge.[8] Those organizations that have been very successful in developing this connection see the effect as a strategic advantage and are unwilling to discuss it, much less publish it. In addition, many organizations are attempting to make the connection but don't feel comfortable reporting the results because of their concern that their processes may not be perceived as adequate or effective.

When it comes to connecting training and development in HRD with strategy, the roles of HRD and human resources (HR) usually enter the picture. From the context of strategic direction, HRD and HR usually closely align with each other. In a study of the current status and future directions of HRD and HR, *Workforce,* the business magazine for leaders in HR, predicted trends, as well as assessed current progress. The magazine identified the strategic roles of both

HRD and HR as one of the most important trends in the field. HRD is focusing more efforts on organizational performance, human capital development, organizational productivity, and intellectual capital. The role of HRD is shifting to one of a strategic business partnership where professionals provide consulting on business unit and corporate performance.[9]

Several new tools, developed to connect organizational measurements to the strategic direction, have been used with the training and development function. One of those is the Balanced Scorecard process (BSC). The BSC translates the business unit's mission and strategy into tangible objectives and measures. The measures represent a balance between external measures for shareholders and customers and internal measures for critical business processes, innovation, and learning growth.[10] Significant evidence exists that many organizations are now using the BSC process as a strategic tool to connect training to the overall strategic objectives of the organization.[11] The feedback and learning dimension of the BSC offers one of the best perspectives for understanding how training and development contribute to business strategy.

A report from Europe and Australia confirms the success with the connection of HRD and strategy. The authors argue that organizations are using a model of strategic HRD, which is concerned with exposing, examining, questioning, and challenging the nature and extent of training and development to facilitate the continuous development of organization capability to support long-term survival.[12] This role and contribution requires the adoption of a proactive approach, and evidence seems to suggest that this approach is being practiced.

Causes and Drivers

The drivers for the progress made to connect training and development to strategy cover several key issues. Although the connection seems to be a logical, rational development of the field, seven important influences emerge from the analysis.

- For training and development to become more effective and produce the desired results, it must be closely linked to the strategic objectives of the organization. Otherwise, it may not add the appropriate value and move the organization where it needs to go. Thus, the concern for the right training at the right time for the right audience to generate the desired results will require a close alignment with strategic objectives.

- At the heart of any strategic direction of an organization are change and change management. Change is the only constant in most organizations, and training and development is often seen as the driver for the organizational change process. This requires the training function to be more closely aligned with strategy as the function organizes, coordinates, implements, and evaluates organizational change.
- The recent interest in the return on investment in training and development has brought more attention to the strategic connection. As senior executives and internal clients demand a measurable return, the training and development function must develop programs with specific business impact objectives. These objectives are derived from an analysis of the business needs of the organization, which are usually defined by the strategic direction. Thus, the requirement for return on investment from training leads to business impact objectives, which are connected to business needs and then to strategy. This chain of events links the training function to the key strategic objectives of the organization.
- The shift from learning and training to a performance-consulting role has increased the connection with strategy. As more training functions attempt to solve business problems and improve business performance, the linkage to strategy becomes clear. Strategy often defines the desired business performance, and training focuses on these performance issues by providing a variety of programs, processes, and services. Thus, the training and performance-improvement process is becoming more directly linked to strategy.
- As the training and development staff members become more sophisticated and professional, they are planning strategically. Training and development functions have mission statements, vision statements, and their own strategic plans, which, by necessity, must support the strategic plan of the organization. Thus, as the training and development department plans strategically, it becomes more closely aligned with the organization's overall strategy.

- Top executives recognize the importance of training and development and the necessity to use it in a strategic role. In some situations, top executives apply top-down pressure to link training and development to strategic direction. For example, some organizations have developed strategies to transform their customer service departments into strategic and competitive weapons. Training and development is one of the most effective processes to achieve excellent customer service. Consequently, training, by requirement, is an important tool to fulfill a major strategic objective.
- Finally, with increased concern about intellectual capital, knowledge-based organizations, learning organizations, and human capital development, top executives are realizing that, to have a competitive advantage, they must acquire, develop, and retain appropriate expertise. This strategic initiative connects the learning process directly to the strategic direction of the organization.

Overall, these major influences have placed considerable pressure on organizations to connect training and development more closely with strategy. The evidence is impressive, and the progress has been significant. However, additional improvement is needed as more organizations attempt to make this dramatic shift.

Trend Description

Strategic Roles

The training and development function is poised to assume several roles in developing and supporting the strategy of the organization. In some organizations, the function assumes only one or more of these roles, while in world-class training and development organizations, it develops all five roles to build a strong linkage with strategy.

1. **Strategic Planning.** The first important role for the training and development function is to develop its own strategic plan. This brings strategy to the department level with a plan that must be closely related to the organization's strategic plan, which begins with a mission statement and contains specific strategies that the training and development staff members can understand

and implement while they strive to stay connected to the strategic direction of the organization.

2. **Strategy Formulation.** The training and development department, an important function in the organization, often helps develop the strategic plan for the organization. In this role, the leader of training and development has a "seat at the table" where strategy is developed and provides important input, raises critical issues, voices necessary concerns, and offers suggestions and solutions to shape the direction. This is perhaps the most critical role of training and development in its linkage to strategy.
3. **Strategy Implementation.** As different parts of the organization implement strategic plans, the training and development function often takes part in the implementation with specific programs, services, and processes. Almost every strategy implementation will include the need for training programs and services because learning and application are essential to achieve the strategic objectives.
4. **Strategic Results.** Training and development programs operate strategically when they drive the important operating and business performance measures. When training and development programs and services succeed, they produce business results, which are usually linked to strategic objectives.
5. **Strategy Training.** A final role assumed by some training and development functions is to teach the strategic planning and implementation process to others in the organization. A dynamic, complex organization requires an adequate level of knowledge and skills with strategic planning and implementation processes. Managers, team leaders, supervisors, and—in some cases—all employees should understand the processes, requirements, tasks, and outcomes of strategic planning. Through consulting services and training programs, the training and development department can build the appropriate expertise.

Developing the Role. Several operational frameworks can be used to develop a strategic role for the training and development organization. In one framework, the creation of the strategic role for HRD requires the assessment of the level of training and development performance in the context of the organization, process in the organization, and the employees in the organization.[13] Figure 2-1 depicts this in the form of specific questions about strategic HRD. These questions are framed for the organization and for the training and development department. They identify specific issues that must be addressed to develop a strategic role in the organization.

Level of T&D Performance

	Organization	Process	Employee
Strategy/ Goals/ Mission	*Organization:* Do the organizational strategy and budget support strategic HRD?	*Organization:* Do the organizational processes have goals regarding strategic HRD?	*Organization:* Are the employee goals linked to a need for strategic HRD?
	T&D Department: Does the T&D strategy support strategic HRD?	*T&D Department:* Do the T&D processes have measurable goals to achieve strategic HRD?	*T&D Department:* Are the T&D staff outputs and standards linked to strategic HRD requirements?

Figure 2-1. *Strategic Human Resource Development.* (Adapted from: McClernon, Timothy R. and Swanson, Richard A. "Redefining HRD's Role in the Corporation: A Case Study on Becoming a World-Class Business Partner," in *In Action: Leading Organizational Change.* Elwood F. Holton and Jack J. Phillips (Eds.), Alexandria, Va.: American Society for Training and Development, 1997, pp. 1–21.)

The development of a strategic role requires a paradigm shift for training and development so that there is more concern for the purpose and direction. As depicted in Figure 2-2, the early focus of the training and development department was on products. The staff developed as many products as possible and offered them to the organization. In a catalog format, packaged in a variety of ways, training and development sold these products with a process similar to selling off-the-shelf items in a supermarket. There was little concern if the program was needed or actually worked. The goal was to have as many products as possible, used by as many groups and individuals as possible.

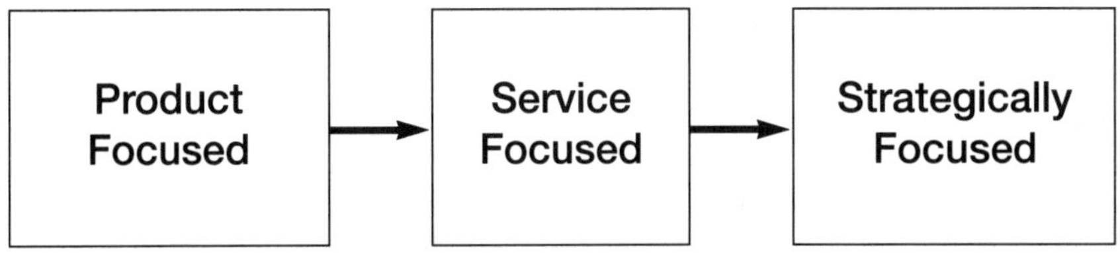

Figure 2-2. *Thinking Strategically.*

The shift to a service-focused training and development function was an improvement. Here, training and development emphasized that products and services must meet the actual needs of the users. The concept of a training client entered the picture, and customer service became extremely important. With various customers identified, the staff focused on ensuring that customers were pleased with the products and services delivered.

As evidenced in this chapter, the training and development (T&D) function is now strategically focused, which means there is concern about products and services meeting organizational needs linked to strategic objectives. The concern goes beyond client satisfaction, ensuring that the products and services are closely linked to important strategies in the organization and that desired results are achieved. This strategic thinking helps ensure that the T&D function provides the appropriate value to the organization and becomes an important business partner to the management team.

Traditional Strategic Planning Model

A variety of strategic planning models reflect the various stages, processes, and steps needed to develop a strategic plan and process for the organization. The model shown in Figure 2-3 is considered one of the more useful and practical models, from the perspective of the training and development function.[14] Each step in the model is briefly described below.

Develop vision. An important part of developing the strategic direction of the training and development department is to develop an appropriate vision that reflects strategy and other shifts in the training and development function. The following vision comes from a large health-care chain and reflects the connection to the strategy as the organization shifts away from the traditional education and training to a performance-consulting role.[15]

> We will exceed the expectations of our business partners by providing world-class performance development processes, expertise, and tools driving superior performance. We will achieve this vision by:
>
> - Consulting with our business partners to assess performance gaps, recommend improvement strategies, and shepherd ongoing performance improvement.
> - Designing, developing, and delivering HRD/performance improvement interventions for work processes and employees—new and old.
> - Evaluating the impact of HRD/performance improvement interventions focused on the organization's stated strategic imperatives of achieving superior customer satisfaction, dominating market share, maximizing profitability, and promoting a culture of winning with highly motivated, well-informed, diverse associates.

Establish mission/purpose. The next step of the model is to develop the specific mission or purpose for the T&D organization, regardless of whether T&D is positioned in a major department, division, unit, subsidiary, or entire company. The mission statement describes why the organization actually exists. It is usually simple, sometimes one sentence, and serves as the organization's reason for being. For example, the mission of Motorola University, one of the most respected, global corporate universities, is as follows:

> To be a major catalyst for change and continuous improvement in support of the corporation's business objectives, we will provide for our clients the best value, leading edge training and education solutions and systems in order to be their preferred partner in developing a Best-in-Class work force.[16]

Set goals and objectives. The next logical step in the strategic planning model is to develop goals and objectives. Goals are usually more general than objectives and reflect an idealized description of where

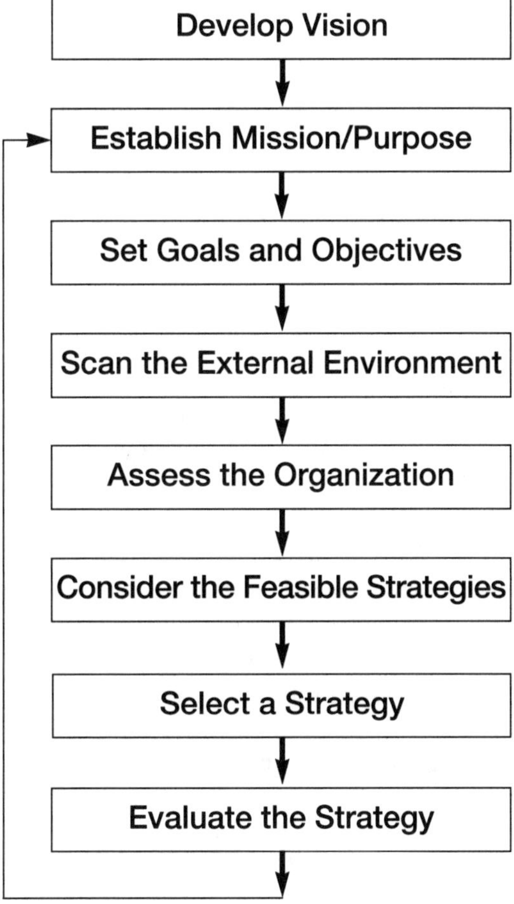

Figure 2-3. *The Strategic Planning Process.*

the organization is going. Objectives usually focus more on specifics, with measures, time frames, and sometimes even particular responsibilities. Training and development goals and objectives should reflect, to a certain degree, the strategic goals and objectives for the organizational units served. Also, they should support the strategic objectives of the overall organization.

Scan the external environment. The next step is to scan the external environment for critical issues that will affect the strategic direction of the organization. For training, this may involve examining the quality of the new employees, the resources for training new employees, the resources for designing, developing, and delivering training, the market conditions that influence workplace skills and competencies, technology developments, and legal and regulatory developments. For a typical organization, the external environment will contain a variety of influences that can provide major input into the strategic planning process.

Assess the organization. In this step, the organization's strengths and weaknesses are detailed. A weakness indicates a specific area where improvement should be made to enhance the effectiveness and efficiency of the education and training function. The strengths are also identified, which are important assets of the function. This step requires an objective viewpoint to determine which issues are actual strengths and weaknesses.

Consider the feasible strategies. The next step is to consider the full range of potential strategies to develop the strategic plans. Feasibility is critical, as well as linkage to the strategic needs of the overall business unit and organization. In this step, all the previous processes are integrated, from vision to mission to goals and objectives, to determine which specific strategies are appropriate.

Select a strategy. The strategy is selected and implemented by following specific schedules, assignments, and responsibilities. The strategic plan translates into operational plans for the training and development function, as specific programs and services are developed and delivered. The implementation involves providing coordination, allocating resources, developing policies, and establishing practices, as the strategy is implemented throughout the organization.

Evaluate the strategy. The final step of the model is to evaluate the success of the strategy. This is a periodic review, sometimes conducted annually. The goal of this step is to gauge the success of the strategy and replan as necessary. Thus, the cycle continues, as adjustments are made and new strategy is developed.

This strategic planning model is appropriate for any type of unit, function, or even individual. It provides a useful framework for the training and development function to perform its different roles.

Operating Strategically

How does the training department become more strategic? Several actions can be taken by the training and development function to more closely link with strategy. Some of these issues relate to trends covered in other chapters in this book. Some actions represent paradigm shifts for the training staff, while others represent actions necessary to develop this special linkage. Ten specific actions are recommended:

Develop a strategic plan. Using a model similar to the one presented in this chapter, the training and development function should develop its own strategic plan. The function will have difficulty linking to the overall strategy if it does not have its own strategic plan. This is often an early step in the process. Developing a strategic plan not only ensures there is a connection but also demonstrates competence in the strategic planning process.

Become proactive with the training and development function. For years the training and development function has operated in a reactive mode, responding to requests from various stakeholder groups. Being strategic requires a proactive role, taking the initiative to develop programs that will support the strategic direction of the organization. The strategic role may not be requested; therefore, training and development will need to take the initiative to become a key player in the strategic direction.

Shift to a performance improvement role. As described in Chapter 4 in this book, the trend of shifting from training to performance improvement is an important step in developing a strategic linkage. Most strategic objectives focus on important business-performance measures, which can be enhanced by the training and development function.

Build partnerships with key managers. As described in Chapter 14, the trend of developing partnerships with other managerial groups is essential to connect to strategy. Key managers formulate and implement major strategic objectives of the organization. Working closely with managers to meet their needs and to rely on them for support, assistance, and direction will help ensure that the training function is connected to strategy.

Become customer-focused. Because customer satisfaction and relationships are usually strategic issues, shifting training programs closer to the customer helps to ensure a closer alignment with strategy. As organizations operate in a more customer-focused environment, the training and development function not only must work with internal customers to meet their specific needs but also must develop programs, products, and services to align with customer contact issues.

Communicate regularly with top executives. Because top executives set strategy, routine communication with them can ensure that training and development services and programs are on target to assist in and achieve strategic goals. Disconnection and alignment problems can be quickly adjusted when top executives are aware of them and when the mechanism is in place to make the adjustment.

Take the pulse of the organization. The work climate must be monitored, and programs must be developed to improve the organization. Some strategic objectives revolve around employee satisfaction, employee involvement, and employee commitment. A favorable and productive work climate is essential and is usually a part of strategy. The training and development function should monitor important measures such as job satisfaction, attitude, organization commitment, and work climate through a variety of feedback mechanisms to make sure that the climate is consistent with management expectations.

Establish programs with core competencies. Most organizations have developed core competencies necessary to position the organization for future success. Some strategic initiatives revolve around developing those core competencies. Many training and development programs should be linked directly to the core competencies whenever possible.

Consider a results-based approach at all levels. Return on investment, business impact, behavior change, and transformation in the work-

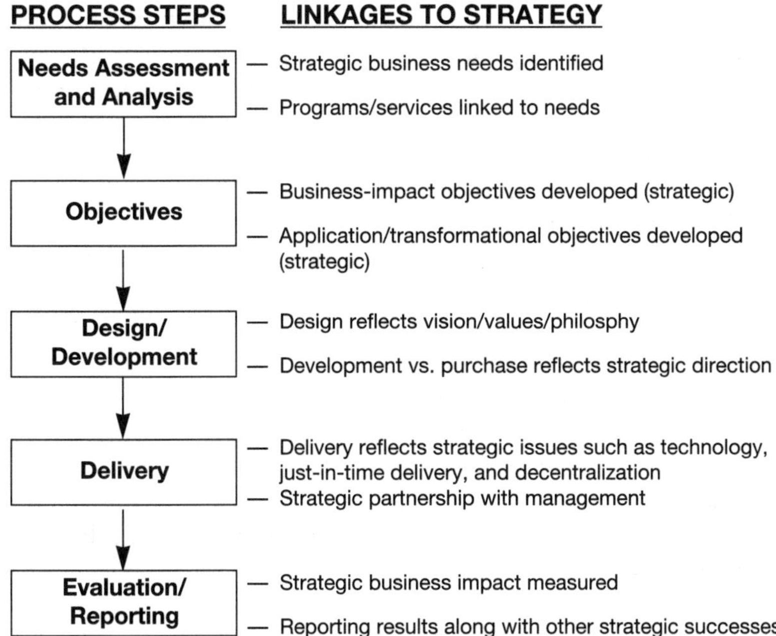

Figure 2-4. *Connecting Training and Development with Strategy, Step-by-Step.*

place are all critical categories of strategy. As the organization focuses on achieving key results measures, the possibility of linkage to the strategic objectives is greatly enhanced. Also, measurable results reported to appropriate target audiences can help ensure that training and development is always invited to the table where strategic issues are discussed.

Link training and development to strategies at all steps of the process. Figure 2-4 shows how training and development can connect with strategies in each major step of the training and development cycle, from needs assessment to evaluation. At the needs assessment and analysis level, the strategic business needs are identified, including specific measures that should be enhanced within the programs. Specific programs and services, which can improve or enhance these measures, are identified in the analysis so that there is a direct linkage between the need and the proposed program.

Objectives developed to drive business impact, application, and transformation are normally strategic and operational. The specific objectives provide the direction necessary to ensure that programs are on target and are helping reach the strategic objectives of the organization. During the design process, each element, module, or activity should reflect the vision, value, philosophy, and beliefs that are in the organization's overall strategic plan. Also, issues such as the development versus purchase of programs may reflect the strategic objective of the organization concerning the use of outsourcing versus internally developed programs.

Delivery reflects such important strategic issues as using technology and having training and development delivered just in time. Managers are involved in delivery issues as programs are implemented in decentralized format throughout the regions and locations. Evaluation provides an opportunity to measure the business impact on strategic measures and report results to appropriate target audiences, along with other strategic successes.

Thus, every step in the training and development cycle presents opportunities for connection to the strategy of the organization.

Trend Consequences

Impact

The shift to a closer link between training and development (T&D) and strategy has been developing for many years. For some T&D leaders this is a logical application of an improvement process that is very familiar to them. If the top training and development executive has enjoyed significant experience in a line operating area, strategic planning is often viewed as a necessary and essential process. Consequently, the shift is easy, and the progress is often more substantial and noticeable.

For other leaders, significant resistance can develop in several different areas. First, a significant paradigm shift must occur with the training and development staff. As described in this chapter, staff members must shift roles and change their thinking and their approach as they assess needs, design and develop programs, deliver products and services, and evaluate the results.

Second, staff members must develop an appropriate understanding of strategic planning and how it can assist the organization. Understanding often reduces resistance and provides the expertise needed to assist the organization with strategic planning issues.

Third, parts of the training and development process may need to change so that the programs align more closely with strategic outcomes. Beginning with the needs assessment, several steps may need adjustment so that strategic initiatives and connections are integrated.

Fourth, HRD staff members will need to build relationships with key clients throughout the organization. These relationships are essential to keep programs and services focused on key goals and objectives in the organization and to build the necessary support to make the programs more effective and efficient.

Finally, the training and development staff members must become more business-minded. They must develop a better understanding of business issues, operational concerns, and external problems confronting the organization, particularly the strategic issues. This often requires more operational and financial knowledge for the entire training and development staff.

Key Questions

Before increasing the connection between T&D and strategy, several key questions should be asked.

Key Questions

1. To what extent do I agree with this trend?
2. How important is this trend?
3. What progress has been made in connecting training and development to strategy within our T&D function?
4. What is the readiness level of the staff to take on a greater strategic role?
5. What resources would be required to connect with strategy to a greater degree?
6. What barriers exist for developing this linkage?
7. What is senior management's viewpoint on connecting training to strategy?
8. To what extent will the key managers support this effort?
9. What will happen if I do nothing?
10. What specific actions will be necessary to develop closer alignment with strategic planning?

Outlook

This trend will likely continue in the future, and it is viewed as necessary by most stakeholders. It has been developing for many years. The drivers for the trend should continue and perhaps intensify in the future. Some consider this trend necessary for the survival of the correctly operating T&D function. Without a strategic connection, the training and development function could diminish to a trivial role in the organization, perhaps through outsourcing with only the essential required training and development processes pursued.

Achieving success with this trend provides several important advantages. Connecting to strategy will build a closer relationship between T&D and the senior management team. This may be one of the most important elements in developing a partnership that is needed to convince senior managers that training can add to the bottom line, as strategic objectives are enhanced by training and development.

Budget and funding are often influenced by the extent to which training and development is linked with strategy or is perceived to be linked with strategy. A clear linkage makes it much easier to obtain the necessary budget. A disconnection will cause problems at budgeting time. Also, strategic training and development ensures that funding for training and development is properly utilized. It ensures that the training and development process is adding value in the areas that matter most—those critically linked to the future of the organization.

Success with this process moves training and development to a vital and critical position in the organization. When training and development has been elevated to an important strategic role, the company views it as necessary to position the organization for the future. In summary, it appears that this trend will continue for years and that the training and development staff should continue to make progress with this important linkage.

References

1. Chau, Jennifer. "SIA: Fifty and Still Soaring." *Singapore Business,* May 1997, pp. 22–25.
2. Yun, Chang Z., Yong, Yeong W., and Loh, Lawrence. *The Quest for Global Quality: A Manifestation of Total Quality Management by Singapore Airlines.* Singapore: Addison-Wesley Publishers, 1996.
3. Marquardt, Michael J. and Engel, Dean W. *Global Human Resource Development.* Englewood Cliffs, N.J.: Prentice Hall, 1993.
4. Shandler, Donald. *Reengineering the Training Function: How to Align Training with the New Corporate Agenda.* Delray Beach, Fla.: St. Lucie Press, 1996.
5. Williams, Teresa and Green, Adrian. *A Business Approach to Training.* London: Gower Publishing, 1997.
6. Nadler, Leonard and Nadler, Zeace. *The Handbook of Human Resource Development,* 2nd ed. New York: John Wiley, 1990.
7. McClernon, Timothy R. and Swanson, Richard A. "Redefining HRD's Role in the Corporation: A Case Study on Becoming a World-Class Business Partner," in *In Action: Leading Organizational Change.* Elwood F. Holton and Jack J. Phillips (Eds.), Alexandria, Va.: American Society for Training and Development, 1997, pp. 1–21.
8. Rothwell, William J. (Ed.) *Linking HRD with Strategy.* Alexandria, Va.: American Society for Training and Development, 1998.

9. Kemske, Floyd. "HR's Role Will Change. The Question Is How. HR 2008: A Forecast Based on Our Exclusive Study." *Workforce,* Jan. 1998, pp. 47–51.

10. Kaplan, Robert S. and Norton, David P. *The Balanced Scorecard: Translating Strategy into Action.* Cambridge, Mass.: Harvard Business School Press, 1996.

11. Moore, Carol A. and Seidner, Constance J. "Organization Strategy and Training Evaluation," in *Evaluating Corporate Training: Models and Issues.* Stephen M. Brown, and Constance J. Seidner, (Eds.), Boston, Mass.: Kluwer Academic Publishers, 1997, pp. 19–40.

12. Fredericks, John and Stewart, Jim, "The Strategy-HRD Connection," *Human Resource Development: Perspectives, Strategies, and Practice,* Stewart, Jim and McGoldrick, Jim (Eds.), London: Pitman Publishing, 1996, pp. 101–119.

13. McClernon and Swanson. pp. 1–21.

14. Rothwell, William J. *Model for Human Performance Improvement: Roles, Competencies, and Outputs.* Alexandria, Va.: American Society for Training and Development, 1996, pp. 18–19.

15. McClernon and Swanson. pp. 1–21.

16. Wiggenhorn, A. William. "Organization and Management of Training," in *The ASTD Training and Development Handbook,* 4th ed. Robert L. Craig (Ed.), New York: McGraw-Hill, 1996, p. 22.

3

NEEDS ASSESSMENT AND ANALYSIS

Trend Definition and Validation

Brief Definition of Trend

Organizations are committing more resources, in the forms of both time and money, toward needs assessment and analysis to ensure that training and development programs are necessary and are linked to business improvement. Several methods are available to pinpoint precise business and job performance needs, in addition to learning needs, and to identify training and non-training solutions.

Case Studies: Izhorsky Zavod and Nestlé

Izhorsky Zavod. Management development has been a critical need in the former Soviet Union since Perestroika, and this is illustrated in Izhorsky Zavod (IZ), a large, state-owned, vertically integrated steel-production facility founded in 1722 by Peter the Great. With more than 26,000 employees, IZ produces steel and alloy products for a diverse group of customers.[1] Before beginning a management development program at IZ, a group of four contract consultants conducted a detailed needs analysis containing three different levels. The first level, an organization analysis, focused on business needs. The next level, a job analysis, concentrated on job performance needs of managers. Finally, the third level, a personnel analysis, concentrated on skills and knowledge deficiencies within the managerial group.

The needs assessment and analysis used detailed interviews coupled with performance records to identify specific needs and potential solutions. The results of the needs assessment led to a recommendation for a nine-week intensive management development program, which was ultimately implemented.

Nestlé. Work-force diversity has prompted many training programs, sometimes with failure or only moderate results. However, the approach taken by Nestlé Beverage Company (NBC) delivered a top-quality program, because of a comprehensive needs assessment process.[2] NBC is a division of Nestlé USA, which is a division of Nestlé SA, the world's largest food company, headquartered in Switzerland. The decision to pursue a needs assessment was made by NBC's diversity advisory board. The purpose was to take a "snapshot" of the current corporate climate to help focus on the issues critical to achieving the company's diversity goals. The comprehensive needs assessment included detailed, one-on-one interviews with a sample of NBC employees. The interview data produced six themes that helped focus diversity efforts on areas that would be of the greatest benefit to the company. The resulting report led to the finalization of NBC's diversity strategy and a diversity workshop for all employees. In addition, NBC initiated other interventions—such as change in recruiting practices, performance management processes, and compensation—as a result of the needs assessment.

Evidence of Trend

A tremendous amount of evidence underscores the existence of this trend and its magnitude within the training and development function. The practitioner survey about global trends revealed a strong agreement among survey respondents regarding this trend, with a response of 3.76 out of 5 (see Appendix 1). Practitioners rated the importance of the trend 4.64 out of 5, making it the fourth most important trend. Clearly, training and development practitioners view needs assessment as a significant trend that has made much progress in recent years. In addition, a survey involving members of the International Federation of Training and Development Organizations (IFTDO) ranked this trend in the top ten critical issues within the thirty-five countries involved in the study.

In a recent survey conducted by the American Society for Training and Development, training and development executives and managers provided input about the most probable trends projected for the next three years.[3] The trend of matching needs with appropriate methods and technologies was listed among the top ten most probable trends.

Studies reporting the progress of the shift from training to performance often reveal an increased emphasis on needs assessment. One of the foundations of the performance consulting process involves bringing more attention to the front-end analysis to determine specific needs. Several studies have indicated an increase in the needs assessment process as the performance analysis process has been implemented.[4]

Organizations are focusing increased attention on evaluation, while additional efforts in evaluation often lead to a more detailed and accurate needs assessment process. Studies that have shown an increased use of evaluations have also revealed additional emphasis on the needs assessment process.[5]

Because of the vital role that needs assessment plays in the training and development process, a failure to address this process properly often leads to ineffective or failed training efforts. Because of these problems, organizations are now placing more emphasis on the needs assessment process as an integral and routine part of the analysis.[6]

A major review of actual practices and case studies reveals a tremendous increase in the use of needs analysis. In addition, multiple methods are being used as organizations improve their assessment processes.[7] Another study, examining the shifting mind-sets of those training and development organizations, also has identified a recent increase in needs assessment and analysis.[8] Finally, a global HRD study found evidence of increased needs assessment across a wide variety of organizations and cultures.[9]

Causes and Drivers

- The training and development process is mature in most organizations, and this maturity is obvious in the developing nations as the training and development function carves out a legitimate place in the organization. As it matures, more attention is placed on improving the basic elements of the process. Needs assessment is one of those key elements that is accepted as a necessary and important part of the process. Unfortunately, in the early development of training, needs assessment is sometimes short-circuited or omitted. As the T&D process matures in an organization, more attention and resources are devoted to it.
- The increased emphasis on the bottom-line contribution and return on investment of the training and development function is driving increased emphasis on needs assessment and analysis.[10] As organizations attempt to evaluate programs at the ROI level, they often uncover deficiencies in the needs assessment process. As a result, more attention and resources shift to needs assessment and analysis.
- The failure of some major training and development projects has often led to faulty or insufficient needs assessment. These failures, when clearly understood and documented, have caused some training and development functions to focus more attention on this critical area. Practitioners are learning from their mistakes.
- The shift from training and development to performance analysis focuses more attention on the needs assessment and analysis process.[11] At the heart of the performance consulting process is a detailed analysis of needs and solutions for those needs. Perhaps more than any other factor, this shift is causing increased resources to be focused on this important area.
- Many high-profile training and development organizations are devoting more resources to the needs assessment and analysis. As these organizations are benchmarked with specific expenditures and staff commitment to needs assessment and analysis, more organizations are beefing up their efforts.[12]
- Finally, many organizations are beginning to realize the actual payoff of the training needs assessment. Consequently, they are allocating additional resources for training needs assessment. In

some organizations, the needs assessment benefits are documented and compared to investment in the process. For example, when the needs assessment and analysis process results in a nontraining solution instead of training (at a lower cost), the net value is documented and becomes an item of the total savings generated by needs assessment and analysis.[13] The actual and potential payoffs are causing some organizations to invest more in needs assessment and analysis.

Trend Description

The needs assessment and analysis process is one of the most critical steps in training and development. Although there has been increased emphasis and additional use of the needs assessment and analysis, much confusion still exists concerning the steps, techniques, methods, and strategies involved in the process. The step is so crucial that some would argue that if a legitimate need for training and development is not established for a program, there will be no economic benefit derived from the program. Consequently, the omission of a needs assessment places the evaluation process in jeopardy.[14]

Needs assessment has traditionally earned its place in the training and development cycle. Almost every training and development process model will include needs assessment as an initial, up-front step. However, the needs assessment and analysis process is sometimes omitted because of pressure to develop a program quickly, because of a lack of resources to conduct the analysis, or because of a lack of understanding of why it is needed. The challenge is to overcome the realistic barriers to its use.

Initiating a Needs Assessment

It is helpful to begin the description of this process by defining four important terms.[15] A **need** is a gap or deficiency existing between the current state and the desired state. The **needs assessment** is the identification of the need and a determination of its importance and cost to satisfy. **Needs analysis** uncovers the cause of the gap that has been identified. A **solution** is a feasible process, program, or activity that will remove the gap or correct the problem.

Several events or situations can initiate a needs assessment.

- New employees enter the organization and need specific training.
- The organization implements new equipment, processes, and procedures.
- New jobs are created, or new responsibilities are developed for current jobs.
- New products are developed, or new processes are implemented.
- The organization undertakes major change programs.
- Management requests a needs assessment or a program that leads to a needs assessment.
- Skills are upgraded, improved, or planned for improvement.
- Significant opportunity for performance improvement exists, or a performance problem has been identified.

Any of these situations can lead to some type of needs assessment. Unfortunately, the process is sometimes omitted or conducted inadequately when management requests a program or when a program has been implemented in other organizations and management wants it implemented. When considering the reasons for the initiation of new programs in an organization, some are legitimate, while others may not be based on an appropriate foundation. There should be concern when any of the following situations drive the development of a new program:

- Management requests it.
- The best-practice or most admired companies are pursuing it.
- The program is a general trend in all organizations.
- The training and development staff thinks the program is needed.

Any one of these situations represents red flags that could translate into problems for the program if a needs assessment is not conducted.

A needs assessment can actually serve several purposes. It can uncover the current level of skills, knowledge, attitudes, and performance and compare that to the desired or optimal level of skills, knowledge, attitudes, and performance. This process essentially identifies the gap. The analysis uncovers the causes of the gap or specific problems and identifies specific solutions to overcome the problem or remove the gap. A needs assessment also identifies potential problems that could surface in the future along with solutions to those problems.

Sometimes a needs assessment is divided into different types of more-specific needs assessments, based on the scope and comprehensiveness of the approach. A job/function needs assessment identifies skill gaps and specific needs for a job, a job family, or a functional unit. For example, a training needs assessment is conducted for new first-level managers. A second type is a performance/problem analysis, which functions to identify the problem, develop causes, and recommend solutions. For example, a performance/problem analysis could uncover specific causes and recommended solutions for the problem of excessive staff turnover. Finally, a macro-level needs assessment identifies needs for the total organization or a large segment of the organization. Changing job requirements are creating new demands for knowledge and skills. For example, a needs assessment on technology identifies specific training needs for the entire work force.

The Steps for Needs Assessment and Analysis

A comprehensive needs assessment and analysis process involves at least fourteen distinct steps as follows:

- Determine the specific purpose and type of needs assessment.
- Identify and select the sources for information for the needs assessment.
- Involve key management in the process and gain necessary commitment.
- Begin with the end in mind, with specific business-impact and job-performance measures.
- Use multiple sources of input and a variety of data.
- Select the data collection methods appropriate for the situation, culture, and resources available.
- Collect data according to a predetermined data collection plan.
- Link business needs to job performance needs, including tasks, behavior, and environment.
- Identify the barriers to successful implementation of the solution.
- Determine specific skills and knowledge deficiencies, if applicable.
- Integrate and analyze all the data.

- Prioritize specific needs in terms of importance and cost to resolve.
- Provide recommendations for specific solutions.
- Communicate results of the needs assessment and analysis to appropriate target audiences.

These steps are comprehensive, and some may be omitted when a simple process is needed or when the stakes are not so high. A shortened version of this process is presented as Figure 3-1, which describes a basic performance assessment and analysis process. This is a basic four-level needs assessment and analysis process that focuses on the business and job performance issues.

The four levels in this model relate to the evaluation levels shown in Figure 3-2. The evaluation levels are the traditional levels developed by Kirkpatrick and reflect the most common framework for evaluation.[16] The levels are described in Chapter 8 in a trend involving systematic evaluation. Information needed to determine the success of a program at each level is derived from specific objectives of the program. For example, the business impact from a training program is developed from measures contained in the impact objectives. The same process applies for application of training on the job and

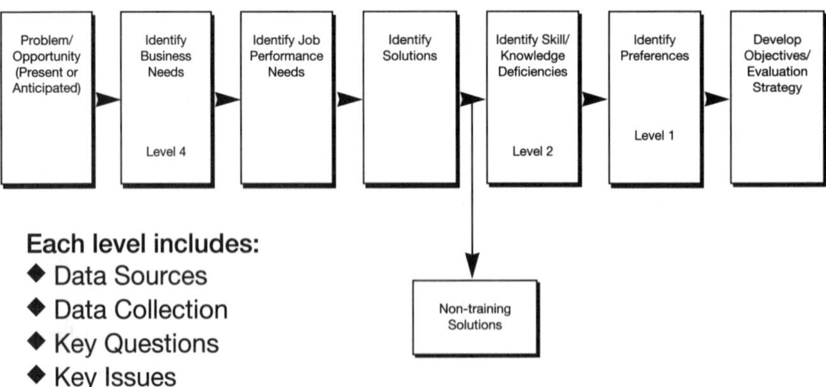

Figure 3-1. *Performance Assessment and Analysis Process.* (Source: Performance Resources Organization, P.O. Box 380637, Birmingham, AL 35238-0637. Used with permission.)

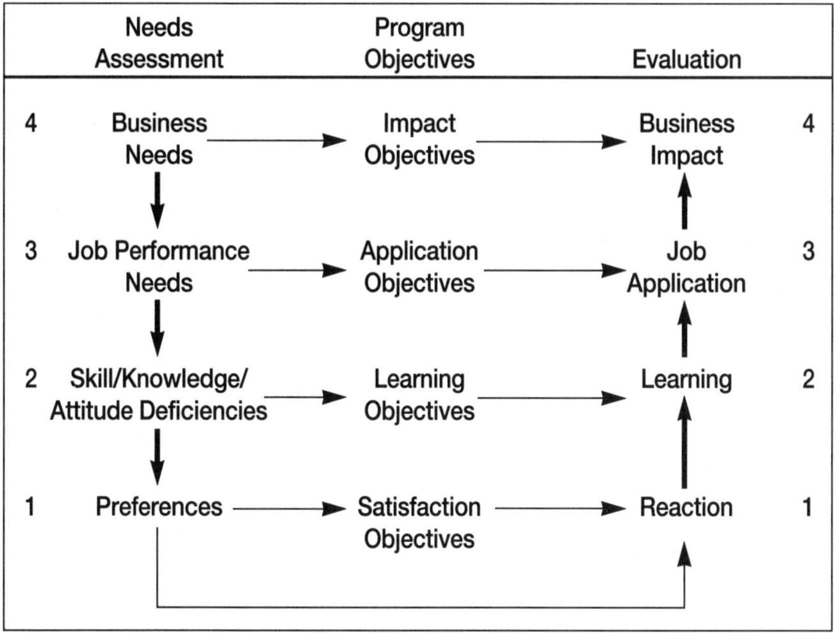

Figure 3-2. Linking Needs Assessment with Evaluation.

learning achieved in the program. Some programs even have reaction or satisfaction objectives, which outline the expected participant reaction to the program.

Program objectives at all four levels are derived from the needs assessment process. For example, the specific business needs uncovered in the needs assessment process will drive the impact objectives and identify the business impact. Also, the job performance needs assessment will uncover changes in tasks, behavior, and procedures needed in the job environment. This will determine the specific application objectives for the program. The skill, knowledge, and attitude deficiencies will determine specific learning gaps, which will appear as learning objectives in the program. Finally, preferences for learning in terms of type of program, location, specific instructor, media, timing, delivery, and content will drive these issues and sometimes appear as satisfaction objectives. Thus, needs assessment is clearly linked to program objectives and evaluation, and these linkages are often referred to as levels of needs assessment, objectives, and evaluation.

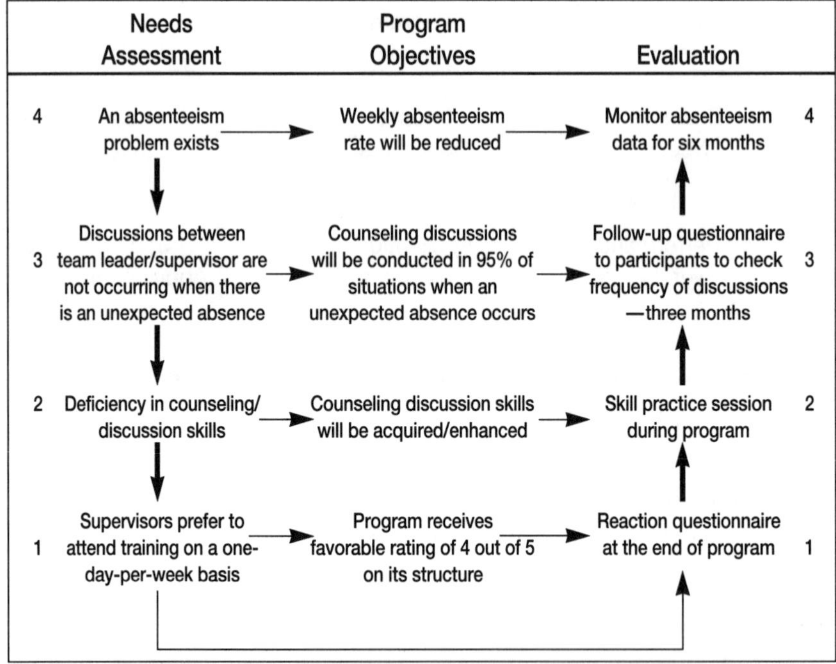

Figure 3-3. Linking Needs Assessment with Evaluation (an example).

An example of this process is shown in Figure 3-3, where an absenteeism problem has been linked to specific supervisory skill and knowledge deficiencies and a program has been developed to overcome them. In this example, the needs assessment and analysis levels clearly drive program objectives, and an appropriate evaluation method is used to collect data to satisfy the requirements for the particular evaluation level.

To develop this process effectively, several key questions need to be asked for each needs assessment level, as shown in Figure 3-4.

Not every needs assessment should be conducted at all levels. The important point is that the value of the information obtained is higher at higher levels, with business needs providing the highest level of information. Frequency of use of needs assessment decreases with the levels (that is, the higher the level, the lower the frequency of use). Preferences are a common type of needs assessment. For example, when a program catalog is distributed to the members of a target

Business Needs	What business-level problems or opportunities exist that need to be improved? What business measures reflect this need? Where are they located? What are the historical values?
Job Performance Needs	What is preventing the business measures from improving? What is not being performed on the job as desired or as needed? What tasks should be performed? What resources are needed?
Skills/Knowledge Needs	What skills and knowledge levels are needed? What gaps exist in skills and knowledge? How can skills and knowledge be acquired or enhanced?
Preference	Which learning activities are preferred? Which delivery mechanisms are desired? What is the appropriate timing?

Figure 3-4. *Key Questions for Needs Assessment and Analysis.*

audience asking them to select the programs they would like to attend in the next six months, this is usually a needs assessment based on preference (Level 1). On the other end of the scale, the analysis of business needs is conducted infrequently, primarily because it is difficult and time consuming. In reality, only a few types of programs should be taken to the Level 3 and Level 4 assessments—programs in which the scope is large and the impact or costs are great. The criteria often hinge on the following issues:

- The anticipated impact of the program and cost savings or profit.
- The perceived life cycle of the program.
- The importance of the program in meeting operational goals.
- Linkage with strategic objectives.
- The expected cost of the program.
- The expected visibility of the program.
- The size of the target audience.

Needs Assessment Methods and Issues

A variety of methods are available to collect data for the needs assessment and analysis. The data collection method revolves around the assessment instrument. The seven most common types of instruments are:

- Questionnaires, which collect a variety of data
- Surveys, which typically collect opinion and attitude data
- A variety of tests to measure skills or knowledge
- One-on-one interviews
- Focus groups
- Observation
- Performance records in the organization

The source of data for the needs assessment is critical to the process. A variety of sources are available, and the seven most common general categories are:

- Participants
- Supervisors of participants
- Subordinates of participants
- Peer groups
- Subject-matter experts
- Organizational performance records
- The training and development staff

Other sources may be appropriate for the specific type of situation and different level of needs assessment. For example, at the business needs level, sources include industry data, benchmarking data, strategic and operational plans, annual reports, business performance data, human resource records, and performance appraisals. At Level 3, sources may include job descriptions, performance appraisals, policies and procedures, job tasks, and subject-matter experts. At Level 2, sources may include tests, simulations, performance reviews, and job descriptions.

Selecting a specific method for the data collection is an important task. The issues that will determine the appropriate method often involve items such as:

- Cost of data collection
- Participant time required
- Training and development staff time required
- Amount of disruption of normal work activities
- Cultural preferences
- Accuracy
- Type of data

In summary, the data collection method for a needs assessment is the most visible and time-consuming process. The method must be selected while recognizing the issues and concerns above. A variety of sources and tools is available, as are excellent examples of tools and processes for needs assessment.[17, 18]

Overall, the needs assessment process involves a variety of steps and many key issues that must be addressed throughout the process. It requires careful planning, data collection from a variety of sources, careful analyses, and thoughtful conclusions to provide the appropriate recommendation. While the needs assessment and analysis process requires resources that some training and development departments may be reluctant to provide, additional investment should result in an improved program and will sometimes prevent unnecessary programs from being implemented.

Communicating Needs Assessment

The results of the needs assessment usually can be presented in several ways. Sometimes the output of the process provides information about the current state of affairs, including problems and opportunities, and specific action may not be required. More often than not, however, the needs assessment will present needs by priority with the most critical needs listed first and the least critical needs listed last. The prioritization is based on either the cost of satisfying the need or the critical importance of the need to the organization's success. This provides a framework to tackle the issues.

Another category of needs assessment results are the recommendations for solutions based on the analysis. Non-training solutions are addressed, as well as training solutions. Finally, the results of the needs assessment are sometimes used to obtain support for the process. The results are usually presented to key stakeholders, in addition to the individuals who supplied information. As a critical component, management must understand the need for a particular solution and realize the factors, that have influenced it. This can perhaps shape the implementation of the solution, as well as determine its success.

Trend Consequences

Impact

A more comprehensive needs assessment process may not be welcome in many organizations. It takes time, adds cost, and often delays the implementation of a requested program. Training and development staff members may not have the appropriate expertise to conduct a proper needs assessment. Also, when management requests a program, some staff members are reluctant to challenge the request and deflect it to a needs assessment. Add to this the viewpoint that needs assessments may not be necessary and are a waste of time. These legitimate barriers to a successful needs assessment process will continue to make it difficult to invest more time and money into the process. However, the potential payoff of additional investment is significant. When linked to evaluation, it becomes quite clear that without the proper needs assessment and analysis, the success of the program is in jeopardy. An effective process may prevent unnecessary programs or result in a radically redesigned program with cost savings. A tally of savings can be generated, which can ultimately be impressive, offsetting the additional investment.

Each barrier to more investment must be overcome for the process to grow and succeed. Perhaps one of the most difficult challenges is to deflect requests for training to an appropriate needs assessment and analysis. Ultimately, the process can be built into the training and development cycle so that needs assessment and analysis becomes an essential part of the process. Also, the management team may need additional information so that it understands the purpose of needs assessment and the team's role to make it successful.

Key Questions

The following key questions should be asked regarding additional needs assessment.

Key Questions

1. Is this a trend in my organization?
2. How important is this trend?
3. How much progress has been made with needs assessment and analysis in my organization?
4. What resources would be required to increase efforts?
5. Specifically, what can we do to increase the needs assessment analysis?
6. Do we have appropriate skills to conduct a needs assessment?
7. Can we obtain additional funding to make the process successful?
8. What barriers exist for the appropriate needs assessment?
9. What would be the reaction of the management group to additional needs assessment?
10. How can I obtain additional support and buy-in for the management team?
11. What happens if I do nothing?
12. Can I measure the payoff of this process?

Outlook

It appears that this trend will continue, although maybe at a slower pace than the other trends. Although some legitimate barriers to making the process more effective exist, it is essential for needs assessment and analysis to be adequately accomplished. The drivers for increased needs assessment will continue to influence additional investment and progress. Other trends will continue to drive this one because the success of evaluation, in particular the return on investment, often depends on a successful needs assessment. Also, because this trend is an integral part of the shift to performance analysis, additional emphasis will be needed. This is definitely a win-win trend but may require careful planning and implementation for it to be effective.

References

1. Wiley, Donna L. "Developing Managers in the Former Soviet Union," in *In Action: Conducting Needs Assessment.* Elwood F. Holton and Jack J. Phillips (Eds.), Alexandria, Va.: American Society for Training and Development, 1995, p. 283.
2. Rasmussen, Tina, "Overcoming Resistance to a Successful Diversity Effort," in *In Action: Conducting Needs Assessment.* Elwood F. Holton and Jack J. Phillips (Eds.), Alexandria, Va.: American Society for Training and Development, 1995, p. 189.
3. *Trends in Human Resource Development.* Alexandria, Va.: American Society for Training and Development, 1997.
4. Shaw, Edward. *The Six Pillars of Reality-Based Training.* Amherst, Mass.: HRD Press, 1997.
5. Barksdale, Susan and Lund, Teri. "How to Link Evaluation to the Business Need," in *Training and Performance Sourcebook.* New York: McGraw-Hill, 1997.
6. Kaufman, Roger. "Needs Assessment and Analysis," in *Human Resources Management and Development Handbook,* 2nd ed. William R. Tracey (Ed.), New York: Amacom, 1994, p. 1160.
7. Holton, Elwood F. and Phillips, Jack J. (Eds.) *In Action: Conducting Needs Assessment.* Alexandria, Va.: American Society for Training and Development, 1995.
8. Shandler, Donald. *Reengineering the Training Function: How to Align Training with the New Corporate Agenda.* Delray Beach, Fla.: St. Lucie Press, 1996.
9. Marquardt, Michael J. and Engel, Dean W. *Global Human Resource Development.* Englewood Cliffs, N.J.: Prentice Hall, 1993.
10. Phillips, Jack J. *Return on Investment in Training and Performance Improvement Programs.* Houston, Tex.: Gulf Publishing, 1997.
11. Robinson, Dana G. and Robinson, James C. *Performance Consulting: Moving Beyond Training.* San Francisco: Berrett-Koehler, 1995.
12. Bassi, Laurie J. and Van Buren, Mark E. "The 1998 State of the Industry Report." *Training & Development,* Jan. 1998, pp. 21–49.
13. Phillips, Jack J. *Accountability in Human Resource Management.* Houston, Tex.: Gulf Publishing, 1996.
14. Phillips, Jack J. *Handbook of Training Evaluation and Measurement Methods,* 3rd ed. Houston, Tex.: Gulf Publishing, 1997.

15. Kaufman, p. 1160.

16. Kirkpatrick, Donald L. "The Four Levels: An Overview," in *Evaluating Training Programs: The Four Levels.* San Francisco: Berrett-Koehler, 1994, pp. 21–26.

17. McClelland, Samuel B. *Organizational Needs and Assessments: Design Facilitation and Analysis.* Westport, Conn.: Quorum Books, 1995.

18. Rossett, Allison. *Training Needs Assessment.* Englewood Cliffs, N.J.: Educational Technology Publications, 1987.

4

PERFORMANCE IMPROVEMENT

Trend Definition and Validation

Brief Definition of Trend

The training and development (T&D) function is shifting its focus to performance improvement, where a variety of training and non-training solutions are implemented to improve performance in the organization. This paradigm shift represents a tremendous change in the way the training and development function is organized, managed, and operated to provide programs and services. Training and development's roles, skills, and outputs are drastically changing as the T&D department's staff members transform into a group of capable performance improvement specialists.

Case Study: Rohm and Haas

A large specialty chemical company with production operations located throughout the world, Rohm and Haas is in an industry with serious global competition. The Rohm and Haas plant in Houston, Texas, provides an example of the type of transformation taking place in the training and development function. The Houston plant, for example, created a network of performance specialists and charged those specialists with the formidable task of changing the plant's prevailing paradigm of training and experience on the job. This was the key to driving adequate performance with a new approach, which considered all the factors that influence human performance.[1]

Each unit in the plant now has a performance development implementer (PDI), who reports to the unit manager and addresses performance issues in the plant. All PDIs are connected by the network, which allows them to share information, address plant-wide initiatives, and build their own knowledge and skills. A performance development manager coordinates the network.

The paradigm shift required developing new knowledge, skills, and competencies for each PDI. The structure of the organization changed significantly, and through a variety of communication strategies and action items, productive relationships were established between the PDIs and key stakeholders throughout the plant. Services changed dramatically from traditional training and development to a variety of performance improvement services and solutions. The result was a network of highly skilled performance specialists who understand and can address common needs of the plants, as well as specific needs in each unit. Basically, the network provides a new lens for examining performance issues.

This case illustrates the tremendous shift in focus for the traditional training and development function as it provides a range of services to improve performance of a work unit, department division, plant, or entire organization.

Evidence of Trend

In the global survey of practitioners, this trend received one of the highest scores for agreement to the existence of the trend, with a rating of 4.25 out of 5 (see Appendix 1). The same practitioners rated the trend 4.37 out of 5 in terms of importance. Practitioners view this distinct trend as important and visible. Perhaps no trend has been more publicized than this trend. Books, articles, and studies describing this process have been plentiful. Many of them are noted at the end of this chapter. Every training and development agenda contains the topic. A special workshop has been developed by the International Society for Performance Improvement to prepare training and development staff members for this transition.

One of the most important studies of this shift is a major research project conducted by the American Society for Training and Development (ASTD) under the leadership of a panel of experts in the training and development and performance improvement fields. In this project, ASTD sought to develop a model for roles and competencies reflecting performance improvement.[2] This model was intended to replace an earlier model of training and human resource development. The expert panel concluded that most major organizations around the globe were making the transition from traditional training and development to performance improvement. After drawing that conclusion, the team developed an official ASTD model for human performance improvement, defining roles, competencies, and outputs. The study also addressed a variety of other issues necessary to make the transition a reality.

A survey of a sample of HRD executives around the globe confirms the transition. In regard to a question about the transition of training to performance improvement, 42 percent of respondents strongly agreed and another 42 percent agreed—84 percent total—that the training department was rapidly changing to fill a performance improvement role. By the year 2000, performance support will replace the typical training department.[3] *Training & Development* magazine, published by ASTD, reported the results of a survey among readers of the magazine. The survey reflected that 40 percent of the respondents believed that changing their professional titles to performance improvement specialist would best describe the work they do. Many departments also are changing their names. Jim Fuller, director of learning and performance technology at the Hewlett-Packard Company, typifies this change.[4] His function represents Hewlett-Packard's research and development efforts in the area of learning and performance with specific responsibility for performance improvement processes, instructional design methods, education evaluation systems, and the application of technology to accelerate learning.

A study from Great Britain illustrating the changing world of training indicated that the training function now offers a wide range of both course and non-course solutions that focus on improving performance.[5] Another study that involved reengineering efforts of the training function identified seven major trends involving business, technology, and training. The No. 2 trend was a shift to more emphasis on performance.[6] The No. 1 trend was structural change of the training function, which is often needed to support the shift to the performance improvement role.

This trend is evidenced by the professional organizations that support the performance improvement process. One major organization, the National Society for Performance and Instruction, has changed its name to the International Society for Performance Improvement (ISPI) to reflect this performance initiative. With more than 10,000 members, ISPI provides a variety of products and services to assist members in their quest to enhance performance in organizations.

Causes and Drivers

Many influences are driving this transition from training to a performance improvement role. The most significant and visible drivers are briefly reviewed below:

- The pressures of competition and the emphasis on efficiency and cost control in all organizations requires more efforts to improve employee performance. The need for formal methods to improve performance represents an important emerging role in businesses, which often ask their training and development departments to become involved in performance initiatives to improve or enhance employee performance.
- The analysis of training-program failure often leads to the conclusion that non-training solutions exist that should have been addressed or corrected for performance to improve. As part of continuous process improvement, the training and development function has addressed these issues. The result is a more formal performance assessment and analysis process. In most situations

where a performance problem exists, training is not the solution.[7] This leads to an awkward situation for most training staff members. Although non-training solutions are needed to correct a problem, the only services they can provide are training programs, which makes it difficult to resolve the problem. The problem must be handed off to some other organization or individual, leaving the client with unmet needs and unsolved problems. The training and development functions have now broadened the range of services they provide to include non-training solutions that complement training solutions.

- A significant amount of training is not transferred to the job, and often many other factors in the work environment must be altered, modified, removed, or minimized for the training to be applied properly. Because of this, many training and development functions have placed more emphasis on performance analysis. A performance improvement role requires more attention to the work environment, sometimes with changes focusing directly on modifications of the workplace, the environment, and support mechanisms. This essentially causes the training department to reach beyond the traditional role of developing programs to a broader role of resolving issues and removing performance inhibitors.
- Key executives and managers in the organization are more accepting of the process of performance improvement as a concept of a one-stop source of performance problems. The notion of a performance improvement function communicates that the emphasis is on improving organizational and departmental performance, something managers have desired for years.
- The implementation of a performance improvement department represents the integration of a variety of different issues, techniques, and elements to bring about radical improvements and changes in the organization. For example, the requirement for measurement and evaluation, including return on investment, causes some organizations to focus more attention on performance analysis to sort out the various causes of performance gaps.

These and other drivers have caused organizations to make the dramatic shift to performance improvement.

Trend Description

Models

Sometimes the first step in analyzing this trend is to examine a performance improvement model. In the ASTD study briefly described earlier, several important models were examined to arrive at what is ultimately labeled the ASTD Human Performance Improvement Process Model.[8] Figure 4-1 shows the simplified model developed in the study, representing six critical steps in the performance improvement process. In the first step, the performance problem or opportunity is thoroughly analyzed to identify a specific performance gap. This step includes an analysis of present performance compared with desired performance, as well as an analysis of the environment, systems, procedures, and processes. The impact of this gap is explored, as well as the cost of continuing with the problem or ignoring the opportunity.

The second step addresses the cause of the gap and examines a variety of potential causes, including reward systems, information flow, capabilites of employees, motivational environment, compensation arrangement, support mechanisms, culture, and local practices. The result is an identification of the specific cause or causes of the performance gap.

The third step is to select the appropriate interventions. Many ways are possible through which performance problems can be resolved, and these possibilities depend on the specific cause, the resources available, and the situation. Job description modifications, policy changes, compensation adjustments, reward systems changes, staffing level modifications, training and development, and implementation of new technology are all potential solutions.

In the fourth step, the performance improvement solution is implemented. The application of the solution may be as simple as changing practices and policies or as complicated as developing and enhancing skills and knowledge. Implementation is carefully scheduled with the appropriate resources, timing, and activities identified.

The fifth step involves managing the change process. The implementation is monitored and steps are taken to make sure the appropriate individuals receive necessary information and that key stake-

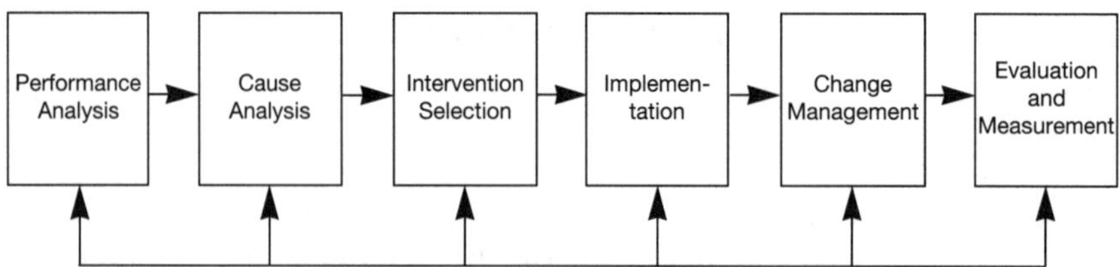

Figure 4-1. ASTD Human Performance Improvement Process Model.

holders are appropriately involved in the process. Building helpful support and buy-in from management and keeping the progress on schedule are critical issues for this step.

The last step, evaluation and measurement, is important and includes data collection through a variety of methods to measure the success of the performance improvement intervention. Different types of data are collected, both qualitative and quantitative, to determine the extent to which the performance improvement process has succeeded in implementing the performance improvement solution, changing job performance, and ultimately driving a positive business impact. Although the measurement and evaluation process is planned in advance, data are collected after process implementation, and the results are presented to key stakeholders.

This model represents a simplified version of the performance improvement process. It has the advantage of condensing a relatively complex process into a series of six steps. Also, it has the validity of development by experts in the field with input from many practitioners.

Paradigm Shift to Performance Improvement

The shift to performance improvement (PI) represents a significant change for all involved in traditional training and development. Table 4-1 represents sixteen important shifts often experienced when an organization transforms training and development into a performance improvement department.

These paradigm shifts represent several important changes in processes, practices, and procedures. The major issues are briefly described next.

Table 4-1
Paradigm Shift to Performance Improvement

Traditional Training Department Characterized by:	Performance Improvement Department Characterized by:
◆ No specific client relationship is established	◆ A client is served throughout the process
◆ No business need for the program	◆ Program linked to specific business needs
◆ No assessment of performance deficiencies	◆ Assessment of performance and causes
◆ Most problems have training solutions	◆ Non-training solutions are common
◆ Services organized around design and delivery	◆ Full range of services to improve performance
◆ Specific objectives focus on learning	◆ Program objectives focused on job performance and business impact
◆ No effort to prepare program participants to achieve results	◆ Results expectations communicated to participants and clients
◆ No effort to prepare the work environment to support transfer of learning	◆ Environment prepared to support transfer performance
◆ Typical job title includes the word *designer* or *trainer*	◆ Typical job title includes the words *performance consultant* or *performance technologist*
◆ Work activities focus on preparation and teaching	◆ Work activities focus on collaboration and consulting
◆ Communication outside the training department is limited	◆ Contacts outside the department are frequent and necessary
◆ No efforts to build partnerships with key managers	◆ Partnerships established with key managers and clients
◆ Department structure contains narrowly focused functions, such as development, delivery, and administration	◆ Department structure contains broad-based functions, such as analysis, consulting, design, and facilitation
◆ Department has a training label and usually reports to a human resource executive	◆ Department has a performance improvement label and usually reports to an operations executive
◆ No measurement of results or cost benefit analysis	◆ Measurement of results and cost benefit analyses are conducted regularly
◆ Planning and reporting on progress is input-focused or activity-based	◆ Planning and reporting on progress is output-focused or results-based

Performance Analysis. As described in the ASTD model, there must be a focus on the performance issues. Business needs must be identified, as well as the work performance issues. Not only are the gaps identified, but the causes are detailed. This is perhaps one of the most important elements of the performance analysis process, which represents a critical paradigm shift for the T&D staff. The result is a clear understanding of the business impact of the opportunity, the specific gaps that exist, and the causes of those gaps.

Solutions and Services. Because the training and development function is now preparing to offer a variety of non-training solutions, services are expanding—shifting from the traditional products centered on structured learning experiences to a full range of performance improvement possibilities. The categories for potential solutions and services can be quite broad, as evidenced by the potential solutions from a leading performance technology model, listed in Table 4-2.[9]

Table 4-2
Potential Solutions from a Performance Technology Model

◆ Coaching	◆ Job/work design
◆ Compensation	◆ Leadership/supervision
◆ Culture change	◆ Performance management
◆ Documentation	◆ Performance support
◆ Environmental engineering	◆ Staffing
◆ Health/wellness	◆ Team building
◆ Job aids	◆ Training/education

For organizations making the switch in the early stages of the performance improvement process, the range of services often is limited. Table 4-3 represents those offered by the PDIs at Rohm and Haas.[10]

Table 4-3
Sample Services PDI Can Provide

Service	Value
Organizational Goals and System Analysis	◆ Provides a check to ensure client's goals align with organizational needs ◆ Provides an overview of external trends, internal climate, and critical systems to help plan more effectively
Problem Analysis	◆ Helps identify the root causes (versus symptoms) of a performance problem so the correct problem is solved ◆ Determines the cost (versus payoff) of solving a problem ◆ Helps identify best solutions to performance problems
Benchmarking	◆ Identifies performance opportunities ◆ Sets standards ◆ Clarifies performance gaps
Performance and Competency Models	◆ Sets an expectation for required performance consistent with the needs of the organization ◆ Provides a performance management tool to increase productivity ◆ Supports alignment of activities with goals
Job and Task Analysis	◆ Supports procedure writing that ensures compliance with mandated regulations and laws ◆ Ensures that training addresses the needs of the job
Training Design and Development	◆ Ensures that training directly supports the solution ◆ Ensures performance improvement
Implementation of Electronic Training Management System	◆ Reduces training costs ◆ Ensures effectiveness of training ◆ Documents that individuals in each job are fully trained

(table continued on page 60)

Table 4-3 (continued)
Sample Services PDI Can Provide

Service	Value
Data Collection and Research	◆ Provides a broader picture of the environment to minimize unexpected performance demands ◆ Provides a more definite understanding of performance issues ◆ Provides baseline data to determine specific impacts
Individual Coaching/ Performance Improvement	◆ Helps identify skill deficiencies and other barriers to successful performance ◆ Identifies strategies between preferred and current proficiencies ◆ Helps bring about a transformation in performance
Evaluation (Impact of Training and Related Efforts on Bottom-Line)	◆ Determines payback for investment of training dollars ◆ Determines whether new skills are being used appropriately
Goals	◆ Provides opportunity to correct problems through ongoing evaluation ◆ Identifies impact on individual performance and organizational effectiveness

Preparation and Expectation. Another important paradigm shift focuses on preparing for the actual intervention or solution, whether a training or non-training solution. Part of the process comes from the specific objectives that are developed to focus on application and business impact. These objectives clearly define what specific changes must be made and what corresponding improvement is expected, moving the process beyond the traditional learning objectives of the training and development function. The designers of the solution, whether a training or non-training solution, will clearly note what changes are expected and the subsequent impact desired. These expectations are communicated directly to participants, as well as clients and others who are directly involved in the process. In addition, the environment is adjusted to support the transfer to the job, whatever the solution. The support groups in the environment are prepared to accept, support, and nurture what was learned so that on-the-job success will be realized, ultimately.

Work Activities and Roles. Work activities change significantly with this paradigm shift. Traditional activities typically focused on conducting a needs assessment, developing and designing materials for a learning experience, and delivering the learning solution in an effective way. The new role focuses on collaboration and consulting. Consequently, job titles now include the words *performance consultant* or *performance technologist,* instead of *designer* or *trainer.* Table 4-4 shows a complete listing of the competencies in the ASTD Human Performance Improvement Process Model. The table lists a total of thirty-eight competencies, with the first fifteen associated with the core competencies involving all human performance improvements. The remaining twenty-three focus on four key roles identified by the ASTD panel of experts: analyst, intervention specialist, change manager, and evaluator. These differ vastly from the traditional training and development roles and titles.

(text continued on page 66)

Table 4-4
Core Competencies Associated with All Performance Improvement Work

1. Industry awareness:	Understanding the vision, strategy, goals, and culture of an industry; linking human performance improvement interventions to organizational goals
2. Leadership skills:	Knowing how to lead or influence others positively to achieve desired work results
3. Interpersonal relationship skills:	Working effectively with others to achieve common goals, and exercising effective interpersonal influence
4. Technological awareness and understanding:	Using existing or new technology and different types of software and hardware; understanding performance support systems, and applying them as appropriate
5. Problem-solving skills:	Detecting performance gaps, and helping other people discover ways to close performance gaps in the present and future; closing performance gaps between actual and ideal performance

(table continued on page 62)

Table 4-4 (continued)
Core Competencies Associated with All Performance Improvement Work

6. Systems thinking and understanding:	Identifying inputs, throughputs, and outputs of a subsystem, system, or suprasystem, and applying that information to improved human performance; realizing the implications of interventions on many parts of an organization, process, or individual; taking steps to address any side effects of human performance improvement interventions
7. Performance understanding:	Distinguishing between activities and results; recognizing implications, outcomes, and consequences
8. Knowledge of interventions:	Demonstrating an understanding of the many ways human performance can be improved in organizational settings; showing how to apply specific human performance improvement interventions to close existing or anticipated performance gaps
9. Business understanding:	Demonstrating awareness of the inner workings of business functions and how business decisions affect financial or non-financial work results
10. Organization understanding:	Seeing organizations as dynamic, political, economic, and social systems that have multiple goals; using this larger perspective as a framework for understanding and influencing events and change
11. Negotiating/contracting skills:	Organizing, preparing, overseeing, and evaluating work performed by vendors, contingent workers, or outsourcing agents
12. Buy-in/advocacy skills:	Building ownership or support for change among affected individuals, groups, and other stakeholders
13. Coping skills:	Knowing how to deal with ambiguity and how to handle the stress resulting from change and from multiple meanings or possibilities

Table 4-4 (continued) Core Competencies Associated with All Performance Improvement Work

14. Ability to see "big picture":	Looking beyond details to see overarching goals and results
15. Consulting skills:	Understanding the results that stakeholders desire from a process, and providing insight into how efficiently and effectively those results can be achieved

Competencies Associated with Specific Roles

There are also specific competencies associated with each role played by those involved in human performance improvement work.

Role 1: Analyst

16. Performance analysis skills (front-end analysis):	Comparing actual and ideal performance in order to identify performance gaps or opportunities
17. Needs analysis survey design and development skills (open-ended and structured):	Preparing written (mail), oral (phone), or electronic (e-mail) surveys using open-ended (essay) and closed (scaled) questions to identify human performance improvement needs
18. Competency identification skills:	Identifying the knowledge and skill requirements of teams, jobs, tasks, roles, and work
19. Questioning skills:	Gathering pertinent information to stimulate insight in individuals and groups through use of interviews and other probing methods
20. Analytical skills (synthesis):	Breaking down the components of a larger whole, and reassembling them to achieve improved human performance
21. Work environment analytical skills:	Examining work environments for issues or characteristics affecting human performance

Table 4-4 (continued)
Core Competencies Associated with All Performance Improvement Work

Role 2: Intervention Specialist	
22. Performance information interpretation skills:	Finding useful meaning from the results of performance analysis, and helping performers, performers' managers, process owners, and other stakeholders to do so
23. Intervention selection skills:	Selecting human performance improvement interventions that address the root cause(s) of performance gaps rather than symptoms or side effects
24. Performance change interpretation skills:	Forecasting and analyzing the effects of interventions and their consequences
25. Ability to assess relationships among interventions:	Examining the effects of multiple human performance improvement interventions on parts of an organization, as well as the effects on the organization's interactions with customers, suppliers, distributors, and workers
26. Ability to identify critical business issues and changes:	Determining key business issues, and applying that information during the implementation of a human performance improvement intervention
27. Goal implementation skills:	Ensuring that goals are converted effectively into actions to close existing or pending performance gaps; getting results despite conflicting priorities, lack of resources, or ambiguity

Role 3: Change Manager	
28. Change-impetus skills:	Determining what the organization should do to address the cause(s) of a human performance gap at present and in the future
29. Communication channel, informal network, and alliance understanding:	Knowing how communication moves through an organization by various channels, networks, and alliances; building such channels, networks, and alliances to achieve improvements in productivity and performance

Table 4-4 (continued)
Core Competencies Associated with All Performance Improvement Work

Role 3: Change Manager	
30. Group dynamics process understanding:	Understanding how groups function; influencing people so that group, work, and individual needs are addressed
31. Process consultation skills:	Observing individuals and groups for their interactions and the effects of their interactions with others
32. Facilitation skills:	Helping performers, performers' managers, process owners, and stakeholders discover new insights

Role 4: Evaluator	
33. Performance gap evaluation skills:	Measuring or helping others measure the difference between actual and ideal performance
34. Ability to evaluate results against organizational goals:	Assessing how well the results of a human performance improvement intervention match intentions
35. Standard-setting skills:	Measuring desired results of organizations, processes, or individuals; helping others establish and measure work expectations
36. Ability to assess impact on culture:	Examining the effects of human performance gaps and human performance improvement interventions on shared beliefs and assumptions about "right" and "wrong" ways of behaving and acting in an organizational setting
37. Human performance improvement intervention reviewing skills:	Finding ways to evaluate and continuously improve human performance improvement interventions before and during implementation
38. Feedback skills:	Collecting information about performance, and feeding it back clearly, specifically, and on a timely basis to affected individuals or groups

(text continued from page 61)

Relationships. Shifting to the performance improvement role results in more focus on building relationships. Inherent with the process is the relationship with the client who desires or needs the performance improvement. The client/consultant relationship flourishes throughout the process. The stakeholders, who have an important concern for or interest in the process, often are routinely involved in communication, information sharing, and problem-solving activities. Performance improvement team members build relationships and use them effectively to solve problems, provide analysis, and implement solutions. The performance improvement specialists must communicate effectively as relationships are built. Because the new roles involve new processes, key stakeholders must understand what the phrase *performance improvement* means and their role in the success of the

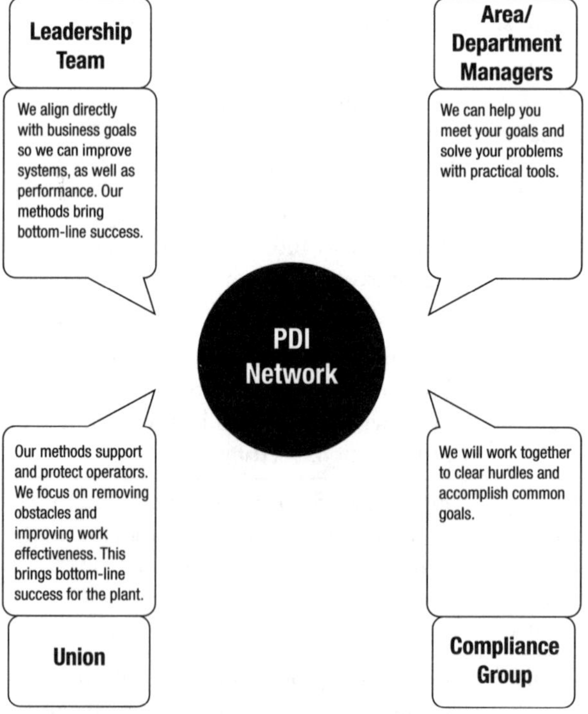

Figure 4-2. *Target Audiences and Key Messages.*

process. For example, in the Rohm and Haas transformation, it was critical for the PDIs to communicate key messages to target audiences. Figure 4-2 shows the four target audiences for these messages and the key message for each audience.

Structure. The structure of the training and development function shifts as the performance improvement role is undertaken. Figure 4-3 shows the structure of a traditional training and development department. This traditional department has analysts who often conduct needs assessments and evaluations, with designers and developers producing or purchasing structured learning programs. Facilitators conduct the programs and coordinators keep the programs organized.

In the performance improvement structure depicted in Figure 4-4, the roles are different. The performance analysis and design group analyzes the gaps and causes, as well as designing or developing the appropriate interventions to solve the problem. Performance consultants implement the solution, sometimes facilitating the process and keeping the process on track throughout implementation. Evaluation is separate, containing the independent and objective evaluation team.

Evaluation. In the performance improvement function, evaluation operates similarly to that role in the training and development function. The primary difference is that an evaluation in a performance improvement function usually includes business impact and job performance data within a five-level evaluation framework.[11] (The levels

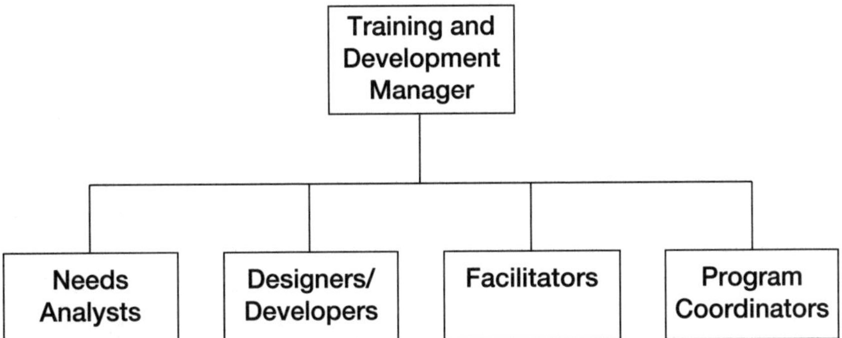

Figure 4-3. *A Structure for a Traditional Training and Development Department.*

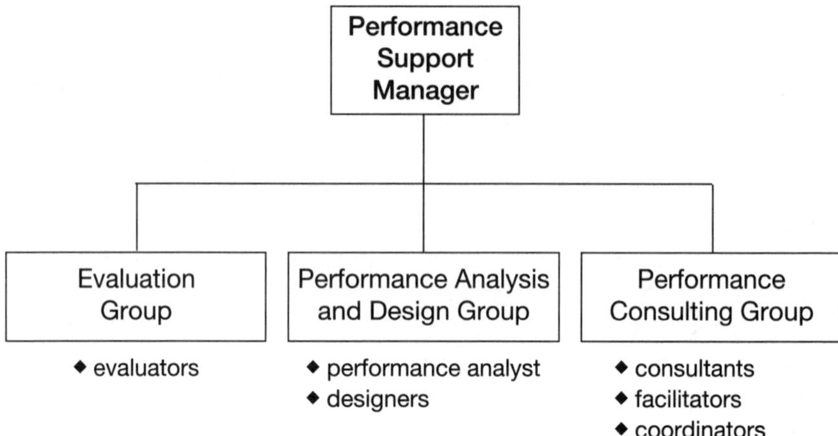

Figure 4-4. *A Structure for a Performance Support Department.*

of evaluation are presented in Chapter 8.) A traditional evaluation stops with reaction data, Level 1. PI evaluators track business impact measures, performance and implementation measures, learning measures, and reaction measures to provide a full range of evaluation information. They also must report these data to a variety of target audiences.

Trend Consequences

Impact

This trend may be slow to develop in some organizations, and some training and development managers actually resist it. The resistance is a function of the current success and perception of the training and development function. In other words, if an organization perceives that its T&D department is ineffective, makes little contribution to the bottom line, and shows no measures of success, that department will have difficulty making a case to expand its role.

This trend often creates a dilemma for training and development departments. On a positive note, the training function expands its range of services to include a variety of non-training solutions. Team members assume different roles with key managers in the organization. However, many training staff members are not equipped for these new roles and are not allowed to offer some of the non-training solutions, such as compensation. Consequently, this process often involves gradual policy changes.[12]

The most significant impact is that new skills must be acquired. A review of the competencies outlined in the ASTD model (see Table 4-4) emphasizes the skills and knowledge the T&D staff needs to be successful with this process. This shift will require substantial training for the staff and, in some cases, may require employing new staff with the required skills. Above all, trainers must become performance technologists.

For some trainers, these new roles may be a radical departure from existing habits. To these seasoned trainers, every performance problem appears to have a training solution, and it may be tempting for them to continue to train when non-training solutions are needed. Consequently, the transition often occurs slowly with much involvement from the staff.

The training and development staff members must learn more about the organization and its problems, opportunities, and performance issues. They must learn the language of operating managers and be able to converse regularly with this group. They must know case strategies, organizational goals, and the current statuses of many projects in the organization. They need to understand how various solutions can help or hinder certain problems and causes.

The training and development staff must communicate the new process to a variety of stakeholders, particularly key managers and clients who need to understand the new approach and framework and what it means to them. Without good explanations and understanding, as well as demonstrations, managers may become skeptical about the process and view it as a new fad floating through the organization.[13] Because the shift from training to performance improvement represents a shift in mind-set and attitude, as well as the development of a new process and set of skills, managers may resist the shift. When a manager asks for a specific training program and the response is an analysis that leads to a non-training solution, some frustration may surface with the manager, particularly if he or she does not understand the process. The key is to communicate routinely and accurately so that resistance is minimized.[14]

Key Questions

The challenge of this issue can be summarized in one preliminary question: Does the training and development department want to be in the performance improvement business? If so, the trend must be managed and coordinated with a decisive timetable. These key questions can be helpful in reaching this decision.

Key Questions

1. To what extent do I agree this is a trend?
2. How important is this trend?
3. How much progress has been made with this trend in my organization?
4. Do I support this trend?
5. Do the key management groups support this trend?
6. What specific skills are needed? Will additional staff need to be added, or can the competencies be built through training and development?
7. What happens if I do nothing?
8. Does top management support this trend?
9. What additional funding, if any, is required to support this trend?
10. What barriers exist in implementing this trend?
11. What specific non-training solutions do I want to offer?
12. How can non-training solutions, not under our control, be handed off to others?

Outlook

This trend will continue during the next few years as organizations look for new ways to improve productivity and boost competitiveness. Not only will the drivers continue to influence the shift to performance, but the benefits of implementing a performance improvement process will be significant. In many cases, this shift reflects a more efficient process by avoiding unnecessary training programs when training is not the solution. Because the intervention focuses directly on business problems, the results are usually significant, desired, and welcomed by the key managers in the organization. Because the true causes of performance will be identified, the chances of improving or overcoming the performance gap are greatly enhanced.

This process also aligns the training and development function more closely with the strategic initiatives of the company and with the key operating executives, greatly enhancing the success of new efforts and initiatives. Additional significant benefits coupled with the increased drivers for the shift almost guarantee that this trend is here to stay.

References

1. Miller, Kathleen. "Reinventing HRD: From Training to Performance Consulting," in *In Action: Leading Organizational Change.* Elwood F. Holton and Jack J. Phillips (Eds.), Alexandria, Va.: American Society for Training and Development, 1997, p. 41.
2. Rothwell, William J. *Model for Human Performance Improvement: Roles, Competencies, and Outputs.* Alexandria, Va.: American Society for Training and Development, 1996, pp. 18–19.
3. Bassi, Laurie J., Benson, George, and Cheney, Scott. "Position Yourself for the Future: The Ten Trends Most Likely to Affect Your Future." Alexandria, Va.: American Society for Training and Development, 1997.
4. Fuller, Jim. *Management Performance Improvement Projects.* San Francisco: Pfeiffer, 1997.
5. Williams, Teresa and Green, Adrian. *A Business Approach to Training.* London: Gower Publishing, 1997.
6. Shandler, Donald. *Reengineering the Training Function: How to Align Training with the New Corporate Agenda.* Delray Beach, Fla.: St. Lucie Press, 1996.
7. Bassi, Benson, and Cheney.
8. Rothwell pp. 18–19.
9. Rosenberg, Marc J. "Human Performance Technology," in *Training and Development Handbook.* Robert L. Craig (Ed.), New York: McGraw-Hill, 1996.
10. Miller p. 41.
11. Phillips, Jack J. *Return on Investment in Training and Performance Improvement Programs.* Houston, Tex.: Gulf Publishing Company, 1997.

12. Robinson, Dana Gaines and Robinson, James C. *Performance Consulting: Moving Beyond Training*. San Francisco: Berrett-Koehler Publishers, 1995.

13. Rummler, Geary. "In Search of the Holy Performance Grail," in *The ASTD Training and Development Handbook,* 4th ed. Robert L. Craig (Ed.), New York: McGraw-Hill, 1996.

14. Langley, Gerald J., et al. *The Performance Improvement Guide: A Practical Approach to Enhancing Organizational Performance.* San Francisco: Jossey-Bass Publishing, 1996.

5

CORPORATE UNIVERSITIES

Trend Definition and Validation

Brief Definition of Trend

Organizations around the globe continue to adopt the corporate university (CU) concept. Although the term *university* may conjure up a vision of a large campus with tenured faculty and a variety of academic programs, the corporate counterpart is much different. The CU concept is a process—not necessarily a place—where all levels of employees, and sometimes customers and suppliers, participate in a variety of learning experiences necessary to improve job performance and enhance business impact. The rationale for developing corporate universities varies. In some settings, the traditional training and development function has been converted to, and sometimes just labeled, a corporate university. At the extreme, some organizations have created a corporate university to meet specific challenges and address change. Although this trend began in North America, it has spread to Europe and Asia and, to a limited extent, the rest of the world.

Case Studies: The Rover Group and Walt Disney Company

The Rover Group. In Great Britain, the Rover Group is committed to becoming the top automobile company in Europe. To achieve this ambitious goal, Rover management realized it must essentially alter the culture of the company. Consequently, in 1990 it launched the Rover Learning Business Group, a corporate university operated as a separate learning company with an annual budget of more than $50 million.[1] With the task of training more than 40,000 employees, the Rover Learning Business Group (LBG) developed several key strategies:

- The Rover Group is renowned in Europe for attracting, retaining, and developing people. The LBG will be an integral part of this strategy.
- The LBG underscores the view that people are the company's greatest assets, as demonstrated in a variety of ways.
- The presence of a corporate university shows employees that the company's commitment to each individual has increased substantially.
- Rover provides recognition to employees as they develop the talents and then use the talents on the job. The LBG will assist in providing this recognition.
- The LBG provides employees an opportunity to earn recognition for their training and education with accreditation from appropriate organizations.
- The LBG improves the competitiveness of the company.

In the early 1980s, the Rover Group was a pioneer in the establishment of open learning as it set up open-learning centers at each of its manufacturing sites. In addition to a variety of training and development programs, the learning centers also provide career counseling and opportunities for face-to-face interaction regarding a variety of career development possibilities.

Rover pays for all training related to the job, but it also subsidizes employees for off-the-job training, even when the learning experience may not be directly related to the job. For example, through the program called Rover Employees Assisted Learning (REAL), up to $175 per year is available to each employee for non-work-related learning experiences. The company feels that the employee will be a better person after taking these courses.

The training and development delivery may be accomplished in one of several ways. Programs may be delivered through in-house facilities, outside providers (such as local universities and colleges), or custom-designed facilities near the work site.

Walt Disney Company. Disney University was established more than forty years ago and is one of the oldest corporate universities. Disney University's ability to stay ahead of the competition on issues related to training, performance, and employee motivation has made it one of the most admired and emulated training organizations in the world.[2] Today it continues to break ground in human performance improvement partially because of the challenges presented to the Walt Disney Company by its growth. Disney World in Orlando, Florida, alone hires 20,000 new employees (cast members) each year, placing unprecedented demands on training. At the same time, the university offers a variety of programs externally through a for-profit operation. Walt Disney wanted to share his business philosophies, which resulted in improved customer service and employee satisfaction. In turn, that led to the creation of Disney University, which the company claims is the first corporate university in the world.

Disney University is centralized within the company's headquarters with many classrooms for training cast members who come to this location. It is also decentralized, as satellite campuses are in place throughout business units across the Disney properties. This decentralization allows cast members to take part in programs near where they will be working with other team members.

Training for new cast members begins early. Pride building starts on Day 1 as every new hire in the theme park spends the first two days on the job at the Disney Traditions Class. Here, new cast members learn about Disney's history, philosophy, and concept for quality guest service. This class is required for every new employee, regardless of level or status. Beyond that, Disney provides a variety of programs involving leadership, management, customer service, quality, and innovation.

Evidence of Trend

The corporate university is highly visible in many organizations. Because of the nature and scope of the concept, many corporate universities are well known to the business community and to other training and development professionals. For example, Motorola University from the Motorola Corporation, Hamburger University from McDonald's, and Disney University from Walt Disney Company are examples of high-profile corporate universities. These universities have become symbols of excellence in training and development, and at times the images of the universities are, often by design, difficult to separate from the images of their companies. Several studies have confirmed the tremendous growth in the corporate university context.[3]

The practitioner survey of global trends revealed that the corporate university concept is a visible trend. Practitioners agreed with the existence of the trend in a score of 3.89 out of 5 (see Appendix 1). Survey respondents rated the importance of the trend 4.01 out of a total of 5, the lowest of the sixteen trends. Still, training and development practitioners view the corporate university as a significant trend that has made significant progress in recent years and that shows additional progress on the horizon. As early as 1985, at least 400 corporate universities existed in North America alone.[4] Since then, on a global scale, that figure could probably be multiplied by ten.

In a major study of universities throughout the world, *The Economist,* a leading business and economic publication from Great Britain, highlighted the importance of the corporate university movement.[5] In discussing the various problems associated with traditional universities and their statuses, the study noted that many large business firms have now created corporate universities, which in part have replaced some of the needs for the traditional university concept. Many corporate universities offer the same services and products as public and private educational institutions, while other corporate universities are only labels.

A study conducted by Deloitte & Touche, one of the big five global accounting and consulting firms, revealed the growing interest in application of corporate universities.[6] Not only did the study show a global proliferation of the corporate university concept, it also showed that those organizations with corporate universities are more successful and the corporate university programs are more likely to be related to strategy as a traditional T&D function.

Another study, conducted by Maritz Performance Improvement and reported in the book, *Learning Partnerships: How Leading Companies Implement Organizational Learning,* revealed the extent and impact of the corporate university process. The study showed that most major organizations have developed a corporate university concept and are converting the training process into a lifelong learning system. According to this study, even the term *corporate university* suggests a scope and sense of a system that wasn't there before the corporate university was implemented, as organizations try to organize and deliver training and development in a more effective, efficient, and systematic way.

The popularity of the corporate university is underscored by the presence of a professional publication devoted exclusively to individuals who are involved in a corporate university. *Corporate University Review,* published six times per year with a circulation of about 30,000, explores topics dealing with the design, development, and improvement of corporate universities. Each issue features several corporate universities, explaining their unique features, challenges, and successes. *Corporate University Review* also publishes current trends and research results that relate to the development of the corporate university concept.8 In addition, major conferences have been developed around the corporate university concept. For example, in a recent two-day conference labeled "Launching and Managing a Corporate University," twenty corporate universities, including those from Sears, AT&T, Amoco, and NCR, presented their recipes for success.[9]

From almost every angle, the evidence is overwhelming that the corporate university concept has spread throughout the world. It has become a fixture in professional training and development in many progressive organizations.

Causes and Drivers

The continued development of the corporate university concept is linked to several of the trends in this book. To a certain degree, the different types of corporate universities that exist today are a reflection of the drivers for the CU concept. The following eight types of corporate universities have evolved because of the drivers that led to the development of the concept.

- In this type of corporate university, CU label is used to bring a higher profile to employee training and development efforts. This approach is sometimes undertaken to increase management support and commitment to the training and development process or to demonstrate to the organization the importance of training and development. Sometimes the training and development staff initiates the conversion to bring more respect to the function. In other cases, sales and marketing staff members may initiate the CU to use it as a showcase in marketing and sales efforts. For example, the corporate university may appear in ads and TV commercials. In a few situations, a corporate university may be a personal project of a top executive who wants a monument to his or her achievements or a legacy to reflect his or her contribution to the organization. Finally, in other situations, the quality function initiates the CU concept as a primary vehicle for presenting quality programs. This type of corporate university, based on the rationale for its development, may represent nothing more than a name change. However, it can still produce some important benefits.
- An attempt to centralize all the training and development functions, at least in a loosely organized way, has led to the development of some corporate universities. As organizations have grown and functions have expanded, training and development units have been created in all parts of the organization, sometimes leading to inefficiencies, duplications, and inconsistencies in training and development standards. To regain some control of a decentralized training and development process, a CU is formed with connection to one individual or one entity. Concurrent with this type of arrangement is often an attempt to make the process more systematic, consistent, and efficient as training is delivered throughout the organization. Sometimes the delivery is still decentralized while design, development, policies, and standards are centralized.
- A few training and development groups want to broaden their scope of operations and offer a variety of programs, some with external college credit and others through alliances with schools

and universities. For example, Dana University, created for the Dana Corporation, the largest automobile parts supplier for North America, represents this type of university.[10] Dana has more than 46,000 employees, as well as sales of $7.6 billion. Dana University offers a wide variety of programs, including an accredited MBA program. The university has a business school, a technical school, a customer school, and an industrial school. This broadened scope has been labeled a corporate university because of its complexity and its similarity to the traditional university setting.

- Some organizations are very pleased with their exceptional customer service, outstanding quality, or unique culture and philosophy. To reinforce and perpetuate this philosophy, they develop and implement the corporate university. This ensures a continued adherence to certain cherished beliefs and values throughout the organization. Disney University is an example of this type of corporate university as it attempts to maintain the tradition established in the early years by its founder, Walt Disney.
- Some organizations develop corporate universities to drive the business by improving sales, building relationships with customers, strengthening ties with suppliers, and contributing to productivity and profitability growth. A desire to enhance business results is the principal force behind the development of the corporate university, and the connection between the university concept and results is taken on faith. An example of this type of university is Land Rover University (LRU), located in Lanham, Maryland. Land Rover makes popular luxury four-wheel drive vehicles, and its sales are growing at a phenomenal 40 percent annual rate.[11] To support this type of growth and ensure that customers connect to the enthusiasm for driving an off-road vehicle, the company created LRU.
- In some situations, a company needs significant change. When the old paradigm is not working, this signals that major restructuring, reengineering, and transformation are in order, and the company develops a corporate university to initiate and manage these major changes. An industry where this is occurring is the electric utility industry. Once a regulated monopoly, the electric utility industry is now deregulated in many countries, causing

utility companies to face stiff competition, unlike the previous environment. As a result, employees must become more customer-focused, examine ways to be innovative and creative, control costs to become more efficient, and develop ways to diversify new product lines. These changes require a significant paradigm shift, and corporate universities are perceived to be the vehicle to make these changes. An example is TVA University in Knoxville, Tennessee. The Tennessee Valley Authority (TVA) is the nation's largest producer of electricity and wants to become the world's leading provider of energy and related services. To realize this vision, TVA must create a work force that is flexible, resourceful, and in tune with strategic objectives. Thus, TVA University was created.[12] TVA University serves the company's 16,000 employees and, through a variety of programs and innovative services, helps employees improve job performance to remain valuable, essential assets and to redirect their energies to create new products and services in the future.

- Because of the tremendous interest in the concept of the learning organization, some organizations have broadened their approaches to learning, making it a continuous part of work life. These organizations have corporate universities with the word *learning* in the names because of the emphasis on learning instead of training. The net result is a full array of learning activities for employees in the classroom, on the job through mentors, off the job in colleges and universities, and at home through the Internet. This approach has also led to innovative processes, bringing learning to the center stage of work. In many of these companies, the learning organization and corporate university concepts merge into one. For example, Bank of Montreal Learning Institute is the corporate university for Bank of Montreal, a large bank with 35,000 employees. The learning institute provides a variety of learning solutions to professional and management employees in a variety of ways, from classroom training to on-the-job assignments and through the use of technology. Bank of Montreal recognizes that learning is its only competitive advantage as it strives to become a full-service North American bank.
- Finally, on a few more occasions, corporate universities have been created to develop the organization of the future. The pur-

pose of this type of corporate university is to act as the primary force for driving and shaping the corporation. For this approach to function properly, it must be supported by top executives and must offer the ideal environment. Upon exploration of situations, the corporate university becomes a safe house or laboratory for questioning, wondering, exploring, and perhaps most importantly, challenging the current business situation. Through a critical mass of externally and internally focused data, coupled with experiential process and support, a few organizations have brought the corporate university concept to this level. Some argue that Motorola University has taken this role in its efforts to develop the business.[13]

Collectively, these drivers have resulted in eight types of corporate universities. In reality, some corporate universities will have overlaps of different types. Developing the university concept is not an easy task. It often involves a complex set of issues, concerns, and tasks, described next.

Trend Description

Basic Issues

As corporate universities evolve and new ones develop, several issues must be addressed regarding core structure and policy. The most critical issues are explored here.

Scope and Mission. One of the first decisions made when developing the CU involves determining the scope and mission. A mission statement is usually developed with input from executives and other key stakeholders. Motorola University was developed to support Motorola and is a respected corporate university with an eighteen-year history and a reputation for being adaptive and flexible, as well as a driver of many basic processes and changes at Motorola. Motorola University's mission has evolved over the years, and its policies, processes, tools, and resources have also evolved. The current mission is:

> To be a major catalyst for change and continuous improvement and support of the corporation's business objectives. We

will provide our clients the best value, leading-edge training and education solutions and systems in order to be their preferred partner in developing a best-in-class work force.[14]

Compliance with the mission will usually add to the scope of programs offered. The typical scope of high-profile corporate universities includes:

- Basic skills and technical training
- Competency base of training and development among major job classes
- Processes and mechanisms to develop shared values and beliefs of the organization
- A variety of partnerships with customers, suppliers, universities, and other significant groups to enhance the success of the organization
- A laboratory for enhancing the quality of training, learning, and performance improvement through a variety of strategic initiatives.

Key Principles. While high-profile, successful corporate universities enjoy many differences, they seem to share many key principles. One major study of fifty successful and high-profile corporate universities identified the following key principles as the foundation of the university infrastructure.[15]

1. Link learning to the strategic needs of the business.
2. Consider the university model to be a process rather than a place.
3. Design a curriculum to incorporate corporate citizenship, contextual framework, and competencies.
4. Train the entire customer/supply value chain, including key customers, product suppliers, and schools that provide tomorrow's employees.
5. Experiment with new ways of reinforcing and transferring learning.
6. Move from instructor-led training to multiple formats of delivering learning.
7. Encourage leaders to be involved with and to facilitate learning.

8. Move from the corporate allocation funding model to self-funding by business units.
9. Assume a global focus in developing learning solutions.
10. Create a measurement system to evaluate outputs, as well as inputs.
11. Utilize the corporate university for competitive advantage and entry into new markets.

Leadership/Governance. A board of directors, board of trustees, board of advisors, or leadership council governs most corporate universities. These advisory groups usually consist of top managers or executives who are deliberately taking an active role in developing the university and maintaining its effectiveness. Figure 5-1 shows the governance structure for Motorola University including the different groups that provide input, specify requirements, and provide feedback. The Motorola board of trustees, made up of senior corporate managers, formulates policies, sets priorities, and allocates resources to the joint ventures of the education and training community.[16] The board reviews Motorola University's performance against strategic plans and formulates action plans accordingly. The regional boards, made up of senior corporate managers, provide geographically specific information, which is combined with additional input from Motorola business units to define and deliver the highest quality and value in training and educational products.

The head of the corporate university may have the title of president, dean, or director. In many cases, the corporate university leader is a key executive with demonstrated success in operations or allied functions in the organization. For example, when General Motors (GM) created the General Motors University in 1997, GM officials appointed Richard "Skip" LeFauve to run the university. Previously, Skip was president of Saturn Corporation, which developed the small international automobile with an impressive reputation for efficiency and customer satisfaction. Because of his record of exceptional experience as an operations executive who built the Saturn organization, GM tapped Skip for this unique challenge. In this position, Skip will report directly to the vice chairman of the board of directors. In making this announcement, GM indicated that it would assemble all of its training and resources under one organization to create the corporate

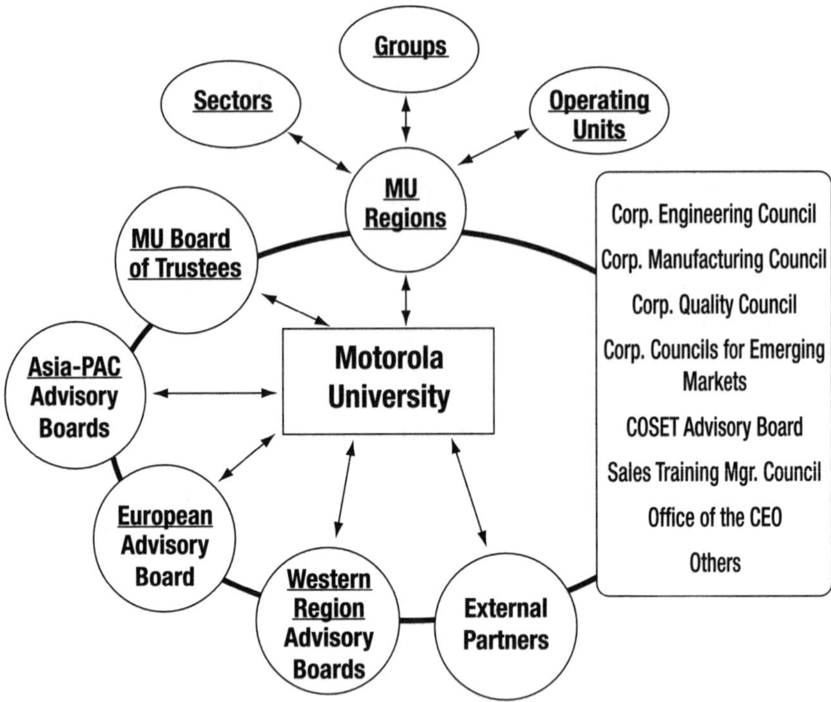

Figure 5-1. Leadership Team for Motorola University.

university. This move by one of the world's largest companies to create one of the world's largest corporate universities demonstrates the importance of training and development in the corporate world.

Structure. Some corporate universities are structured functionally around products and services delivered or offered by the corporate university—for example, technical training, leadership development, performance consulting services, customer service, team development, and professional development. Others organize around product lines of the organization. For example, a corporate university from a large international bank is divided into four colleges, supporting basic product lines: the commercial bank, the investment bank, the consumer bank, and the trust bank. Other structures often follow traditional organization of the training and development function but can vary with policies and practices of the organization. For example, the extent to which training and development is centralized or decentralized can dictate the corporate university structure.

Policy. The corporate university leadership, in concert with the governing boards or committees, must set the basic policies of the university. Some policies are broad, to provide a fundamental direction; others are more detailed, exploring specific issues and processes to be addressed. For example, policies define the extent to which the corporate university is decentralized. Centralized design and development of programs with decentralized delivery and implementation is common. Another issue is the make-versus-buy decisions for major programs. In some situations, it is more cost-effective to purchase most programs while developing only those unique programs necessary to support the corporate mission and values. Still another typical policy decision involves staffing levels, including the type of faculty. Most corporate universities recruit faculty from the operating areas, either as rotational assignments or on part-time duty. This approach increases the effectiveness of the programs and increases the relevance of training and learning while conserving resources. Other policies may focus on the experience and competencies of the staff, as well as the specific standards of program development, delivery, and follow-up evaluation.

Location. The location of corporate universities is crucial, and many companies often place them at or near the headquarters facilities. Other companies prefer their CUs to be in remote, peaceful settings to facilitate learning and minimize distractions, usually in a large campus environment. Examples include Xerox's Document University, Andersen Consulting's Center for Professional Education, and McDonalds' Hamburger University. Still in others, the corporate university is located throughout major facilities with a small headquarters staff to provide policy and coordination. For example, Nortel Learning Institute, supporting Northern Telecom, has a small headquarters staff in Toronto, Canada, with most of the learning institute staff located in major facilities throughout the organization. These basic issues must be addressed appropriately, after careful consideration, to ensure that the corporate university meets the needs of the organization. And from the beginning, the corporate university is developed the way the senior executive team has planned.

What to Teach. Corporate universities offer a variety of programs, usually covering a small number of categories. These categories often are grouped into corporate citizenship, conceptual framework, and core competencies.

The corporate citizenship category focuses on developing the culture of the organization by offering programs and activities that underscore its values, traditions, and beliefs. For example, Intel University (supporting Intel) offers a string of programs aimed at developing values such as:

- **What Makes Intel Intel?**—A four-hour course about history, products, and culture
- **Intel's Operating Philosophy and Economics**—A three-hour course about corporate objectives and finance
- **All About Intel: Marketing and the Customer**—A four-hour course covering key markets, customers, and distribution
- **Intel Management by Objectives**—A four-hour course in which employees learn to write performance objectives
- **All About Intel: Performance and Systems Manufacturing**—A four-hour course that takes Intel employees through the manufacturing process
- **All About Intel: The Intel Product Line**—A four-hour course that explains product development
- **The Intel Culture Course**—An eight-hour course examining Intel's unique culture, values, and philosophy.[17]

These innovative programs usually involve all employees and are unique for that organization.

The conceptual framework category focuses on basic business issues, including the industry and competition. It describes key customers and product lines and often focuses on the best practices in the industry, including those who exhibit best practices. These programs attempt to stimulate the desire to build world-class, or best-in-class, practices for the organization.

Core competencies can vary but often fall into the categories of learning skills, basic skills, personal skills, business language, creative thinking and problem solving, leadership and visioning, and self-development and self-management.

Building Partnerships

The corporate university develops partnerships with a variety of groups. As shown in Figure 5-2, as many as eight groups are identified and developed. Partnering with employees and with managers is traditional in most corporate university settings. CU leadership recognizes that the university programs will not succeed unless employees take the initiative and assume the responsibility for their own learning and development. Consequently, some corporate universities develop detailed statements regarding the responsibilities of the CU, employees, and managers. Some even develop formal written agreements requiring signatures of employees, university representatives, and managers. This helps clarify basic concerns and confusion about responsibilities and places much of the burden for learning on those who can make it happen—employees and their managers.

Figure 5-2. Potential Partnership Arrangements.

Customers represent a growing target group of a corporate university. Some organizations, such as Motorola and Xerox, have discovered a critical need to provide training for customers, and consequently the corporate university provides customer education and training. Working with this critical part of a business brings the corporate university directly into the supplier-customer chain. These companies realize that successful training provides a competitive edge and brings the customer closer to the organization's product, processes, and philosophy.

Training suppliers is perhaps one of the newest partnerships to develop, and one of the most comprehensive processes comes from Saturn University. The automaker launched a complete curriculum for suppliers, which is available for the more than 300 suppliers that provide products directly to the company.[18] Typical courses include:

- Introduction to Saturn Culture
- Doing Business with Saturn
- Obtaining Quality, Piece-by-Piece
- Decision Making
- Packaging for Saturn Suppliers
- Value Management
- Equal Partners Program
- Value Change Analysis
- Dedicated Logistics and Transportation System
- Manufacturing Gain
- Leadership and Team-Building

These and other programs provide an opportunity to enhance the success and quality of the supplier, bringing the supplier closer to the company's philosophy and values.

Colleges and universities offer excellent sources of talent and resources for corporate universities. Vocational and secondary schools provide a stream of qualified new employees to staff plant and service locations. Many corporate universities partner with local colleges or universities to offer specialized courses, non-credit courses, and specialized degree programs. Some even offer advanced degrees through their partnership arrangement. For example, Saturn Corporation offers an MBA program for employees in a partnership arrangement with Middle Tennessee State University. Corporate universities also partner with local and secondary schools to assist them in developing qualified new employees for major employment centers. The CU may provide equipment, technical assistance, curriculum development, and instruction.

In some situations, the corporate universities partner with other specialized groups. For example, when the CU facilities are not owned by the organization, a partnership arrangement should exist with the property owner and operator of the facilities. Many organizations prefer not to tie up significant investments in buildings, and so they enter into a leasing management arrangement instead. The CU must develop an effective, long-term, win-win relationship with these key partners. In other situations, a training supply firm or contractor may provide the training design, development, and delivery services. The corporate university will usually develop a partnership arrangement to offer these programs through a long-term contractual arrangement. For example, Chevron partnered with a training development firm to develop and deliver most of its technical training at the Chevron Technical University.[19]

Auxiliary Services

Beyond the core programs offered by the university and the various partnerships developed, some corporate universities take active involvement in several auxiliary types of services. Many organizations realize that selection is perhaps the most critical issue when developing the proper corporate culture. For some employees, no amount of training can overcome basic deficiencies that may exist. In these firms, the CU coordinates and manages the selection process. This helps ensure that new employees are recruited to mesh with the desired culture and requirements. The employee is then introduced to the organization through the university's regular programs.

Some corporate universities provide a variety of recognition programs for employees to reinforce company culture, beliefs, and value systems, while recognizing performance. Recognition can come in a variety of ways and is often fostered through providing information to develop recognition programs, providing appropriate materials and processes for recognition, providing direct recognition from the university itself, and finally through teaching managers how to actually provide the recognition.

Finally, the corporate university often serves as a learning laboratory to explore new ways of learning and more effective processes for transferring learning to the workplace. Figure 5-3 shows a variety of different ways in which the corporate universities experiment with the learning process, all aimed at improving on-the-job performance.

Interest in learning by doing is increasing as experiential learning and on-the-job learning develop. Corporate universities are exploring ways in which informal learning can take place, particularly as employees learn from team members and team leaders. Alternative methods of learning, including a variety of technology applications and just-in-time learning strategies, are being explored and delivered. Finally, to ensure that learning is used successfully on the job, corpo-

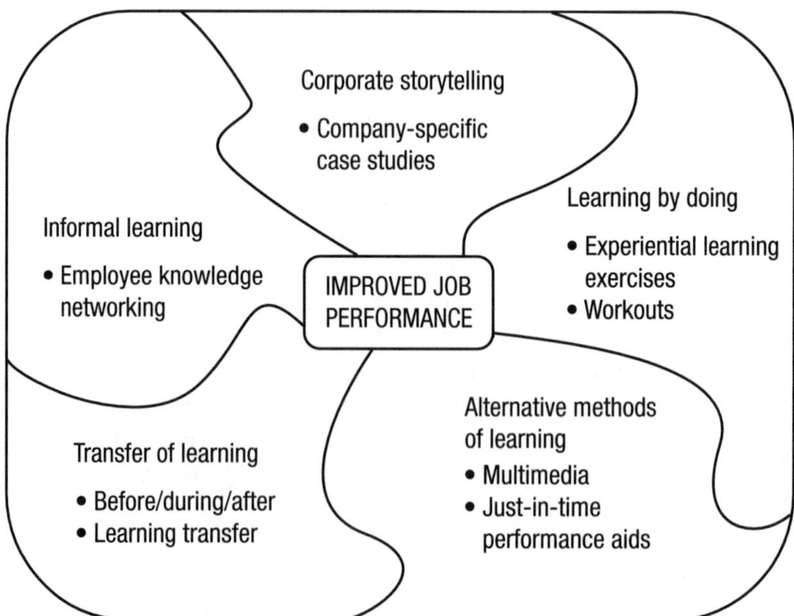

Figure 5-3. *Experiment with New Ways to Learn.* (Source: Meister, Jeanne C. *Corporate Universities: Lessons in Building a World-Class Work Force,* rev. and updtd. ed. New York: McGraw-Hill, 1998.)

rate universities are tackling the transfer-of-learning issue, using a time frame of before, during, and after the learning activity to develop strategies.

Quality and Accountability

Two key challenges of corporate universities are how to maintain quality processes and how to ensure that the university is accountable to the various stakeholders. Accountability and quality surface in several ways, utilizing a variety of information. For example, accountability is addressed in these ways:

- By developing objectives to ensure that all programs begin with the end in mind and with clear direction in terms of learning, application, and business-impact objectives
- By ensuring that programs are actually needed and are presented to the appropriate audience at the right time
- By establishing the proper strategies and support to transfer learning to the job
- By ensuring that key managers support the goals, mission, and objectives of the corporate university
- By developing internal partnerships necessary to ensure success in all steps of the training and development cycle
- By managing the costs of the corporate university to ensure that it operates efficiently, providing value-added resources
- By obtaining direct feedback from a variety of stakeholders concerning the perceived effectiveness and success of programs, processes, and activities
- By providing routine follow-up to ensure that there is transfer of learning to the job as envisioned when the program was designed and developed
- By connecting the training and development to specific business results, ensuring that a linkage occurs between major programs and important business measures
- By developing the return on investment for a selected group of programs to ensure that the university provides an appropriate return on the investment
- By pursuing a program of continuous process improvement for all the activities, steps, and processes used in the corporate university

- By guaranteeing top quality and relevance of all programs as they are designed, developed, delivered, and implemented
- By reporting the appropriate information about accountability, quality, and relevance to selected target audiences and key stakeholders

These, and other, accountability issues must be addressed by corporate universities so that they are able to maintain their current resources and grow along with the organization.[20]

Profit Opportunity

Some universities have taken advantage of profit potential either by pursuing a profit-center concept for internal programs or by developing programs and services for external distribution to generate revenue for the organization. Several corporate universities have considered the possibility of an internal profit-center, and a few of them have developed a true profit-center arrangement.[21] In this context, the corporate university charges the organization a fee for each product or service delivered. The fee is usually competitive, compared with that of external programs of a similar type. The fees collected offset the expenses of the corporate university to generate a break-even situation, or an actual profit. In a true profit-center arrangement, the operating divisions or units have the autonomy to use the corporate university or other external suppliers.

Some corporate universities supplement revenue by offering programs externally. Motorola, for example, offers many of its programs on a public basis to generate revenue. Disney University generates significant revenue through a variety of programs designed to teach the Disney approach.

Some organizations go beyond courses and actually provide consulting services, including program design, development, and evaluation. Xerox and American Airlines, for example, provide these types of services to external clients. A few corporate universities develop special products and make them available for customers. For example, Bell Atlantic Learning Center, the corporate university for Bell Atlantic, the largest telephone company in the United States, provides a variety of training products to external customers. Most of the products are technology-based training products, and the external sales represent an attempt to recover part of the tremendous capital investment necessary to develop these products for the 65,000 employees internally.[22] Bell Atlantic actively markets at least twenty products in the categories of courseware, electronic performance support systems, and multimedia development software to external suppliers.

Finally, some corporate universities lease their facilities externally to provide additional revenue, particularly facilities being underutilized by the current organization. For example, Aetna Insurance, Andersen Consulting, American Airlines, and Xerox all lease facilities to external clients.

Trend Consequences

Impact

The corporate university concept tremendously impacts the traditional training and development function. The level of interest in this trend, from the senior management perspective, is based on an organization's progress with the corporate university concept. When organizational leaders are deciding what to do about this concept, actions usually fall into three areas.

- If a corporate university exists, the action may be to maintain the current structure, staffing, and programs so that the CU can withstand budget cuts, scrutiny, and criticisms while providing necessary programs.
- If a corporate university exists, the action may include expanding the current scope and operations of the university.
- If a corporate university concept has not been implemented, leaders should consider launching a new corporate university. This difficult decision will require much analysis.

Regardless of which decision is chosen, certain issues must be addressed. The type of corporate university desired (or currently in process) should be examined relative to the eight types listed earlier. Which type is desired when compared to the type that is available or planned? The investment is another important issue. Corporate universities usually require extensive resources in buildings, equipment, and staff. Is the investment necessary or appropriate? Also, the corporate university is a high-profile process, and some training and development departments do not want the risk of having a highly visible department. Visibility brings accolades when things are going great but criticisms when they are not going so well.

Corporate universities can become disconnected from the major operating units, particularly if a great distance exists between the university setting and the major operational facilities. This problem is compounded when no representatives or satellite components of the university reside in those operational areas. Employees may attend the university and then feel no obligation to apply what they learned to their jobs, miles away. In addition, the distance can create a disconnect in the program design, content, and relevance.

Management support is critical for the corporate university concept to continue to flourish. Management involvement in all phases and processes of the corporate university is important. Managers must willingly send employees to programs and involve them in learning activities. Senior management commitment is necessary because commitment usually translates into funding for the university. Without adequate overall management support, the university concept can fail.

Finally, a comprehensive measurement and evaluation process must be in place to address accountability issues and show the contribution of the corporate university. Otherwise, the value may be questioned, and the contribution will not be fully understood or appreciated. Perhaps this is the greatest challenge for corporate universities and for those organizations considering them. Otherwise, the corporate university could be discontinued, as was the case for the Burger King University (BKU) a few years ago. The restaurant chain was in a slump and, because it could see little or no value for the university, closed BKU. Under new leadership at the top, the Burger King University is open again.[23]

Key Questions

Several key questions should be addressed when considering the launch of a corporate university or the expansion of a CU's scope.

Key Questions

1. To what extent do I agree with this trend?
2. How important is this trend to me?
3. What type of corporate university do we need in the future?
4. Do I have top-management commitment to invest in a corporate university (or expand it)?
5. Am I willing to raise the profile of the training and development function?
6. What resources will be needed to launch or expand the corporate university?
7. What specific services will be provided in the future that are not provided now?
8. What barriers will exist to launching or expanding the corporate university?
9. What would be the reaction of the staff to the expansion or implementation of the corporate university?
10. What happens if I do nothing?
11. What skills and capabilities are required for implementing and maintaining the corporate university concept?
12. Is the management support appropriate to make the corporate university concept successful?

Outlook

It appears that this trend will continue to develop because of the tangible and intangible benefits of the corporate university concept. However, if implementation of the concept is perceived as a fad by some organizations, growth may be inhibited in the future. In addition, most corporate universities will continue to exist in their current forms. The greatest challenge for a corporate university is to show its value to the organization as it continues to grow and prosper. If its value is questionable and it is not perceived as part of the strategic and operational framework of the organization, it could very well disappear. However, many current leaders of corporate universities are outstanding individuals who bring a wealth of operational experience from the executive level. Under their leadership, the concept is likely to continue to gain acceptance. Very successful leaders will continue to be high profile and set the pace for others.

This trend may not be appropriate for every organization. The concept of a corporate university differs vastly from the traditional training and development function, and unless it has the full support of the entire management group and unless mechanisms are in place to ensure that the university has a proper direction and alignment, it will not flourish.

References

1. Marquardt, Michael J. and Engel, Dean W. *Global Human Resource Development.* Englewood Cliffs, N.J.: Prentice Hall, 1993, pp. 132–133.
2. Demsford, Lynn E. "At Disney, Education Underpins Excellence." *Corporate University Review,* May/June 1996, pp. 14–21.
3. Meister, Jeanne C. *Corporate Quality Universities: Lessons in Building a World Class Work Force.* Chicago: Erwin Publishing, 1994.
4. Eurich, Nell P. *Corporate Classroom: The Carnegie Foundation for the Advancement of Teaching.* Princeton, N.J.: Princeton University Press, 1985, p. 48.
5. "Universities: Inside the Knowledge Factory." *The Economist,* Oct. 4, 1997, p. 19.
6. Demsford, Lynn E. "Best Practices and Corporate Universities Go Hand in Hand." *Corporate University Review,* July/Aug. 1997.
7. Mai, Robert P. "Corporate Universities Drive Organizational Learning." *Corporate University Review,* Mar./Apr. 1996, p. 14.
8. *Corporate University Review,* Enterprise Communications Inc., 1165 Northchase Parkway, Suite 350, Marietta, Ga. 30067.
9. Program offered by the International Quality and Productivity Center, 150 Clove Road, P.O. Box 401, Little Falls, N.J. 07424-0401.
10. Forcinio, Hallie. "Dana University Ensures That Employees Find a Better Way." *Corporate University Review,* Mar./Apr. 1997, pp. 20–29.
11. Smith, Ethan. "Business Driven Corporate Universities Take Many Forms." *Corporate University Review,* Mar./Apr. 1997, p. 12.
12. Demsford, Lynn E. "TVA University." *Corporate University Review,* Nov./Dec. 1996, pp. 22–23.

13. Fresina, Anthony J. "Three Prototypes of Corporate Universities." *Corporate University Review,* Jan./Feb. 1997, pp. 18–20.

14. Motorola. "1996 Annual Report."

15. Meister, Jeanne C. *Corporate Universities: Lessons in Building a World-Class Work Force,* rev. and updtd. ed. New York: McGraw-Hill, 1998.

16. Wiggenhorn, A. William. "Organization and Management of Training," in *The ASTD Training and Development Handbook,* 4th ed. R. Craig (Ed.), New York: McGraw-Hill, 1996, pp. 19–46.

17. Meister, 1994, p. 77.

18. Demsford, Lynn E. "Saturn University Created to Offer Suppliers Staff Training." *Corporate University Review,* Jan./Feb. 1997, p. 6.

19. O'Neal, Dan E. M., Morris, David R., and Tooley, Norman E. Jr. "Chevron Technical University—Teaching Tomorrow's Engineers Today." *Corporate University Review,* Jul./Aug. 1997, pp. 24–25.

20. Phillips, Jack J. *Return on Investment in Training and Performance Improvement Programs.* Houston, Tex.: Gulf Publishing, 1997.

21. Phillips, Jack J. *Handbook of Training Evaluation and Measurement Methods,* 3rd ed. Houston, Tex.: Gulf Publishing, 1997.

22. Demsford, Lynn E. "Going Public." *Corporate University Review,* July/Aug. 1997, pp. 6–7.

23. Smith, Ethan. "Birth and Rebirth. The Reopening of BKU: Burger King's Belief in Training." *Corporate University Review,* Sept./Oct. 1996, pp. 14–19.

6

TRAINING AND DELIVERY

Trend Definition and Validation

Brief Definition of Trend

The delivery of training and development is rapidly changing in all types of organizations. The use of traditional classroom training is declining and is being replaced by a variety of methods designed to deliver more relevant training, including coaching, mentoring, structured on-the-job training, just-in-time training, individualized development plans, job aids, performance support tools, and peer training. In addition, a variety of technology-supported delivery techniques are now being used regularly.

Case Studies: Saudi Arabian Airlines and Honda Motor Company

Saudi Arabian Airlines. Founded in 1943, Saudi Arabian Airlines serves more than one hundred cities in fifty countries and flies three million passengers per year. As with many companies in the Gulf Region, it has expanded rapidly in the past ten years while experiencing a shortage of qualified local nationals to fill key management positions. Consequently, Saudi Arabian Airlines must invest heavily in training and development to develop a sufficient level of Saudi managers. Specific training programs relate to the unique culture of the organization and the country.[1] The training program for marketing managers, described in the next paragaph, serves as a model for all Saudi Arabian Airlines training programs.

After identifying the competencies needed and selecting candidates, the training staff developed a thirty-month marketing management program that addresses subjects such as marketing and economics, business management, financial accounting, cost accounting, reservations, ticketing, and customer service. After completing the theoretical training in each area, each trainee was required to complete a specific on-the-job training experience. During this part of the program, the managers and supervisors for the various assignments provided feedback on the trainees' performances. The program was based on the whole-part-whole principle in which trainees initially received exposure to the whole operation, then worked on individual tasks in real job situations, and finally reviewed the entire operation. Part of the success of the program lies with its feedback process, which communicates the success and effectiveness of each assignment to the trainee. Feedback is also provided to trainees' immediate managers and training administrators with regard to training needs, progress, and proposed course revision. Saudi Arabian Airlines considers this on-the-job training experience to be a cornerstone of its overall HRD strategy.

Honda Motor Company. Honda Motor Company has 119 facilities in forty-six countries. Honda of America employs 10,000 people at four plants in three locations. These associates, as Honda calls them, produce automobile parts, automobiles, and motorcycles. Most of the traditional training and development for the associates is provided under the umbrella of the Associate Development Center (ADC).[2] Previously, the center filled the traditional role of teaching in a classroom setting. All departments viewed the ADC as a place to go to learn because it had the responsibility for producing learning outcomes. Since then, the role of the ADC has shifted from teaching to facilitating learning and its application in the workplace. This shift occurred because of the loss of skill transfer from traditional training.

To illustrate the shift in Honda's ADC, a course on troubleshooting was redesigned to add a coaching module. Previous presentations of the troubleshooting course had no impact on actual jobs, as follow-up evaluations showed. Although the associates did learn the skills and knowledge, they did not apply them at the work site. Consequently, the recommended changes in the program were twofold. First, the classroom delivery was reduced and partially replaced with on-the-job application modules. This allowed the associates to apply in the afternoon what they had learned in the morning. The second change involved increasing reinforcement and support on the job through the addition of process coaches. Selected associates were trained to provide process coaching. The process coaches focused on learning coaching skills rather than learning process skills for problem solving. They were asked to help others stick to the process and not actually do the work for them. The process coach's major responsibility was to establish an environment on the plant floor that supported transfer of learning from the classroom.

This redesigned effort greatly improved the success of the troubleshooting course. Additional evaluation revealed significant instances of application of the process, as well as valuable improvements toward the business impact. This shift from traditional classroom learning to on-the-job process coaching reflects the typical transition that has taken place in Honda's ADC.

Evidence of Trend

The evidence of this shift in delivery comes from a variety of sources and studies. In the global survey of practitioners, the extent of agreement with the existence of the trend scored 4.26 out of 5, representing a visible trend (see Appendix 1). The importance of the trend scored high, with a rating of 4.39 out of 5. Clearly, practitioners view this trend as representing a tremendous shift in the way training is delivered in an organization.

A survey of HRD executives conducted by the American Society for Training and Development (ASTD) underscores this shift in training delivery.[3] Survey respondents represented HRD executives across the globe. Among the trends listed were the following:

- Increased pressure for just-in-time delivery of HRD services and programs
- A shift in delivery from training professionals to managers, team leaders, and technical workers
- Increased interest in facilitating learning via existing or new informal networks

The ASTD also developed its top ten trends for training and development based on combinations of studies.[4] Among the trends identified was that training and development departments are finding new ways to deliver services. The study also underscored the increased use of electronic learning technologies, highlighting a tremendous jump in the use of technology between 1996 and 1997. The most dramatic increase was use of the company intranet, which jumped from 14 percent of organizations using the medium in 1996 to 45 percent in 1997. By the year 2000, intranets are expected to be the No. 1 nontraditional method of training delivery. Sixty-four percent of organizations use computer-based training, while 56 percent use videoconferencing. Forty-three percent now use interactive television. Obviously, organizations are experiencing a phenomenal use of electronic learning technologies as an alternative to classroom delivery.

A major study of human resource executives identified several key issues in work-force development.[5] The study showed that training is now delivered just in time wherever people need it, using a variety of technologies. The survey viewed current work-force development trends, as well as predictions for the next ten years.

A major study on the reengineering of the training function indicated that just-in-time training is one corporate reality whose time has come.[6] The report showed that the traditional training function, to a large degree, has discarded a wide variety of archaic practices and now meets new training needs of the rapidly changing organizations through a variety of new media and delivery. Part of this report described the virtual training organization that many organizations are adapting. A virtual training organization will offer a menu of learning options customized to the individual's needs and delivered on a just-in-time basis, primarily through the use of technology.

A study from the Conference Board concerning the status of training and development, particularly management T&D, revealed some changes in its delivery.[7] The study, which involved more than one hundred leading corporations across the world, showed that 76 percent of organizations use one-on-one instruction through coaching and mentoring, whereas 74 percent use action learning. Fifty-seven percent used job rotation through some type of planned progression, while 38 percent of the companies used self-study. The Conference Board's study, compared with previous studies, underscored the shift in the way training is delivered.

Another study, illustrating how organizations sustain high performance in bad times, revealed the use of several performance management practices.[8] These organizations, which are highly successful and global in scope, credited part of their success to the use of two nontraditional training and learning delivery methods. Forty-two percent of these organizations used individual development plans, while 39 percent used coaching and mentoring programs.

Another study, reporting from the perspective of improving the quality of training, identified several key trends including one that revealed that organizations were exploring new and unique methods of delivering training and education services.[9] This trend underscored the declining use of the traditional classroom experience for training, which is being rapidly replaced by a variety of processes that move the learning closer to the job, sometimes using technology.

The training and development function is undergoing rapid change, and some experts indicate that the profession is essentially reinventing itself. One major report reached several important conclusions after the collection and integration of trends across the globe:[10]

- The focus of learning activities is shifting away from isolated skill building and information transfer to performance improvement and support, often near the job site.
- The focus on models and methods of learning is shifting from the teacher's or facilitator's perspective to that of the learner or participant.
- More learning is occurring just in time and directly in the context of the job or task, sometimes at the job site.

- The use and success of self-directed learning and team learning are increasing dramatically.
- Group training events are being used less to transfer information or to teach skills and more to motivate and bond groups and clarify direction and purpose.
- Learning is more likely to occur with the help of some form of technology.

Of all the important developments, these trends highlight the primary issues presented in this chapter.

Finally, the Benchmarking Forum of the American Society for Training and Development, which is a large group of high-profile global organizations with a track record for progressive training and development, reported shifts in the delivery of training and development.[11] From 1994 to 1995 alone, these organizations reported a reduction in traditional classroom use from 78 percent to 69 percent. Future projections call for further reductions. The study also indicated that delivery will continue to decentralize, with almost half the training and delivery decentralized already.

Clearly, the evidence from these studies, along with many others, illustrates the dramatic changes taking place in the delivery of learning and training. The process is being restructured dramatically, and the next section highlights the reasons for the changes.

Causes and Drivers

Several important drivers have influenced the shift in training and development. Although the shift has been occurring incrementally for many years, it recently exploded with the use of technology and the emphasis on learning and learning transfer.

- Perhaps the most important driver for this shift is the explosive growth of the use of technology with training, learning, and performance improvement. Although the technology has been available for some years, recently it has become economical and feasible for most organizations to shift to using delivery mechanisms involving technology. Chapter 15, reflecting trends in technology, further explores the tremendous growth in technology and its influence on training and delivery. Even organizations with relatively modest training budgets can use technology to deliver training. In addition, training can be delivered effectively in remote locations through new technology that was not available a few years ago.

- Inefficiencies in learning with traditional training and development caused some organizations to focus more efforts into new ways of learning. In a traditional environment, lecture and discussion have been the principal methods, and many studies have shown that these are not effective for acquiring skills and knowledge. Other techniques are much more effective, even in diverse cultures.[12] Thus, as organizations examined different approaches to learning utilizing appropriate research, the shift to other innovative and more efficient techniques occurred.
- The cost of providing traditional training and development continues to grow. Classroom facilities are becoming more expensive. Travel expenses continue to escalate. The time commitments for traditional training are significant. The days of traveling a long distance, taking weeks away from the job, and sitting all day in a classroom environment are disappearing. HRD executives are realizing that, to produce cost-effective learning solutions, they must reduce to a minimum the learning time of the participant, the time away from the job, and travel costs. Also, an elaborate facility for classroom training may prove too expensive for many organizations. Consequently, the cost of traditional training delivery forced many organizations to consider alternative processes.
- The effectiveness of training has come into question from many viewpoints. Not only is learning with traditional methods inefficient, but the transfer of learning to the job is sometimes diminished in the traditional training process. Because participants are physically removed from the job, sometimes by great distances, many opportunities exist for a disconnect to occur between what has been learned and what is utilized on the job. Support mechanisms are often not in place, and the transfer process is often inadequate. To improve the effectiveness of training to drive specific outcome measures, traditional processes are being supplemented or replaced by a variety of alternative delivery methods.

- Many organizations have a keen interest in delivering training near the work site, preferably integrated with the actual work to be done. When this occurs, several important benefits are derived:

  1. Training is more likely to be transferred directly to the job because the training occurs near or at the site.
  2. The training is usually more relevant because it directly relates to the work being done.
  3. Adjustments in the training process can quickly be made as problems are uncovered and solutions are identified.
  4. The training and learning often involve the manager or the supervisor of the participant. This involvement often adds value in terms of reinforcement and support of the training.

  Collectively, these benefits are pushing training closer to the job site and away from traditional delivery methods.
- Finally, the shift in responsibility of training and development is altering the way training is delivered. As presented in Chapter 7 as another trend, managers and training participants are assuming a greater role in the responsibility of training in their divisions and work units. As part of the responsibility, they are often involved in a variety of delivery mechanisms that differ from traditional delivery methods. When managers accept this responsibility, they become more actively involved and will support methods that bring training closer to the job and reduce the time participants spend away from actual work. When participants assume more responsibility for learning, they will become more involved in self-directed learning, self-study, and just-in-time training activities.

Collectively, these six drivers have created tremendous influence to shift from the traditional delivery to a variety of alternative delivery methods. Several of these methods are described next.

Trend Description

The image of a classroom quickly comes to mind when people think of training and development. But the classroom is just one setting available to trainers. Each of the methods described below has specific advantages and can be implemented with little expense to the organization—and without using a classroom.

Job Rotation

Some organizations use a formal job-rotation program to develop employees in current assignments and prepare them for future roles. The most common type of job rotation involves two or more people exchanging places, with each taking on new responsibilities. For example, in the inspection department of one manufacturing firm, several supervisors inspect employees' work at different stages in the process. These supervisors rotate systematically to wrestle with different types of inspection and quality-control problems. In one hospital, management trainees rotate through all major departments and stay in each for one month. A variation of job rotation, called internal lateral replacement, involves filling vacancies with transfers from within the department, eliminating the need for the extensive orientation that would be required for someone brought in from outside.

A part-time or temporary job rotation allows two people to train each other in certain job duties. For example, one organization temporarily assigns district sales representatives to work at headquarters when corporate staff members are on vacation. This provides additional training for district sales representatives while improving the cooperation and working relationship between field and headquarters staff.

Finally, if budget and organizational settings permit, an extra employee can be allocated for a permanent training slot. One person may be kept in the work unit to learn as many jobs as possible. This extra employee is usually preparing for the next opening. The extra employee also can be cross-trained or used to relieve others involved in cross-training. One manufacturer keeps an extra production supervisor in each major department—usually a newly promoted supervisor who fills in when someone is on vacation or a short leave of absence.

Job rotation has several advantages both for the organization and for managers who initiate it. A manager has more flexibility to make assignments when more than one person can do a job. The operation continues to run smoothly while the company prepares employees to assume other jobs and advance their careers. Job rotation prepares replacements for jobs that eventually will have to be filled. It even allows an employee to develop a replacement for his or her own job, thus eliminating the anguish of a promotion deferred because a prepared successor was not available. What's more, job rotation helps the organization objectively identify those who have the ability and skills to be promoted to other jobs.

In addition to the advantages for the organization, the individual also benefits from the challenges of job rotation. It prevents stagnation on the job and lets employees learn more about other positions and other aspects of the organization. Because different experiences teach different lessons, employees may develop skills and abilities not required for current assignments. Overall, job rotation can raise self-esteem, increase skills, and help develop careers.

On-the-Job Training

Although job rotation is an important type of on-the-job training (OJT), many other types of training activities can actually occur on the job. To be effective, on-the-job training should be planned, which is sometimes referred to as structured on-the-job training. In practice, most of the training that occurs is on-the-job training, and early efforts to train employees all occurred on the job, sometimes under the direction of an immediate supervisor. Research shows that on-the-job training in a structured and planned format can increase the effectiveness of training.[13] Setting up on-the-job training involves several key elements:

- First, the specific training needs of participants have to be uncovered to determine if on-the-job training is appropriate, feasible, and desired.
- Both the learner and the trainer have to be prepared for their assignments. Trainers may be part-time trainers in the organization, or in some cases they may be full-time on-the-job trainers.
- A specific plan needs to be developed to show what should occur at what time. The sequencing, timing, and expectations of each step should be clearly detailed. Specific goals should be set that are measurable so that the completion of each step can be observed and verified.

- Work tasks must be examined to see how on-the-job training can fit into the current work profile. OJT should be as non-disruptive as possible and, at the same time, connected to and supporting the current job task.
- As the plan is followed, progress reports should be required in some way to measure the success and readjust the strategy if possible.
- The process should be evaluated to see how much learning has occurred and the extent to which it has been transferred into routine job assignments.

Self-directed Learning

Most jobs require some self-directed learning or self-development for success. The employee must be motivated to learn new skills, technology, and methods. Many organizations recognize their obligation to make learning opportunities available and to stimulate interest in those opportunities. At the same time, they emphasize self-directed learning. Highly motivated employees, eager to learn more about their jobs, will take advantage of this approach to learning. Others will follow if encouraged—or required—to do so.

Organizations use several approaches to self-directed learning. Some provide a suggested reading list; others develop a prescribed program with assignments and follow-up meetings. This reading material must be related to the job and written for easy comprehension. This reading-list approach seems to work best if top management sets the example and develops its own reading schedule.

Perhaps the most appropriate way to use self-directed learning is through the use of technology. Whether in the form of online World Wide Web–based training, a CD-ROM, or other types of technology, self-directed learning can be an important part of the technology and media mix. In these technology options, employees can select the modules or courses they need, when they need them, sometimes even in the comfort of home.

Self-study courses commonly are used as a self-teaching technique. These allow the learner to proceed at his or her own pace, learning one topic before going to the next. Reinforcement and repetition are used to ensure that the employee fully understands the material. Self-teaching has two major advantages:

- It requires the active involvement of the employee. He or she responds to a question-stimulus after the presentation of small amounts of information.
- It provides immediate feedback about the quality of the participant's response. Participants are immediately provided with correct answers and can compare their responses with the preferred answers.

Local evening courses are another approach to self-study. They help employees sharpen skills, as well as build expertise in a variety of topics. Many courses are available at local colleges and universities.

Individual Development Plans

Because much development is individual in nature, some training and development can be efficiently accomplished on an individual basis. One such approach involves the use of individual development plans (IDPs), which are developed around what the employee needs to know to perform more effectively and/or to prepare for movement to other jobs. IDPs may be developed for all employees or restricted to selected groups. One organization, for example, limits this approach to those employees it considers to have high potential for advancement, *high potential* being defined as "the ability to advance two job levels in five years."

Individual development plans outline various experiences, specific training and educational programs, special projects, and other learning activities planned for a predetermined period of time. Ideally, these plans are developed with the help of the HRD staff. These individual plans are most effective when:

- The employee has direct input into determining what the IDP should contain.
- The manager is directly involved in the assessment of the employee's education and training needs and in the preparation of the IDP.
- Employees are given some responsibility for monitoring their own progress related to the IDP.
- Employees receive immediate, objective feedback on their progress.

- HRD staff support is provided to ensure that the IDPs are developed and reviewed on a timely basis and that the process is accomplished in a consistent manner.
- The IDP is modified as necessary after periodic progress reviews.
- The IDPs remain confidential and are available for review by those who have a need to know.

Individual development plans come in a variety of formats. The plan usually has several target dates and is reviewed periodically, such as every six months. The specific items are initiated and monitored by either the manager or the HRD department.

The primary benefit of this approach is that it recognizes individual differences in the training and education needs of employees and subsequently provides a tailored plan to meet those specific needs. In the places where this approach has been used, the reaction has been extremely favorable.[14]

Mentor Relationships

Mentoring, an intriguing and increasingly common approach to development, exists informally in almost every organization. Some organizations capitalize on this principle, encourage the practice, and develop formal guidelines.

A mentor helps another individual with career development. Specifically, mentors teach, guide, advise, counsel, and sponsor supervisors, as well as serving as role models. The mentor may or may not be in the same department, division, plant, or location as the supervisor. Mentoring requires establishing a relationship with an experienced, influential superior. For the relationship to be productive, there must be a good match between the mentor and the person being mentored. They both must be willing participants. In addition, the mentor must enjoy helping supervisors achieve their goals within the organization. An awareness of what constitutes mentoring will allow many veteran managers to utilize their daily interactions to develop employees. The impact can be far greater than many expensive formal management or employee development efforts.[15]

A word of caution: Employees learn from poor role models as well as good ones. In practice, most successful managers have worked for several memorable bosses and have learned what *not* to do from role models almost as often as they have learned what to do. Therefore, the supervisor with several mentors holds an advantage over the supervisor with a single mentor, regardless of the competence of the mentor.

On-the-Job Coaching

On-the-job coaching provides a practical and sometimes informal approach to training. Usually conducted by the middle manager, this technique presupposes that the vast majority of learning will occur on the job as a result of guided experience under the direction of effective managers. Coaching is not a one-time effort but a continuous process that involves discussions between the manager and the employee. The manager (coach) observes the employee, provides feedback, and plans specific actions to correct performance deficiencies. Because the process is repeated regularly, employees feel less anxiety toward coaching than toward typical performance appraisals. Realistic performance feedback is vital, but somehow managers confuse coaching with criticism and consequently avoid the process. Employees must thoroughly understand their duties and the standards by which they are evaluated. They must know and understand the goals, targets, and mission of their department, division, or organization. Performance feedback must be frank, open, and straightforward, and participants must know when their performance is good and when it is unacceptable. The participants' managers are in the best position to provide this feedback.[16]

Coaching should not be confused with cheerleading. A coach should provide positive reinforcement and motivation. However, coaches usually attempt to raise the morale of employees only when low morale is a critical issue. A mistaken belief exists that only fast-track employees and marginal performers need coaching. In reality, all employees need coaching, including the large group of average performers. Coaching helps new employees become more productive in a short period of time. Coaching also helps marginal performers improve their performance to an acceptable standard. It helps average employees excel by identifying strengths and weaknesses and developing necessary skills. For the super-performers, coaching helps maintain their outstanding performance records and helps them advance to other jobs in the organization.

Although employees may come to view their coaches as role models, the coaching process does not provide leadership. A coach does not carry the ball. Instead, the coach helps the employee with a performance problem, but the coach does not solve the problem.

Effective coaching does not happen by itself. Top management must encourage it, and role models must exist throughout the organization.

Special Projects and Assignments

Special projects and assignments to develop employees, although infrequently used, can be effective. This approach involves assigning special, non-routine job duties to build skills needed in the employee's current job, as well as to prepare the employee for assignments in the future. Typical projects include:

- **Short-term assignments.** Examples are special investigations, such as analyzing a problem, exploring the feasibility of a new method, procedure, or technique, and installing new equipment.
- **Task forces.** These may implement a new management information system in the organization, tackle a serious quality problem, or design a program to train new employees.
- **Special assistance to schools and colleges.** A supervisor might help a local vocational school develop a new curriculum, serve on an advisory committee, or teach a business course in high school.
- **On-loan assignments for volunteer and nonprofit organizations.** The full range and scope of activities are almost unlimited. Projects or assignments should be selected on the basis of the training and educational needs of the employee and the employee's willingness to participate in such activities.

Action Learning

Closely aligned to the project assignments discussed above is a process called action learning. This process of facilitating learning varies considerably from traditional training. Action learning is a continuous process of learning and reflection, often supported by colleagues with the intentions of actually accomplishing something. Through action learning, individuals learn with and from each other by working on real problems and reflecting on their own experiences.

Typically, an action learning application would involve three to four weeks of actual training in the classroom supplemented by a project. The projects are challenging, meaningful, and represent problems or opportunities that need to be addressed. Participants work in teams, utilizing the knowledge and skills they discussed and learned in order to complete the project.[17]

Electronic Learning Technologies

As discussed earlier, the area that is growing most in terms of alternative delivery of training is the use of electronic learning technologies to deliver information and facilitate the development of skills and knowledge. Technology allows training and learning to be delivered virtually anywhere, particularly through multiple sites at the same time. Technology also allows for delivery on demand for the learner, compared with the set schedule of traditional training. Figure 6-1 illustrates this point. Traditional classroom training is at point A in the figure, whereas electronic technologies move up to B and C in the figure.[18]

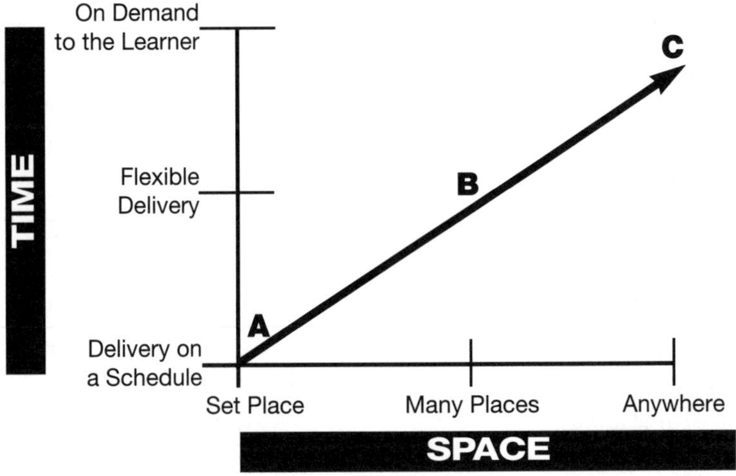

Figure 6-1. *Classroom Training vs. Technical Training.*

The use of technology for training delivery has mushroomed and includes a variety of processes. A major survey, illustrated in Table 6-1, shows the use of technology in a two-year period along with a projection of its relative rank of use in the future. It becomes clear that the Internet and intranets are quickly becoming important opportunities to deliver training in a variety of ways. Additional information about technology is presented in Chapter 15, which discusses the trend of increasing technology in training and development.

Table 6-1
Use of Electronic Learning Technologies

LEARNING TECHNOLOGY	PERCENTAGE USING TECHNOLOGY IN 1996	PERCENTAGE EXPECTING TO USE TECHNOLOGY IN 1997	RANK IN THE YEAR 2000
Computer-based training (CBT): disk/hard drive	55.2	63.5	9
Video-teleconferencing	53.1	56.3	5
CBT: CD-ROM/CD-I	42.7	54.2	10
Interactive television/video (including satellite)	37.5	42.7	6
Multimedia: CD-ROM/CD-I	29.2	37.5	7
Internet/World Wide Web	27.1	47.9	3
CBT: LAN/WAN	21.9	41.7	4
Computer teleconferencing	14.6	22.9	8
Intranet	13.5	44.8	1
Multimedia: LAN/WAN	12.5	24.0	2
EPSS	4.2	13.5	11
Virtual reality/ electronic simulation	1.0	2.1	12

Source: ASTD's National HRD Executive Survey, *1997.*

Peer Training

A special type of on-the-job training involves the one-on-one training opportunity often referred to as peer training. Peer training is training performed by a peer employee or team member. It is an organized and planned approach to develop other persons using one-on-one instruction. The processes for developing peer training and team member training are similar to the on-the-job training discussed earlier, and the types of efforts and projects reflect the job rotation method discussed previously. Organizations using peer training report significant success with the process when it is organized and follows a structured format.[19]

Just-in-Time Training

The concept of providing training at the right time to the right employees on the appropriate schedule and containing the right materials is not a new concept. It has been the desire of every training and development organization. However, because of the structure of traditional training, just-in-time training has been difficult to achieve. With new delivery methods moving training and development to the job site and using a variety of technology options, organizations are able to provide just-in-time training. An organization that accepts the principles of just-in-time training makes a commitment to create the conditions to help employees, customers, distributors, and suppliers keep up with breaking change by providing them with timely information and instruction. Just-in-time training is grounded in adult learning theory, which has shown that adults are most keenly motivated to learn when they are grappling with immediate work problems or struggling with life-changing situations.[20] This process not only involves the actual method of delivery at the location of training, but it also examines a process that develops and responds to needs. Further, it involves examining communications and scheduling of training, ensuring that no item is lost and that the training is not provided too early or too late to be effective. This concept will continue to be a hot topic as time pressure becomes critical and the need for new skills becomes urgent.

Conclusion

This section has illustrated some of the more common approaches to alternative delivery methods. Collectively, they illustrate a wide variety of possibilities as organizations struggle with delivering training and learning in a cost-effective way on a timely basis, while causing the least disruption possible and producing the most effective, efficient outcomes. The possibilities are almost unlimited, as organizations develop creative approaches to combine a variety of delivery methods.

Trend Consequences

Impact

As with many of the other trends, this one has been developing for many years. However, in recent years it has mushroomed considerably with the development of technology. Most training and development staff welcome this transition and have actually explored different ways of making training and development more efficient, responsive, and timely. However, some resistance may exist among individuals who prefer to be stand-up trainers. They may want to do the process the old way, in which they are most comfortable. Helping these people make the transition from traditional delivery will require education, coaching, and ultimately some goal setting.

This trend will also require some additional funding, particularly when using technology as an alternative delivery method. Technology is expensive, both because of the delivery mechanisms and the development of programs and materials. Most organizations attempt this transition on a gradual basis, bringing technology in at a deliberately slow pace so that it does not dramatically influence the budget at any one period.

Alternative delivery will also require communication and training for the target audience and support group. The individual participants and their immediate supervisors need to understand how alternative delivery works and their roles in the process to make it successful. For most of them, selecting alternative delivery methods will be welcome news, as the process often provides them with more pleasing options, reduces their time commitment, and maximizes learning. However, participants may resist because they have become accustomed to the traditional classroom training. This is particularly likely in cases where organizations have been delivering training at resort locations. A one-week-long program with social activities and recreational opportunities provides a relaxing opportunity and a break from the job routine. Therefore, if individuals attend programs for the wrong reasons, alternative delivery may not be attractive and may even be resisted.

Senior management usually welcomes this alternative delivery because it reduces the cost of facilities and the cost of delivering training, at least in most cases. Senior management usually supports the process and provides the necessary commitment to make it work.

Key Questions

Several important questions need to be addressed as the training and development function considers additional alternative delivery methods or increases the extent to which specific methods are utilized at the present time. The following questions may be helpful.

Key Questions

1. To what extent do I agree with this trend?
2. How important is this trend to my organization and me?
3. How much progress have we made in each of the non-traditional delivery methods?
4. What resistance to continued development of alternative delivery processes will we experience?
5. What resources are required to expand alternative delivery?
6. Which methods will be most effective?
7. What will happen if I do nothing?
8. What barriers will arise as alternative delivery methods are pursued?
9. What is top management's perception of alternative delivery?
10. Is senior management committed to developing alternative delivery?

To expand the third question above, it may help to develop a table to capture progress and plans. Figure 6-2 illustrates a chart that may be used for that purpose.

Alternative Delivery Status in Planning

Alternative Delivery Method	Status	Plans Next Year	Plans Next Three Years	Comments

Figure 6-2. *Determining Progress and Developing Plans.*

It is recommended that Figure 6-2 be used as a planning document to decide which areas will need the most attention in the future. Careful attention to planning and routine progress reporting are helpful to keep the process on track.

Outlook

This trend should continue in the future and perhaps even accelerate as technology continues to develop and becomes more economical and feasible. The drivers for this trend will continue to provide major influences on alternative delivery. Although some resistance exists in certain areas, the advantages of alternative delivery far outweigh the disadvantages, and most organizations will continue to make tremendous progress with this shift. On the positive side, alternative delivery does have several significant benefits. Learning can be more efficient, programs can be more effective, costs can be reduced, clients will be more satisfied because of the responsiveness of the process, and disruption of normal work activity will be minimized. These significant benefits can be achieved with this process only if it is carefully planned, organized, utilized, and understood by those who must use and support the process.

References

1. Marquardt, Michael J. and Engel, Dean W. *Global Human Resource Development.* Englewood Cliffs, N.J.: Prentice Hall, 1993, pp. 130–131.
2. Jones-Morton, Pamela. "Process Coaching: Honda of America's Model to Enhance the Transfer of Knowledge," in *In Action: Transferring Learning to the Workplace.* Mary L. Broad (Ed.) and Jack J. Phillips (Series Ed.), Alexandria, Va.: American Society for Training and Development, 1997, p. 231.
3. Van Buren, Mark E. *National HRD Executive Survey.* Alexandria, Va.: American Society for Training and Development, 1997.
4. Bassi, Laurie J., Cheney, Scott and Van Buren, Mark E. "Training Industry Trends." *Training & Development,* Nov. 1997, pp. 46–59.
5. Kemske, Floyd. "HR's Role Will Change. The Question Is How. HR 2008: A Forecast Based on Our Exclusive Study." *Workforce,* Jan. 1998, pp. 47–51.

6. Shandler, Donald. *Reengineering the Training Function: How to Align Training with the New Corporate Agenda.* Delray Beach, Fla.: St. Lucie Press, 1996.
7. "Companies Are Revamping Management Development." *Corporate University Review,* Nov./Dec. 1996.
8. Bassi, Laurie J., Benson, George and Cheney, Scott. "Sustaining High Performance in Bad Times." Alexandria, Va.: American Society for Training and Development, 1997.
9. Diech, Elaine. *TQM for Training.* New York: McGraw-Hill, 1994.
10. Gallagan, P.A. "Reinventing the Profession." *Training & Development,* June 1996.
11. Bassi, Laurie J. and Cheney, Scott. "Benchmarking the Best." *Training & Development,* Nov. 1997.
12. Knowles, Malcolm, Holton, Ed, and Swanson, Richard. *The Adult Learner: The Definitive Classic on Adult Education and Training,* 5th ed., Houston, Tex.: Gulf Publishing, 1998.
13. Rothwell, William J. and Kazanas, H. C. *Improving On-the-Job Training: How to Establish and Operate a Comprehensive O.J.T. System.* San Francisco: Jossey-Bass, 1994.
14. Rylatt, Alistair and Lohan, Kevin. *Creating Training Miracles.* San Francisco: Pfeiffer, 1997.
15. Bell, Chip R. *Managers As Mentors: Building Partnerships for Learning.* San Francisco: Berrett-Koehler Publishers, 1996.
16. Blanchard, Ken and Shula, Don. *Everyone's a Coach.* New York: Harper Business, 1995.
17. Tunheim, Katherine A., Skoglund, Judith and Cottrell, Dorothy. "Action Learning," in *In Action: Designing Training Programs.* Donald J. Ford (Ed.) and Jack J. Phillips (Series Ed.), Alexandria, Va.: American Society for Training and Development, 1996, pp. 271–287.
18. Bassi, Cheney and Van Buren, pp. 46–59.
19. Nilson, Carolyn. *Peer Training: Improving Performance One by One.* Englewood Cliffs, N.J.: Prentice Hall, 1994.
20. Rothwell, William J. *Just in Time Training: Assessing the Instrument.* Amherst, Mass.: HRD Press, 1996.

7

SHARED RESPONSIBILITIES

Trend Definition and Validation

Brief Definition of Trend

The responsibility for training and development is shared between several important groups in the organization. Among the groups are the participants, the immediate managers of the participants, key managers in the organization, and a variety of individuals and groups involved in design, development, analysis, coordination, and delivery of the training and development programs. Although these groups of people have always had the responsibility for training, organizations are deliberately shifting responsibility and are preparing them to accept responsibility.

Case Studies: Saturn Corporation and the AIB Group

Saturn Corporation. General Motors (GM) created Saturn Corporation in 1984 to develop and produce small cars that would be competitive in the global market in quality and costs. Today Saturn has more than 9,000 employees producing highly competitive automobiles for the world market. At the heart of Saturn's success is a tremendous commitment to training and development. Saturn invests more than $10 million each year in training and education, and that figure excludes the salaries of participants during training.[1] Saturn estimates that its total investment in training and development for a team member's career, including salary, is approximately $2 million. Team members share in the responsibility for training by committing to participate individually in a minimum of seventy-two hours of training each year or else risk losing a significant percentage of their salaries under a unique risk-reward compensation system.

To increase team members' level of commitment and enhance the opportunity of success to team members, Saturn has implemented a comprehensive training accountability system. Eleven groups, explained later, share the responsibility for success of training programs. Five of the groups represent leadership groups, beginning with the Saturn Action Council, an organization similar to the board of directors. Other leadership groups include the team leader, manufacturing training leader, training coordinator, and other leaders who coordinate functions of a business unit. The remaining six are more specialized groups that focus on training responsibility. These groups include the People Systems Training and Development department, the course owner, the course developer, the trainer, the training point person, and the measurement specialist. (For further clarification of these groups, see Figure 7-1.) Collectively, these eleven groups address the appropriateness of training, the quality of the training design, the delivery methodology, and the application on the job. Saturn believes that going through this comprehensive multiple-responsibility model will reap training benefits needed to continue to make automobiles that are high quality and affordable.

The AIB Group. Formed in 1966 as the Allied Irish Bank, the AIB Group now has more than 10,000 employees with operations in the United Kingdom, Belgium, Singapore, the United States, and Australia. The company's philosophies for training and development launched AIB into a worldwide success story. G. B. Scanlon, AIB's chief executive officer, publicly challenged the staff to change the way they think about learning and development so they can make the company the premiere Irish financial services organization, capable of competing worldwide.

Part of the philosophy AIB developed entails a list of responsibilities for employees, titled Charter for Employee Development. This list contains four basic principles:

- Professional development is a top priority of each employee.
- Training and development should complement and be driven by business plans.
- Self-development is a primary responsibility of employees.
- Employees have a responsibility for the individual and collective development of colleagues.[2]

AIB realizes that most learning can, and should, occur through the day-to-day work activities under the responsibility of each employee. Each employee must accept responsibility for his or her own development by learning from others and from successes and mistakes. Working as part of a team, or task force, employees are asked to seek feedback on performance and get advice from others. During their annual reviews, all employees must answer two basic questions, "What have I done in the past twelve months to improve my professionalism and that of my colleagues?" and "What positive action will I take in the next twelve months in my self-development and that of my colleagues?"

The Saturn and AIB Group cases individually point out that training and development is not just a responsibility of the traditional training and development function. Rather, responsibility is shared by many groups, each of which must be aware of the duties and be prepared to assume them in an effective way.

Evidence of Trend

Although various groups have been held responsible for training and development for some time, today the specific responsibilities are more detailed and are more clearly communicated. Much evidence indicates that the groups discussed above are accepting the responsibility. The practitioner survey of global trends revealed that practitioners agree with the existence of the trend in a score of 4.14 out of 5 (see

Appendix 1). Survey respondents rated the importance of the trend as 4.28 out of a total of 5. Clearly, training and development practitioners view this as an important trend with much visibility.

Several studies show that the effectiveness of the transfer of training to the workplace is greatly enhanced when managers are actually involved in assuming responsibility for training and development. These studies show that without the effective involvement of managers and the removal of other impediments, as much as 58 percent of training will not be transferred to the job.[3] Fortunately, these same studies indicate that organizations, recognizing the important role of managers, include them in transfer activities, both before the actual training is conducted and after training, in some type of follow-up role.

Many international studies show that the effectiveness of training increases significantly when managers are involved in a coaching or supporting role.[4] More organizations are recognizing this important issue and are assigning responsibility directly to managers.

Surveys of large training-organization and corporate-university practices revealed more and more instances of specific responsibilities being defined by organizations.[5] For example, in Nortel, a large global telecommunication company, specific responsibilities for training and development rest not only with the Nortel Learning Institute, the provider of education and training, but also with business units, the participants, and participants' immediate managers.

A British study of the changing world of training found that the main responsibility for training lies with the individual and the immediate managers, not with the training and development department.[6]

Organizations implementing change programs are realizing that success is greatly enhanced when managers are involved in change training.[7] Consequently, change programs regularly feature the active role of the manager in the training and development cycle.

The training function has been going through cycles of decentralization and centralization. For the most part, the primary rationale for decentralizing the training and development function was to move the process closer to the operating managers who request and use the training. Consequently, training and development functions have been decentralized into many operational units.[8]

Studies showing the changing structure and nature of managers' jobs have reflected dramatic shifts in their direct responsibility for training other managers.[9] One major study shows that training and development duties are considered to be among the core competencies of managers.[10]

Overall, much evidence exists that this responsibility is being structured by a variety of groups, particularly the managers in the organization.

Causes and Drivers

Long before formal training and development was initiated, training was accomplished by employees trying to learn their jobs and by supervisors who, out of necessity, had to teach employees how to do the job. Eventually, as formal training and development grew, the responsibility for designing, developing, and delivering training became centralized in a formal training function. As a result, the individual participants and their immediate managers assumed less responsibility in the process, deferring it to the formal structure. Only recently have companies attempted to bring responsibility back to the original owners and distribute it among several individuals. The drivers for this process are logical and practical:

- Involvement of a variety of stakeholders in the training and development process is the best way to ensure the success of training. The desire to have successful and more relevant training is creating a greater need to actively involve others in the training responsibility.[11]
- Training and development is more realistic, practical, and job-related when key members of the management group design, develop, coordinate, or deliver it. This has caused some organizations to bring a variety of management groups into the process and have those groups assume important responsibilities.
- Assigning specific responsibilities to participants, managers, and others is an important way to develop ownership for the training and development process. If individuals feel they are responsible, at least partially, they will have more ownership and buy-in for a process.
- In the quest to become more responsive and sensitive to specific client needs, responsibility for training and development has been pushed out to line and operating organizations. This direct involvement will ensure that training is properly focused, delivered in a timely manner, and designed for a specific need.[12]

- In an effort to create their own success, managers are assuming the responsibilities for training and development. These managers realize that, for them to create and sustain a competitive advantage, they must take a strategic role. Training and development is an important part of that effort.[13]
- As more organizations transform, the role of effective training becomes critical. Ineffective training has been blamed for the failure of many transformational efforts.[14] To ensure that the proper change programs are effective, managers are taking a more active role in the process.
- Managers are realizing that the most important and effective way they can develop a competent, successful staff, capable of driving the business to meet new challenges and developing replacements for key jobs, is to assume responsibility for training themselves. Coaching, mentoring, and role modeling are ways in which managers address this responsibility.[15]
- Finally, the budget crunch is causing some organizations to accomplish more with fewer resources. This means that many other individuals in the organization have to take both direct and indirect training responsibilities, as the need of sharing training and development duties becomes necessary for economics' sake rather than as a luxury.

Trend Description

The Stakeholders

Many individuals have a stake in the success of training and development. Essentially, every group of individuals who have input into the design, development, delivery, application, and support of training has some specific responsibilities for T&D's success.

Perhaps the model of Saturn Corporation, described earlier, illustrates the range of possibilities for stakeholders.[16] That model, as shown in Figure 7-1, identified eleven stakeholder groups as having important responsibilities for ensuring the success of training and development.

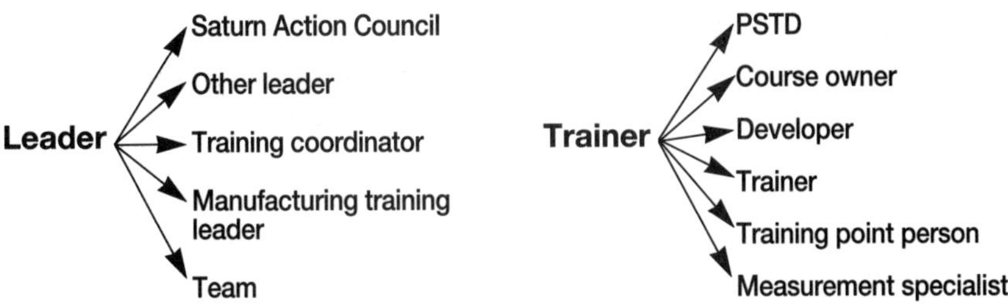

- **Saturn Action Council member** (comparable to a board member in other companies): Sets strategic direction; writes strategic business plan; approves major business decisions for Saturn
- **Other leader:** Coordinates functions for a business unit, module, special project team, resource team or manufacturing team
- **Training coordinator:** Coordinates training schedule and executes training-related administrative responsibilities for, and among, business units
- **Manufacturing training leader:** Identifies and responds to manufacturing training needs; communicates needs to centralized training function; accesses necessary training resources; reports to manufacturing leadership
- **Team member:** Performs basic business functions, either resource support or manufacturing functions, to support Saturn business plan
- **People Systems Training and Development (PSTD):** Provides centralized training support in the form of training design, development, facilitation, and measurement support for the entire organization; sets direction for training
- **Course owner:** Owns the course; ensures the course is designed and developed to specifications and is revised as needed; ensures certified individuals are available to teach the course when it is offered
- **Developer:** Designs, develops, and revises courses
- **Trainer:** Facilitates and delivers classroom course to trainees
- **Training point person:** As team member, helps other team members develop their individual training plans (ITPs); enrolls team members in courses; helps track completion of required training hours
- **Measurement specialist:** Designs, administers, and tracks formative course evaluations; compiles and communicates evaluation results to various training stakeholders

***Figure** 7-1. Training Responsibilities at Saturn Corporation.*

Although somewhat complex, these eleven groups can be condensed into four distinct groups that have the primary responsibility for training and are explained in this section. The four groups are:

1. The participants involved in training and development programs
2. Immediate managers of participants, who need to reinforce training in a variety of ways
3. The managers and executives who must allocate resources, request training, and provide overall direction for the training and development activities
4. Those involved in needs assessment, design and development, facilitation, and program coordination

These four groups, illustrated in Figure 7-2, represent the primary focus of the remainder of the material in this chapter. The four issues that are not enclosed in boxes in Figure 7-2 (goals and expectations, organizational culture, policies and practices, and measurement system) are factors that will have some influence on results. These are secondary influences that may need improvement.

Participants. Until recently, participants of training programs were rarely held accountable for producing results on the job. Participants

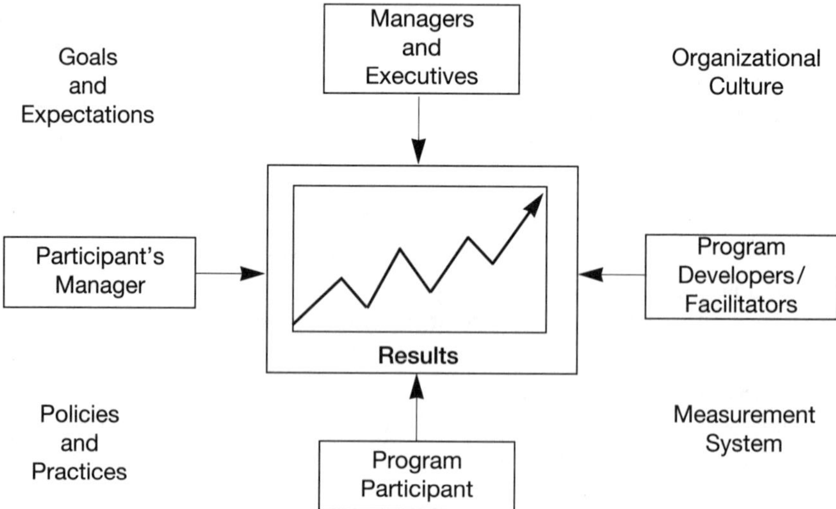

Figure 7-2. Groups That Share Responsibility for Training Results.

often shifted the pressure to the facilitator or supervisor to be responsible for results. If the materials were not interesting and the subject matter was not easy for participants to learn to apply on the job, they often chose not to use the training. Now, organizations are shifting that responsibility directly to participants in a variety of ways.

Participants are an excellent group to whom responsibility for results should be charged. They are often highly motivated during and immediately after a training program. Many studies show that, individually, participants can achieve tremendous success with the application of training on their own, without support and reinforcement from others.[17] Assigning responsibilities to participants complements other initiatives of employees. Companies are empowering employees to take on more responsibility and provide more input into the direction of their own work and to that of coworkers. Also, companies are challenging participants to grow and learn in a variety of ways and to apply developed skills and knowledge from one organization to the next.[18] Thus, it seems natural that organizations formally charge employees with the responsibility for obtaining results. Figure 7-3 outlines the responsibility for participants in programs from Nortel, a large telecommunication company based in Toronto, Canada. As the figure shows, Nortel charges the participants with a broad range of responsibilities for their own training and development, particularly as they attend formal programs or take computer-based training.

Some organizations take the responsibility a step further. In addition to participants clearly understanding what they should accomplish, participants are asked to identify specific barriers that may prevent them from applying what they have learned and to devise ways in which they can either remove each barrier or minimize its effect. Thus, participants not only have to apply what they have learned but also identify and overcome obstacles.

Responsibility for learning is communicated to participants before, during, and/or after the training program. Some organizations communicate the responsibilities at the beginning of each program, sometimes as participants register to attend. Other organizations write the responsibilities in the beginning of each participant workbook. Others place the responsibilities in employee handbooks, policy manuals, and various newsletters and brochures. Still others communicate the training responsibilities during the employee orientation program so that everyone clearly understands them.

Participant responsibilities:

- Participate fully in learning solutions as driven at the business unit level.
- Choose an individual learning solution with his or her manager based on needs discovered in performance review discussions and/or business unit objectives.
- Enter into the program/intervention with an open mind, being willing and eager to learn new concepts and material.
- Take responsibility for success of attendance/involvement in the learning solution.
- Commit full effort before, during, and after the learning solution.
- Apply learning on the job.
- When requested, provide information and feedback about the success of the learning and the barriers to implementation.
- Partner with management to identify and help remove barriers for application.

***Figure** 7-3. Example of Participant Responsibilities at Nortel.*

Immediate Managers of Participants. Probably no group has more influence on the success of training than the immediate managers of those individuals who attend training. This is particularly true when participants learn new skills. The new skill is awkward until it becomes routine practice and becomes internalized into normal work activity. Participants need encouragement, support, and sometimes advice about effectively using these new skills on the job. Ideally, they would like to be rewarded for efficient, effective use of the skills. Before attending a program, participants often want to know the manager's perception and expectation of the program. Up-front discussions of expectations and requirements is the most critical element of transferring training to the job. Thus, a powerful role for the management team is to have pre-program discussions, as well as follow-up activities. Figure 7-4 shows specific responsibilities for managers in a large banking organization. The responsibilities match those in job descriptions and focus not only on efforts to support training but also on efforts to provide direct reinforcement for skills and knowledge acquired.

Participants' managers have the responsibility to:

- Partner with their employees in enrolling in training programs intended to improve business performance.
- Discuss the training program with the participant prior to attendance/involvement to determine expected outcomes.
- Conduct a personal follow-up for the program results.
- Reinforce behavior after the program has been implemented and provide positive feedback and rewards for successful application of the training program.
- Assist in the planned formal follow-up activities of the training program.
- Be proactive in identifying and removing barriers to the application of training programs.

Figure 7-4. *Manager Responsibilities at a Large Bank.*

Managers and Executives. Another powerful group responsible for training and development is the managers and executives who request training, provide funding for training and development projects, and provide overall guidance and direction for the training staff. This influential group has many direct responsibilities that build commitment and support and provide direct involvement in the process.

Management commitment refers to allocating the appropriate resources and providing the proper direction to the training and development effort. Figure 7-5 shows the ten commitment areas for top executives, written in the form of basic responsibilities. When properly implemented, this commitment will have a tremendous influence on the success of training efforts.

Management support can come in a variety of ways but often involves the actions and behavior of middle management toward the training and development effort. Figure 7-6 describes ideal management support, which is sometimes translated directly into a responsibility.

Direct involvement in the process also has a powerful influence on the success of training. In some organizations, direct management involvement is required as a responsibility or immediate goal. Involvement can range from participating on advisory boards to actually con-

The Ten Commitments for Top Managers

For strong top-management training and development commitment, the chief executive officer should:

1. Develop or approve a mission for the training and development function.
2. Allocate necessary funds for successful training and development programs.
3. Allow employees time to participate in training and development programs.
4. Become actively involved in training and development programs and require others to do the same.
5. Support the training and development effort and ask other managers to do the same.
6. Position the training and development function in a visible and high-level place on the organization chart.
7. Require that each training and development program be evaluated in some way.
8. Insist that training and development programs be cost-effective and require supporting data.
9. Set an example for self-development.
10. Create an atmosphere of open communication with the training and development manager.

***Figure** 7-5. The Ten Commitments for Top Managers.*

ducting programs. As described in Chapter 14 in a trend about developing partnerships with managers, involvement can take on as many roles as there are steps in the training and development cycle.

Training and Development Staff. The most obvious responsibility in training and development comes from the T&D staff. While it is usually clear that facilitators have some responsibilities for results, the role of other groups within training and development is vital to the overall success of the program. For example, the individuals who conduct the training needs assessment must clearly identify specific

Ideal Management Support

The manager:

- Encourages employees to be involved in training and development programs.
- Volunteers personal services or resources to assist the training and development function.
- When appropriate, makes an agreement with employees before they become involved in training and development programs.
- Reinforces the behavior change objectives of training and development programs.
- Meets all responsibilities and duties for making training and development programs successful.
- Assists in determining the results achieved from training and development programs.
- Provides rewards and recognition to participants who achieve outstanding accomplishments with training and development program participation.
- Makes unsolicited positive comments about the quality and effectiveness of training and development programs and services.

***Figure** 7-6. Ideal Management Support.*

problems and situations linked to skill and knowledge deficiencies so that the success of training can be properly judged after participants have completed the program.

Program designers and developers have a responsibility to focus content and learning activities on results dictated by the application and impact objectives, described in Chapter 8. When programs focus on the application and impact objectives, this enhances the possibility of their success. Finally, the facilitators have the important role of keeping the process on track and focused on outcome objectives. The skill practices, role-plays, discussions, and examples and exercises used in the program focus on specific results. In addition, the facilitator will communicate expectations, discuss follow-up activities and barriers to applications, and explain how results should be monitored and reported. Collectively, the training and development staff has not only the primary responsibility to provide training but also the responsibility to ensure that the training focuses on results.

Shifting the Responsibility

In recent years, evidence has surfaced that training and development organizations are deliberately shifting responsibility to the various groups outlined in this section. Two important questions quickly surface: How can this responsibility be shifted? Even though responsibility may be assumed, how do we make the various stakeholders aware of their duties and prepare them to meet them? Eight important methods have been successful in shifting this responsibility:

- **Changing job descriptions.** The most fundamental and, perhaps, the most permanent way to ensure that stakeholders know their responsibilities well is to include those duties in job descriptions and competency models. This ensures that participants are aware of their responsibilities and will regularly review performance based on them.
- **Integrating the performance of training and development into performance review and pay plans.** This may be one of the most effective ways to ensure that the various stakeholders meet their responsibilities in a successful manner. For example, in the case of Saturn, discussed earlier, all employees' bonuses are tied to their involvement in training and development programs. In other situations, a part of the annual merit increase for managers is determined by their performances regarding goals established around the training and development effort.
- **Requiring active involvement in the training and development process.** Some organizations set specific goals for participation in training. For example, at the Southern Company, one of the world's largest utilities, the former chief executive officer (CEO) set a minimum number of days during which he would actually conduct training and development programs. His major commitment was to meet what he referred to as a significant responsibility to train and develop others. He also required similar types of commitments from the other executives.

After completing this workshop, each manager should:

- Realize the potential for HRD/PI to help achieve departmental, division, and company goals and add economic value to the organization.
- Define and describe his or her responsibility for HRD/PI development.
- Identify and understand the various elements of the HRD/PI process.
- Identify areas for personal involvement in the HRD/PI process.
- Develop specific behaviors to support and reinforce program objectives.

***Figure** 7-7. The Manager's Role—Workshop Objectives.*

- **Rewarding those who do outstanding jobs of meeting training and development responsibilities.** These types of rewards are usually non-monetary and go to individuals outside the training and development function. Typical recipients of rewards might include a participant who excels in the application of training, supervisors who reinforce training and coach the application of the process, and middle managers who show effective support for the training efforts. These rewards can come in the form of publicity and newsletters, memos and letters directed to individuals, plaques and certificates, announcements at meetings, specialty advertising items, or other ways.
- **Communicating duties, responsibilities, and expectations regularly.** Through memos, handouts, brochures, and training materials, explain the various responsibilities and remind stakeholders of their roles in the training and development process. For example, Dana University, a major corporate university, provides participants with a list of their responsibilities in each package of handout materials.
- **Providing job-aids, manuals, and other documents to explain responsibilities.** Documents can include policies and procedures,

manuals, checklists of specific actions necessary to support training, useful guides, and other aids that will help ensure that each stakeholder understands the process and his or her role in it. Along with this action, each stakeholder must have the actual opportunity to discharge the responsibilities.

- **Training stakeholders to meet their responsibility.** In some situations, stakeholders attend special programs designed to illustrate their roles in training and development. For example, at Illinova University, the corporate university of a major gas and electric utility, managers attend a special program to learn more about their particular role in the training and development function. This one-day workshop, titled "The Manager's Role in Results-based Training," demonstrates how managers can meet the objectives outlined in Figure 7-6. Through exercises, skill practices, and cases, the managers more clearly understand their role and build necessary skills to support and reinforce training.
- **Finally, holding managers accountable for training and development.** When training is not successful, the various stakeholders should be asked to explain the reasons. When training is successful, they should be informed and asked to explain the elements that led to the success. But more importantly, they should realize that they are accountable for this process.

Trend Consequences

Impact

Training and development leaders may not welcome this trend. In essence, they may see it as a trend forcing them to give up control of the training and development effort. A few training and development managers are concerned about the potential consequences of this shift: deterioration of training and development, inefficiency that duplication of effort can generate, and inconsistency that can come from having a variety of people involved. These concerns can be alleviated if the training manager will delegate responsibilities to others. Some training and development managers feel the need to keep full control of the training and development department and are unwilling to delegate it to a group of managers who may be ill-prepared to assume the responsibilities or may not want them in the first place. This may be a legitimate barrier. However, in those efforts where this shift of responsibility has been highly successful, the status, influence, and image of the training and development function was enhanced considerably.[19]

This trend will require training and development managers to be proactive in these efforts. Not many managers will step up and ask for this responsibility. Only on rare occasions will they actually seize the effort and take it away from the training department. More than likely, the training and development manager must initiate the effort and plan for the transition in a careful and methodical way, ensuring that each group is prepared for the responsibility.

In some cases, the very stakeholders may not want this responsibility. Some managers are too busy now to take over additional duties. In a few organizations, managers resisted this effort because they perceived it as another responsibility dumped on them as the organization tries to become lean and mean by trimming back the training and development function. The major problem is that the managers are already overworked and are not prepared for this assignment.[20] If the managers perceive that the training responsibility is being merely dumped on them, the shifting process will not succeed.

The shift in responsibility requires additional efforts from the training and development staff and perhaps actual training programs to prepare others for this responsibility. As indicated above, a special workshop for managers not only is appropriate but is recommended in most cases.[21] This additional workshop will take time and effort to conduct, which ties up resources that could be used to train others. However, the payoff should outweigh the sacrifices of this effort.

The shift in responsibility may result in the loss of control of training and development. If other managers take control of the training effort and ignore the training and development staff, even greater problems may be created. Ideally, it should be a coordinated effort even though other managers are involved and, in certain cases, are completely responsible for the training. Pushing responsibilities to managers can breed duplication of efforts and generate inefficiencies as different departments and divisions purchase or develop the same programs. Also, inconsistencies may surface, as one program is presented one way in one division and another way in another division.

All these legitimate concerns can be managed if the process is organized and coordinated appropriately.

Finally, this shift in responsibility needs support from the top executives. They must model the behavior necessary to encourage others to assume their responsibilities. They must set the example for assuming more duties and meeting those goals in an effective and successful way.

All these issues are legitimate problems that can inhibit the shift of responsibility to all the stakeholders. It is important for the training and development staff to see the payoff of this effort to continue to make progress.

Key Questions

The following key questions serve as guidelines to explore the use of this trend.

Key Questions

1. To what extent do I see this as a trend in my organization?
2. How important is this trend to me?
3. How much progress has been made in shifting this responsibility?
4. Which stakeholders are actually responsible for training in this organization?
5. Which stakeholder group has accepted the responsibility the most? Which one has accepted it least?
6. What barriers must be overcome to shift this responsibility?
7. Do the particular stakeholder groups want this responsibility? Will they resist it?
8. What resources will be required to make this shift?
9. What preparation is needed for the training and development staff to shift this responsibility?
10. What preparation is needed for the various stakeholder groups to assume more responsibility?
11. What resources are required to make this process successful?
12. Does top management support this transition?
13. What will happen if I do nothing?

Key Questions (continued)

14. How long will it take to make this shift?
15. What will be the payoff if all stakeholders assume the responsibility?
16. Will there be a reduction in staff once the responsibility has shifted?

Outlook

It appears that this gradual trend occurs throughout major organizations. Essentially, the shift brings training back to its original days, when more responsibility was absorbed by the immediate supervisors. From a management perspective, the change makes good sense. Also, from a resource allocation perspective, the change is necessary to conserve resources and increase efficiency. Finally, to ensure that training and development is successful, this responsibility shift is absolutely essential. The primary drivers for this trend will continue in the future, although the trend may be slow to develop in some organizations. It is important for the training and development function to prepare for this trend rather than to have it forced on them in an improper and untimely manner.

References

1. Wall, Sharon and White, Eleanor. "Building Saturn's Organization-wide Transfer Support Model," in *In Action: Transferring Learning to the Workplace.* Jack J. Phillips and Mary L. Broad (Eds.), Alexandria, Va.: American Society for Training and Development, 1997, p. 165.
2. Marquardt, Michael J. and Engel, Dean W. *Global Human Resource Development.* Englewood Cliffs, N.J.: Prentice Hall, 1993, pp. 130–131.
3. Broad, Mary L. and Newstrom, J. *Transfer of Training.* Reading, Mass.: Addison Wesley, 1992.
4. Marquardt and Engel. pp. 130–131.
5. Meister, Jeanne C. *Corporate Universities: Lessons in Building a World-Class Work Force,* rev. and updtd. ed. New York: McGraw-Hill, 1998.

6. Williams, Teresa and Green, Adrian. *A Business Approach to Training.* London: Gower, 1997.
7. Robbins, Harvey and Findley, Michael. *Why Change Doesn't Work: Why Initiatives Go Wrong and How They Can Try Again and Succeed.* London: Orion Publishing Group, 1997.
8. Shandler, Donald. *Reengineering the Training Function: How to Align Training with the New Corporate Agenda.* Delray Beach, Fla.: St. Lucie Press, 1996.
9. Stone, Florence M. and Sachs, Randi P. *The High-Value Manager.* New York: Amacom, 1995.
10. Yukl, Gary. *Skills for Managers and Leaders.* Englewood Cliffs, N.J.: Prentice Hall, 1990.
11. Pepitone, James S. *Future Training: A Roadmap to Restructuring the Training Function.* Dallas: AddVantage Learning Press, 1995.
12. Shaw, Edward. *The Six Pillars of Reality-Based Training.* Amherst, Mass.: HRD Press, 1997.
13. Floyd, Steven W. and Wooldridge, Bill. *The Strategic Middle Manager: How to Create and Sustain Competitive Advantage.* San Francisco: Jossey-Bass, 1996.
14. Farmer, Neil and Lankester, Bob. *Total Business Design.* Chichester, England: John Wiley and Sons, 1996.
15. Bell, Chip R. *Managers As Mentors: Building Partnerships for Learning.* San Francisco: Berrett-Koehler Publishers, 1996.
16. Wall and White.
17. Phillips, Jack J. *Handbook of Training Evaluation and Measurement Methods,* 3rd ed. Houston, Tex.: Gulf Publishing, 1997.
18. Peters, Tom. *The Tom Peters Seminar.* New York: Random House, 1994.
19. Bell.
20. Wall and White.
21. Phillips.

8

SYSTEMATIC EVALUATION

Trend Definition and Validation

Brief Definition of Trend

Organizations are taking a more systematic and methodical approach to the overall evaluation of programs and services. This systematic approach involves developing evaluation goals and timetables using standardized data collection processes, defining roles and responsibility, and applying consistent approaches for analyzing and reporting. With significant planning, a systematic approach ensures that evaluation receives the proper emphasis throughout the design and development process.

Case Study: Nortel

Nortel, a telecommunication company based in Toronto, Canada, with operations across the globe, adopted a systematic, methodical process of evaluating all the learning solutions, programs, and services offered by Nortel's Learning Institute. The systematic process requires that needs assessments be conducted with all major requests for learning solutions, and that application and impact objectives be developed for each learning solution. Program designers, owners, and coordinators have significant responsibilities for evaluation along with various stakeholders, including business unit managers, program participants, managers of participants and instructors, facilitators, and support staff. Nortel established the targets shown in Table 8-1 to reflect the percentage of learning solutions evaluated at each level (levels are explained later in this chapter).

Table 8-1
Evaluation Targets at the Nortel Learning Institute

Level of Evaluation	Percent of Learning Solutions Evaluated at This Level
Level 1, Reaction	100%
Level 2, Learning	50%
Level 3, Application	30%
Level 4, Business Impact	20%
Level 5, Return on Investment	10%

As part of Nortel's systematic evaluation processes, the company developed detailed guidelines to provide direction and ensure consistency. Evaluation guidelines provide for standardization of processes and adoption of specific methods for collecting data, isolating the effects of learning solutions, converting data to monetary values, determining how costs are collected, and identifying target audiences for communication resources. According to Nortel, this systematic approach ensures that evaluation is planned appropriately and built into all processes. This approach provides the appropriate framework for measuring the strengths and weaknesses of the process and for reporting impact.

Evidence of Trend

Evidence of this trend comes from many areas. The practitioner survey of global trends shows that this is a highly visible trend, with practitioners indicating agreement with the existence of the trend with a score of 4.57 out of 5 (see Appendix 1). The importance of the trend is rated 4.69 on a scale of 5, representing the third most important topic. Clearly, training and development practitioners view this as a very important trend that has made much progress in recent years.

The status of evaluation, as reported in the industry report from *Training* magazine, highlights the extent of evaluation success in the United States.[1] As shown in Table 8-2, the use of evaluation at different levels is extensive, revealing a systematic and methodical approach to this assessment. Although the results from *Training* magazine may be overstated, they underscore the important gains that have been made conducting evaluations at Level 2, Level 3, and Level 4.

Table 8-2
Status of Training Evaluation

Level	Percent of Organizations Measuring at This Level	Percent of Courses Measured at This Level
Level 1: Training Reaction	86%	83%
Level 2: Learning	71%	51%
Level 3: Behavior	65%	50%
Level 4: Business Results	49%	44%

Source: Training, *Oct. 1996, p. 63.*

Additional evidence of this trend appears in the work of the American Society for Training and Development (ASTD) Benchmarking Forum, where measurement and evaluation is exposed as one of the important issues facing the group.[2] The forum consists of a group of large, high-profile organizations. Many of the organizations in the forum are multinationals with operations around the world that have a strong commitment to training and education. Collectively, they are developing best practices. In a recent report, the forum indicated that developing systematic approaches to evaluation is one of its most pressing concerns and goals.

Perhaps the evidence of the trend is most visible in publications and articles that offer and encourage a systematic approach. At last count, at least twenty-five books have been published to reflect this approach. Evaluation is ASTD's hottest publishing topic. Articles about systematic evaluation make their way each month into training and development magazines in each major country.

Systematic evaluation is usually on all major conference agendas. In recent years, presentations about evaluation at major national and international conferences increased dramatically. Some conferences devote themselves exclusively to this topic, with titles such as "Performance Measures in Training," "Measuring Training's Effectiveness," "Evaluating Your Investment in Improvement Training and Development," and "Measuring the Success of Performance."

Finally, the adoption and widespread use of Don Kirkpatrick's four-level framework worldwide underscores the significant increases in interest in systematic evaluation.[3] The Kirkpatrick levels of evaluation, discussed later in this chapter, have become the standard framework for training and development and performance improvement functions.

Causes and Drivers

Several influences created this important, significant trend. The most critical are highlighted below:

- Multiple clients must be satisfied with the training and development process. This satisfaction requirement drives different types of evaluation. For example, participant feedback and learning measures are primarily designed to check the satisfaction of participants, who represent an important group of customers. On-the-job application, business impact, and return on investment (ROI) measures are primarily undertaken to satisfy other clients, namely the sponsors who support, request, and fund training and development initiatives. To satisfy all customers, evaluation data at different levels, collected in a systematic process, are necessary.
- A systematic approach is necessary to ensure that training and development processes are efficient and effective and that the strategy is appropriate for the program. Evaluation must be utilized to determine if the processes are appropriate and efficient at the same time. In addition, evaluation is necessary to determine if the outcomes meet the organizational objectives and requirements.

A one-shot evaluation will not fulfill this need. Evaluation must be planned and carefully executed by following a systematic process. This approach ensures that all issues, concerns, and key elements are tightly integrated in an organized and methodical way.

- Built-in evaluation has a much better chance of success with a systematic approach. Evaluators realize that, to obtain the highest quality and quantity of information necessary to make decisions, evaluation must be designed into the T&D process from the beginning. After the needs assessment process is completed, objectives at different levels are established, which guide the design and delivery process. Built-in evaluations ensure that the process is conducted in a timely and effective manner and that the various involved groups accept their responsibilities.
- The accountability requirement for all processes and functions in an organization encourages evaluation to be more complete and thorough. Because there are so many processes and programs involving increased costs and time requirements within an organization, evaluation of training and development must be consistent and routine. The reactive approach to evaluation is no longer appropriate. Evaluation information is needed by all stakeholders, and the most appropriate way to accomplish this is through a systematic logical approach.

To achieve success with measures and evaluation, the entire staff must share the responsibility for evaluation. Otherwise everyone will perceive it as someone else's responsibility. A systematic approach helps ensure that these responsibilities are appropriately assigned and distributed.

Trend Description

A systematic evaluation process involves five major elements:

- Adapting evaluation around a framework of levels with specific targets for each level
- Building evaluation into the process, from the beginning of the initiative to the collection of data
- Assigning various responsibilities to all parties involved in the evaluation process

- Developing specific policies and procedures to provide a consistent and standardized approach to evaluation
- Developing specific skills necessary to achieve a systematic evaluation effort

Each element is briefly described below.

Levels of Evaluation

Training evaluation is a complex issue that involves a variety of components, methods, and techniques. In simple terms, a framework is needed to place evaluation in specific categories or levels. Almost forty years ago, Don Kirkpatrick developed a four-level evaluation model.[4] In recent years, the framework was updated to include the concept of ROI.[5] The revised framework, presented as Table 8-3, shows the levels of evaluation and the measurement focus.

Table 8-3
Measurement Focus Among Levels

Level	Measurement Focus
1. Reaction and Planned Action	Measures participant satisfaction with the program and captures planned actions
2. Learning	Measures changes in knowledge, skills, and attitudes
3. Application	Measures changes in on-the-job behavior
4. Business Results	Measures changes in business impact variables
5. Return on Investment	Compares program benefits with the costs

In addition to levels of evaluation, a target-setting or goal-setting scheme must be created to determine the extent of evaluation at different levels. No organization has the resources to evaluate every program at each level. More importantly, that magnitude of concentrated measurement effort is not needed in any organization. A practical and economical approach to evaluation is needed, reflecting the extent of evaluation desired at each level. This requires a sampling process to select only a few programs for ROI calculations. An illustration of this target-setting process was presented earlier in this chapter (see Nortel targets in Table 8-1).

Level 1, Measuring Reaction and Planned Action. Measuring reaction from training is absolutely essential. With today's customer service focus in organizations, gaining direct feedback from a key customer (that is, program participants) is important to measure satisfaction with the different parts of the program. In addition, this feedback provides needed input on the strengths and weaknesses of the training process, including issues such as program content, duration, handout materials, videos, exercises, simulations, games, and the learning environment. This level of evaluation is critical with new programs, which need initial feedback to make adjustments.

An important addition to this evaluation level is the participants' input on specific action items planned in the program. A series of questions posed to participants can pinpoint how participants plan to implement what they learned. This step actually assists the transfer of learning to the workplace, as this approach requires participants to develop specific steps to apply the material. Planned actions are appropriate for any type of training program.

Because it is necessary to collect feedback from all groups, gain important insight into the strengths and weaknesses of the learning process, and determine specific action plans, Level 1 feedback is often collected from 100 percent of participants in all programs. The length of a program and the definition of what constitutes a training program may alter this 100 percent target. Programs shorter than one hour, informational briefings, and awareness sessions may not require a formal Level 1 feedback process.

Level 1 feedback does have serious weaknesses. Many studies confirm a lack of correlation between overall participant satisfaction and actual learning and subsequent application of the program material. Thus, Level 1 data are not a good predictor of training effectiveness. Although feedback is essential to measure satisfaction from this group of customers, reaction data serve as an overall evaluation of the program. Consequently, additional levels of evaluation are needed in order to thoroughly measure learning, application, and business results.

Level 2, Measuring Learning. In most training and development programs, participants are expected to learn new skills. Learning objectives usually focus on knowledge and skill acquisition or enhancement and sometimes attitude changes. With increased emphasis on building learning organizations, the issue of measuring learning through training and development programs is especially important. However, some organizations find it difficult to capture the extent of learning, particularly because formal, objective testing is not considered acceptable or desirable in many situations. Consequently, a variety of methods were devised to assess skill and knowledge changes informally. Although objective testing is important, informal, subjective methods include self-assessments, team assessments, facilitator assessments, performance testing, simulations, case studies, skill practices, role-plays, and exercises.

Fifty to 90 percent of programs are usually targeted for learning measurement. Specific criteria are developed to select the programs in which learning will be measured. Measuring learning is necessary when participants must gain prescribed knowledge and skills essential for job success. Situations in which competency building, major change, and transformation are under way, may require high levels of learning assessment. In instances where a large body of technical information must be accumulated, knowledge assessment becomes critical. Also, when safety and compliance issues are linked to learning tasks and skills, measuring learning is critical and essential.

Although a very important part of evaluation, measuring learning provides no assurance that participants will apply skills and knowledge on the job. Some studies show that as much as 60 percent to 90 percent of what participants learn they do not transfer to the job.[6] Consequently, the next level of evaluation is needed to determine the specific application of knowledge, skills, and attitude changes.

Level 3, Measuring Application. Perhaps one of the most critical issues of training and development is the transfer of acquired skills and knowledge to actual on-the-job application. A Level 3 follow-up evaluation determines the extent of job application and illustration. A follow-up evaluation takes time, adds cost to the training and development process, and is often disruptive. These three issues alone keep many organizations from appropriately using application evaluation.

Fortunately, a follow-up evaluation can be conducted in many ways. Table 8-4 shows the most common ways to collect data for Level 3 and Level 4 evaluations. The challenge is to select a method that fits the organization's culture, budget, and time constraints. More information on data collection methods can be found in other resources.[7]

Table 8-4
Collecting Post-Program Data: The Methods

	Level 3	Level 4
◆ Follow-Up Surveys	✓	
◆ Follow-Up Questionnaires	✓	✓
◆ Observation on the Job	✓	
◆ Interviews with Participants	✓	
◆ Follow-Up Focus Groups	✓	
◆ Program Assignments	✓	✓
◆ Action Planning	✓	✓
◆ Performance Contracting	✓	✓
◆ Program Follow-Up Session	✓	✓
◆ Performance Monitoring		✓

Because of the costs and inconvenience of Level 3 evaluation, a target lower than Level 2 is usually planned. The increasing emphasis on building competencies has generated more interest in measuring improvements in competencies on the job. For most organizations, a 30 percent follow-up is appropriate. This smaller percentage means that companies should establish criteria to select programs for Level 3 evaluations. For example, training and development programs are targeted for a Level 3 evaluation when they are considered critical to the organization's success, represent significant investments, or involve large target audiences. Also, programs in which skill application is critical to the goals of the organization usually are targeted for a Level 3 follow-up (for example, customer service skills or compliance with government regulations).

For many programs, a check of skill application is sufficient for the evaluation process. For others, however, a connection with actual business performance is desired. When business impact is needed, the next level of evaluation is necessary to determine performance improvement in the work unit.

Level 4, Measuring Business Impact. Most managers are interested in knowing how training and development actually improves the business in bottom-line performance terms they readily understand, such as increased productivity, improved quality, reduced cycle times, and enhanced efficiency. The difficulty in making this connection stems from the origin of most training and development initiatives. Some needs assessment processes do not link skills and knowledge deficiencies to business performance problems or business opportunities.

Recognizing that many factors can influence a particular business performance measure, evaluation at this level must include a method to isolate the effects of the training program from other influences. A variety of methods to accomplish this task are available, and additional information on these techniques can be found in other sources.[8]

Because of the increased time requirements, additional cost, and complexity of measuring business impact, a target lower than Level 3 evaluation is appropriate. For most organizations, a 10 percent level is recommended (that is, 10 percent of all program offerings should be subjected to a business impact evaluation). With this relatively low level of activity, it is essential to define specific criteria to determine which programs should receive a Level 4 evaluation. In addition to the requirements for a Level 3 evaluation, Level 4 requirements include items such as the linkage of the program to strategic objectives, the size of the target audience, and the life cycle and visibility of the program.

Although the Level 4 business impact evaluation is extremely important and pushes training evaluation to the level desired in many organizations, it still falls short of what is considered an ultimate evaluation. It is possible for a program to positively impact business performance but still represent a negative ROI. In this situation, the cost of the program has exceeded the monetary benefits. Because of this situation, the return on investment—the ultimate level—should be calculated for a few select programs.

Level 5, Measuring ROI. Return on investment has been used to evaluate performance of business ventures for many years. The construction of new plants, purchase of new equipment, acquisition of a branch, and development of a new product line all are subjected to an

ROI methodology, which captures the payoff of the investment. Today, more organizations are developing the same evaluation for major training and development expenditures.

The development of ROI requires two additional steps: converting Level 4 business impact measures to monetary benefits and capturing the actual program cost. Because these additional steps are required, a very small number of programs are recommended for Level 5 evaluation. A common target for many organizations is 5 percent of all programs offered annually. For example, an organization with twenty-five programs offered an average of four times a year has a potential of one hundred programs for which it could calculate an ROI. A 5 percent target means that the organization would subject five of these one hundred programs to a Level 5 ROI analysis.

Because of this low number of ROI studies, the criteria needed to select the programs become extremely important. The criteria should be developed with input from senior managers, and the programs selected should have senior management approval. Programs may be targeted for Level 5 ROI when they represent major investments, involve large audiences, or have high visibility. The criteria used to select programs for Level 3 and Level 4 analysis may also apply to Level 5. This type of analysis is usually reserved for programs closely linked to the company's operational and strategic objectives.

Built-In Evaluation

Evaluation should be built into the training process, from the needs assessment to the follow-up data collection. Built-in evaluation can be

1. Conduct a Needs Assessment and Develop Tentative Objectives
2. Select Evaluation Method/Design/Strategy
3. Determine and Develop Program Content
4. Design or Select Delivery Methods
5. Implement or Conduct Program
6. Collect Data and Analyze Results

Figure 8-1. *Process for Developing and Delivering a Training and Development Program.*

best explained by referring to a process model. Figure 8-1 shows a typical process for developing and delivering training, as well as development programs. Step 1 during the needs assessment identifies specific data that reflect users' needs (Level 4), job performance needs (Level 3), and knowledge and skills deficiencies (Level 2). This analysis helps develop tentative objectives for each of these three levels to reflect the learning acquired in the program, the specific application on the job of what was learned, and the corresponding impact in the business unit.

Step 2 finalizes the evaluation strategy. Here, a deliberate attempt is made to determine how the program will be evaluated and at what levels the specific instruments and specific timing of data collection are detailed. If an ROI analysis is planned, the methods for isolating the effects of training and the methods of converting data into monetary values are determined. Other key issues, such as cost, can be captured. Anticipated intangible benefits and communication target audiences are also identified.

Step 3 develops program content. Because of very specific objectives showing learning application impact, content will revolve around those specific issues. Exercises, skill practices, and role-plays, as well as guidelines and documents, will reinforce the overall objectives of the program.

At Step 4, the specific delivery method can enhance the way the material is transferred to the job and used. Some delivery methods enhance transfer, while others can impede it. At this point, focus on the most likely method that will ensure that the results are enhanced.

At Step 5, programs are conducted, and facilitators are provided with specific objectives that consequently focus directly on learning, application, and impact outcomes. In essence, the facilitator is teaching the ultimate outcomes, which enhances the likelihood of success.

Finally, at Step 6, data are collected as dictated in the evaluation strategy, and the results are then analyzed. With clear focus and adequate planning, data collection and analysis become an easy final step in the process.

Assigning Responsibilities

As a first step in the process, one or more individuals should be designated as the internal leader or champion for the process. As in most change efforts, someone must take the responsibility for ensuring that the process is implemented successfully. This leader serves as a champion for measurement and evaluation and is usually the one who understands the process best and sees the vast potential for the contribution of the process. More importantly, this leader is willing to show and teach others.

The evaluation leader is a member of the training and development staff who usually has this responsibility full time in larger organizations or part time in smaller organizations. The typical job title for a full-time leader is manager of measurement and evaluation. Some organizations assign this responsibility to a team and empower that team to lead the effort. For example, one company selected five individuals to lead this effect as a team.

Defining the specific responsibilities for the staff is critical because individuals may be unclear as to their specific evaluation assignments. Responsibilities apply to two general groups. The first is the measurement and evaluation group for the entire training and development staff, because all staff members usually have duties assigned to them. Typical responsibilities for this group include the following:

- Ensuring that the needs assessment includes specific business impact measures
- Developing specific application objectives (Level 3) and business impact objectives (Level 4) for each program
- Focusing the content of the program on performance improvement and ensuring that exercises, case studies, and skill practices relate to the desired objectives
- Keeping participants focused on application and impact objectives
- Communicating rationale and reasons for evaluation
- Assisting in follow-up activities to capture application and business impact data
- Providing technical assistance for data collection, data analysis, and reporting
- Designing instruments and plans for data collection and analysis
- Presenting evaluation data to a variety of groups

Although involving each member of the staff in all these activities may be inappropriate, individuals should have at least one responsibility as part of their routine duties. This assignment of responsibility keeps measurement and evaluation from being separate from major training and development activities. More importantly, it brings increased accountability to those who develop and deliver the programs.

The second group with specific responsibilities is the technical support function. Depending on the size of the training and development staff, it may help to establish technical experts who provide assistance with measurement and evaluation. When this group is established, everyone must understand that the experts are not there to relieve others of evaluation responsibilities but to supplement technical expertise. Some firms find this approach to be effective. For example, Andersen Consulting has a measurement and evaluation staff of thirty-two individuals who provide technical support for the education and training function. When this type of support is developed, this group's responsibilities revolve around six key areas:

- Designing data collection instruments
- Providing assistance for developing an evaluation strategy
- Analyzing data, including specialized statistical analyses
- Interpreting results and making specific recommendations
- Developing an evaluation report or case study to communicate overall results
- Providing technical support in any phase of the ROI process

The assignment of responsibilities for evaluation also needs attention throughout the evaluation process. Although the training and development staff must have specific responsibilities during an evaluation, it is not unusual to require others in support functions to have responsibility for data collection. These responsibilities are defined when a particular evaluation strategy plan is developed and approved.

Revising/Developing Policies and Procedures

Another part of systematic evaluation is revising (or developing) the organization's policy concerning measurement and evaluation. Evaluation policy is often a part of policy and practice for developing and implementing training and development programs. The policy statement contains information specifically for the measurement and evaluation process. It is frequently developed with the input of the training and development staff and key managers or clients. The policy addresses critical issues that will influence the effectiveness of the measurement and evaluation process. Typical topics include adopting the five-level model presented in this chapter, requiring Level 3 and 4 objectives in some or all programs, and defining responsibilities for training and development. Table 8-5 shows the topics included in the measurement and evaluation policy of a large firm in South Africa.

Table 8-5
Results-based Internal HRD Policy
(excerpts from actual policy for a large firm in South Africa)

1. Purpose
2. Mission
3. Evaluate all programs, which will include the following levels:
   a. Participant satisfaction (100%)
   b. Learning (no less than 70%)
   c. Application (50%)
   d. Impact (usually through sampling) (10%) (highly visible, expensive)
4. Evaluation support group (corporate) will provide assistance and advice in measurement and evaluation, instrument design, data analysis, and evaluation strategy.
5. New programs are developed following logical steps beginning with needs analysis and ending with communicating results.
6. Evaluation instruments must be designed or selected to collect data for evaluation. They must be valid, reliable, economical, and subject to audit by evaluation support group.
7. Responsibility for HRD program results rests with trainers, participants, and supervisors of participants.
8. An adequate system for collecting and monitoring HRD costs must be in place. All direct costs should be included.
9. At least annually, the management board will review the status and results of HRD. The review will include HRD plans, strategies, results, costs, priorities, and concerns.
10. Line management shares in the responsibility for HRD programs. Evaluation, through follow-up, pre-program commitments, and overall support.

(table continued on page 156)

Table 8-5 (continued)
Results-based Internal HRD Policy

11. Managers/supervisors must declare competence achieved through training and packaged programs. When not applicable, HRD staff should evaluate.
12. External HRD consultants must be selected based on previous evaluation. Central data/resource base should exist. All external HRD programs of more than one day in duration will be subjected to evaluation procedures. In addition, participants will assess the quality of external programs.
13. HRD program results must be communicated to the appropriate target audience. At a minimum, this includes management (participants' supervisors), participants, and all HRD staff.
14. HRD staff should be qualified to do effective needs analysis and evaluation.
15. Centralize the data base for program development to prevent duplication and serve as program resource.
16. Union involvement is required in total training and development plan.

Policy statements provide guidance and direction for the staff and others who work closely with evaluation. They provide an opportunity to communicate basic requirements and fundamental issues regarding performance and accountability. More than anything else, they serve as a learning tool to teach others, especially when they are developed in a collaborative and collective way.

Guidelines for measurement and evaluation are important to show how to utilize the tools and techniques, guide the design process, provide consistency in measurement and evaluation, ensure that appropriate methods are used, and place the proper emphasis on each part of the evaluation process. Guidelines are more technical than policy statements and often contain detailed procedures showing how the process is actually undertaken and developed, including forms, instruments, and tools. Table 8-6 shows the table of contents of evaluation guidelines for a multinational company. As this table of contents reveals, the guidelines are comprehensive and include significant emphasis on ROI and accountability.

Table 8-6
Table of Contents of Evaluation Guidelines for a Multinational Company

Section 1:0:	Policy
Section 1:1:	The Results-based Approach of the Learning Institute
Section 1:2:	Evaluation at All Levels—Total Satisfaction Is the Goal
Section 1:3:	Implications
Section 1:4:	Communication
Section 1:5:	Implementation Issues/Targets
Section 1:6:	Payoff
Section 2:0:	Responsibilities
Section 2:1:	The Learning Institute—Overall
Section 2:2:	The Learning Institute—Teams and Primes
Section 2:3:	Business Units
Section 2:4:	Participants' Managers
Section 2:5:	Participants
Section 3:0:	Evaluation Framework
Section 3:1:	Purpose of Evaluation
Section 3:2:	Levels of Evaluation
Section 3:3:	Evaluation Targets
Section 3:4:	Types of Evaluation Data
Section 3:5:	Hard-Data Categories
Section 3:6:	Soft-Data Categories
Section 3:7:	Results-based Model for Implementing New Learning Solutions
Section 3:8:	The ROI Process
Section 4:0:	Level 1 Evaluation Guidelines
Section 4:1:	Purpose and Scope
Section 4:2:	Areas of Coverage—Standard Form
Section 4:3:	Optional Areas of Coverage
Section 4:4:	Administrative Issues
Section 4:5:	How to Use Level 1 Data
Section 5:0:	Level 2 Evaluation Guidelines
Section 5:1:	Purpose and Scope
Section 5:2:	Learning Measurement Issues

(table continued on page 158)

Table 8-6 (continued)
Table of Contents of Evaluation Guidelines for a Multinational Company

Section 5:3:	Techniques for Measuring Learning
Section 5:4:	Administration
Section 5:5:	Using Level 2 Data
Section 6:0:	Level 3 Evaluation Guidelines
Section 6:1:	Purpose and Scope
Section 6:2:	Follow-Up Issues
Section 6:3:	Using Follow-Up Questionnaires and Surveys
Section 6:4:	Action Planning and Follow-Up Assignments
Section 6:5:	Follow-Up Interviews
Section 6:6:	Follow-Up Focus Groups
Section 6:7:	Administrative Issues
Section 6:8:	Using Level 3 Evaluation
Section 7:0:	Level 4 and 5 Evaluation Guidelines
Section 7:1:	Purpose and Scope
Section 7:2:	Business Results and ROI Issues
Section 7:3:	Monitoring Performance Data
Section 7:4:	Isolating the Effects and Learning Solutions
Section 7:5:	Converting Data to Monetary Values
Section 7:6:	Developing Costs
Section 7:7:	Calculating the ROI
Section 7:8:	Using Level 4 and 5 Evaluation Data

Preparing the Staff

One group that will often resist evaluation is the training and development team who must design, develop, and deliver training. These team members often see evaluation as an unnecessary intrusion into their responsibilities, absorbing precious time and stifling their freedom to be creative. On each key issue or major decision, the staff should be involved in the process. As policy statements are prepared and evaluation guidelines developed, staff input is absolutely essential. Staff members will have difficulty criticizing something they helped design and develop. Through meetings, brainstorming sessions, and task forces, the staff should be involved in every phase of developing the framework and supporting documents for evaluation.

One reason staff members may resist evaluation is that it will fully expose the effectiveness of their programs, putting their reputations on the line. They may fear failure. To overcome this, the evaluation should clearly be positioned as a tool for learning and not a tool to evaluate training staff performance, at least during its early years of implementation. Staff members will not take interest in developing a process that the organization will use against them.

Several obstacles to the implementation of evaluation will usually be uncovered. Some of these are realistic barriers, while others are often based on misconceptions. Each should be explored and addressed.

The training and development staff usually has inadequate skills in measurement and evaluation and needs to develop some expertise in the process. Measurement and evaluation is not always a formal part of staff members' preparation to become trainers or instructional designers. Consequently, each staff member must be provided with step-by-step training to learn how measurement and evaluation works. In addition, staff members must know how to develop an evaluation strategy and specific plan, collect and analyze data from the evaluation, and interpret results from data analysis. Sometimes a one- to two-day workshop is needed to build adequate skills and knowledge to understand the process, appreciate what it can do for the organization, see the necessity for it, and participate in a successful implementation.

Trend Consequences

Impact

From the viewpoint of all parties involved, this is a welcome trend. Systematic evaluation is a necessary process to ensure that all stakeholders have the information desired and to clearly pinpoint the success of training.

The increased usage of systematic evaluation may require additional funding for the evaluation process. It may help to consider the current funding level for evaluation as a percentage of the total training and development budget. In most organizations, this number is less than 1 percent of the total training and development budget. This figure is developed by adding the direct and indirect evaluation costs and dividing the sum by the total direct expenditures for training and development (which usually includes all expenditures other than the participants' salaries for their time in training). A more systematic evaluation process may require that this percentage be increased to 4 percent or 5 percent. The payoff should be a more effective training and development process, possibly overshadowing the additional funding. In essence, no additional funding is usually required; the budget is just rearranged to allocate more funds for measurement and evaluation.

A systematic approach also requires the T&D leader to pay more attention to the training and development staff and communicate information about evaluation more frequently. This can reduce the resistance to increased evaluation. To ensure that increased evaluation is effective, the management group usually acts as a part of this systematic evaluation, and the participants will assume more responsibilities in the future.

Key Questions

When considering this issue, the following questions should be addressed:

Key Questions

1. Do I agree with this trend?
2. How important is systematic evaluation to my department?
3. How much progress has been made toward systematic evaluation?
4. Will my staff support this trend?
5. If not, what must I do to make systematic evaluation more evident?
6. What will happen if I do nothing?
7. What specific resources will be necessary?
8. What targets for evaluation levels will be appropriate?

Key Questions (continued)

9. Is built-in evaluation possible?
10. Do policies and procedures need to be developed or revised?
11. Who is the champion of this process?
12. Which responsibilities need to change?
13. Which skills need to be developed?
14. Will the management group support this trend?

Outlook

It appears that this trend will continue, as the drivers and causes for the trend will likely intensify, forcing more organizations to take a systematic approach to evaluation. Because a systematic approach brings more efficiency and effectiveness to the evaluation process, this approach will be needed more in the future.

References

1. "Industry Report." *Training,* Oct. 1996.
2. "Benchmarking Budgets." *Training & Development,* 1997.
3. Kirkpatrick, Donald L. "The Four Levels: An Overview," in *Evaluating Training Programs: The Four Levels,* 2nd ed. San Francisco: Berrett-Koehler Publishers, 1998.
4. Kirkpatrick, Donald L. "Techniques for Evaluating Training Programs." *Journal of ASTD, Vol. 11,* 1959, pp. 3–9.
5. Phillips, Jack J. "Level Four and Beyond: An ROI Model," in *Evaluating Corporate Training: Models and Issues.* S. M. Brown and C. Seidner (Eds.), Norwell, Miss.: Kluwer Academic Press, 1997.
6. Broad, M. L. and Newstrom, J. W. *Transfer of Training.* Reading, Mass.: Addison Wesley, 1992.
7. Phillips, Jack J. *Handbook of Training Evaluation and Measurement Methods,* 3rd ed. Houston, Tex.: Gulf Publishing Company, 1997, p. 161.
8. Phillips, Jack J. "Was It the Training?" *Training & Development,* Vol. 50, No. 3, Mar. 1996, pp. 28–32.

9

MEASURING ROI

Trend Definition and Validation

Brief Definition of Trend

An important trend of increased accountability for training results made the measurement of return on investment (ROI) a routine part of evaluation processes in many organizations. Senior executives are requiring results in terms they understand and appreciate. An ROI calculation clearly shows the ultimate value of training when benefits are compared with the cost of (or investment in) programs. Because the actual number of ROI calculations is small relative to the total number of possibilities, a convenient sampling process is used to select the appropriate programs for this ultimate level of evaluation.

Case Studies: NYNEX and DHL

NYNEX. Created by the merger of New York Telephone and New England Telephone and now merged with Bell Atlantic, NYNEX became interested in implementing the ROI process in response to increased pressure from senior executives to calculate the actual return on investment in a variety of training programs. The training and development (T&D) staff pursued the ROI process and implemented a methodology to develop a limited number of ROI calculations throughout NYNEX. T&D established specific criteria to select the programs to target for ROI calculations, including the following:

- A predetermined number of employees per year must participate in the program.
- The minimum course life must be one year.
- The program must have high impact and visibility.
- The program must relate to a critical job function or cover a critical subject matter.

Follow-up evaluations collect data on a post-program basis, usually three to six months after participants complete the program. NYNEX uses the ROI information in a variety of ways to improve programs, build a productive partnership relationship with key managerial groups, and increase the respect for the training and development function. As of 1997, NYNEX had a target of developing eighteen ROI studies per year, representing a very comprehensive approach to the ROI process.

DHL Worldwide Express. A package-delivery company based in Brussels, Belgium, DHL enjoys No. 1 market share in most countries it serves except the United States. The manager of training and development for Europe and Africa accepted a challenge from the president of DHL to bring additional accountability to the human resource function and, more specifically, to training and development. The manager searched for the appropriate process to measure the actual return on investment for a variety of training programs. After reviewing several models in Europe, Asia, and North America, the manager selected an ROI process offered by Performance Resources

Organization. An initial two-day ROI workshop was conducted to expose key training managers at DHL to the concept of ROI. After this introduction, a representative manager from each major European and African country participated in a certification process to build comprehensive skills that dealt with how to measure return on investment using the same ROI formula as the representatives used with other investments. As part of the certification process, each manager pursued ROI studies for critical programs in the company. Collectively, DHL training managers are building a data base of ROI studies about major programs, showing the actual ROI expressed as a percentage.

As these two situations illustrate, the ROI process is becoming a routine part of many organizations as they pursue the ultimate level of evaluation.

Evidence of Trend

Measuring the return on investment in training and development consistently earned a place among the critical issues in the HRD field during the past five to ten years.[1] The topic appears routinely on conference agendas and at most professional meetings. Journals and newsletters regularly embrace the concept with increasing print space. At least a dozen books provide significant coverage of the topic, and at least three are devoted exclusively to the subject. Even top executives stepped up their appetites for ROI information.

The practitioner survey of global trends showed that the ROI is a visible trend with a level of agreement with the existence of the trend receiving a score of 4.02 out of 5 (see Appendix 1). The importance of the trend was rated 4.71 out of 5, which makes this the second most important trend. These high ratings of the ROI process give firm evidence of the significance practitioners place on the trend and their recognition of its progress in recent years.

The status of the ROI process among practitioners in the field is difficult to pinpoint. Senior HRD managers are reluctant to disclose internal practices, and even in the most progressive organizations, they confess that they have made too little progress. In the past, it was difficult to find cases in the literature illustrating how an organization attempted to measure the return on investment in HRD. Recognizing this void, the American Society for Training and Development (ASTD) undertook an ambitious project to develop a collection of cases that represent a variety of examples of measuring ROI. To find the cases, ASTD contacted more than 2,000 individuals for the initial volume, including practitioners, authors, researchers, consultants, and conference presenters. The response was encouraging. More than 150 individuals from several major countries requested specific guidelines as they explored the possibility of developing cases.

To have their cases accepted for publication, authors had to be willing to detail specific steps, issues, and concerns involved as the ROI was developed. In the final analysis, forty individuals expressed willingness to submit cases, and ASTD halted the acquisition process when it received thirty cases. Ultimately, ASTD selected eighteen of those cases for the casebook *In Action: Measuring Return on Investment,* published in 1994.[2] The casebook was the American Society for Training and Development's best-seller in 1995, 1996, and 1997, outselling more than 250 titles. Because of the reaction and response, ASTD repeated the process and published Volume 2 in 1997.[3] Volume 3 is planned for 1999.

One of the most interesting signs of progress with training evaluation and measurement comes from the annual Industry Report compiled by *Training* magazine.[4] In 1996, *Training* surveyed more than 40,000 training managers and specialists to determine the status of evaluation at different levels. The study revealed that 49 percent of organizations measure the success of training at the business results level, which usually reflects ROI. Those organizations evaluate 44 percent of courses at the ROI level.

ROI is now receiving increased interest from the executive suite. Top executives who watched their training budgets grow without the appropriate accountability measures are frustrated and, in an attempt to respond to the situation, have demanded a return on the training investment. The payoff of training is becoming a conversation topic in senior executive circles. As evidence, the theme of the summer 1995 issue of *William and Mary Business Review* was "Corporate Training: Does It Pay Off?"[5] Distributed to corporate leaders and executives, the *William and Mary Business Review* special summer issue focuses on an important topic facing corporate executives to stimulate intellectual and practical debate of prevailing management concerns. In summer 1995, the *William and Mary Business Review* provided a critical examination of the ROI topic by assembling diverse points of view from members of academic and professional communities within ten articles. "Measuring Training's ROI: It Can Be Done!" was the lead story.[6]

Virtually every function in an organization is being subjected to increased demands for accountability. Functions that were previously assumed necessary and immeasurable (such as public relations) now must show a contribution.[7] This is especially true for staff support functions. Even internal auditors, who several years ago never dreamed of being held accountable for their success, are now adapting measurement processes and, in some cases, turning audit functions into profit centers. In this respect, training and development is just one of many functions responding to pressures to show their contributions in measurable terms.

Causes and Drivers

In all areas of the HRD field, the pressure to measure ROI is increasing. The issue is a hot topic in developing countries, as well as in fully developed nations. Sooner or later, every organization will face this concern. The pressure to measure the results from training may come from line managers, internal customers of HRD who must support HRD, or top executives who must allocate resources to those functions that are contributing to the bottom line. Several important drivers are visible. Collectively, they provide evidence of the pressure for increased use of ROI.

- Clear evidence of the increase in training and development budgets exists. In the United States, budgets for 1997 went up 5 percent for 1998. The number of individuals trained in 1997 was 56.6 million, an 8 percent increase from 1996 and one of the largest increases in recent history.[8] Budgets are also increasing in other countries, particularly where training expenditures are tied to government legislation. As budgets increase, so does the need for accountability. Large (and growing) budgets become bigger targets for critics. When training and development receives significant funding increases, it usually happens at the expense of other functions of the organization. As the percentage of operating expenses allocated to training increases, the budget will continue to be a target of people who question the size of the budget and its relationship to organization effectiveness. These situations place pressure on the training and development staff to show that the function achieves results.

- Many organizations use training and development as a competitive weapon to create a distinct market advantage. In some situations, training is seen as **the** most critical competitive weapon. Whether the organization is experiencing tremendous growth, restructuring, right-sizing, or changing markets and locations, training is seen as an important vehicle to implement these changes. Ambitious training and development efforts, linked with competitive strategies, enable organizations to increase market share, introduce new products, improve delivery and customer service, reduce cost, become more efficient, improve response times, and increase productivity. When training takes on this highly visible role, there is pressure for accountability.[9] Executives and other stakeholders want to measure and hold accountable all competitive tools and initiatives.
- ROI applications have increased because of growing interest in organizational improvement and change. Some organizations have tried almost any trend that appeared on the horizon. Unfortunately, many of these change efforts failed. The attempt to improve the organization resulted in a passing fad.[10] The training and development function often gets caught in the middle of this activity, by either supporting or coordinating the new effort. Although the ROI process is an effective way to measure the accountability of training, it was rarely used in the past.
- Fourth, the business management mind-set of many HRD managers causes them to place more emphasis on economic issues within the function. Today's training manager is more aware of bottom-line issues in the organization and is more knowledgeable of operational and financial areas, often having spent some time in those areas. This new, enlightened manager often takes a business approach to education and training, and the ROI issue is a part of this strategy.
- The restructuring and reengineering experience and the threat of outsourcing caused many education and training executives to focus more clearly and directly on bottom-line issues. Many education and training processes were reengineered so that programs align more closely with business needs and so that maximum efficiencies are achieved in the various stages of the HRD cycle.

These change processes brought more attention to evaluation issues and resulted in measuring the contributions of specific programs. The threat of outsourcing forced some education and training managers to more closely align programs to organizational objectives and to measure successes so that management can understand the contribution to the organization.

- Complete implementation of the ROI process requires a thorough needs assessment and significant planning. If these two elements are in place, organizations can avoid passing fads doomed for failure.[11] Utilizing the ROI process will expose new programs that do not produce positive results. Early awareness will allow managers to make appropriate adjustments to the programs.
- Chief executives, struggling to make their organizations profitable and viable, are demanding accountability with all expenditures. They encourage, and sometimes require, the training staff to measure the return on all training investments. In some cases, executives issue ultimatums to either show value or reduce operating budgets, as happened at IBM.[12] In other cases, senior executives employ subtle hints and suggestions. Even executive education programs offered by universities, which were previously untouchable on the accountability issue, are expected to result in a positive return.[13]

These drivers occur in all types of organizations and place renewed demands on training and development staffs to show their contributions in measurable, quantitative terms. This pressure creates a need to calculate the ROI for at least a few programs so that management will have confidence that all programs produce adequate returns. Most practitioners view return investment as an extension of the four-level evaluation framework described in the previous chapter. Essentially, ROI is the fifth level of evaluation, where the actual monetary benefits of the training and development program are compared with the cost of the program.[14] This ultimate evaluation shows the organization if the initiative represented was a sound investment.

The desire to achieve the ultimate level of evaluation drives many ROI calculations. Practitioners, managers, and other stakeholders take interest in this ultimate level. For years, managers have used the concept of return on investment to show the financial payoff of investments in equipment, buildings, and new product lines.[15] They understand the concept clearly and feel comfortable with the evaluation data. Now managers want the same evaluation process applied to other types of investments, such as education and training.

Trend Description

The calculation of the return on investment begins with the basic ROI process model shown in Figure 9-1, which simplifies a potentially complicated process.[16] The model provides a systematic approach to ROI calculations and meets the criteria for an effective ROI process. The model also emphasizes the fact that this is a logical, systematic process that flows from one step to another.

A step-by-step approach keeps the process manageable so the users can address one issue at a time. Applying the model provides consistency from one ROI calculation to another. Because of the time and costs involved in an ROI analysis, only a small number of programs are evaluated at this level, usually 5 to 10 percent.

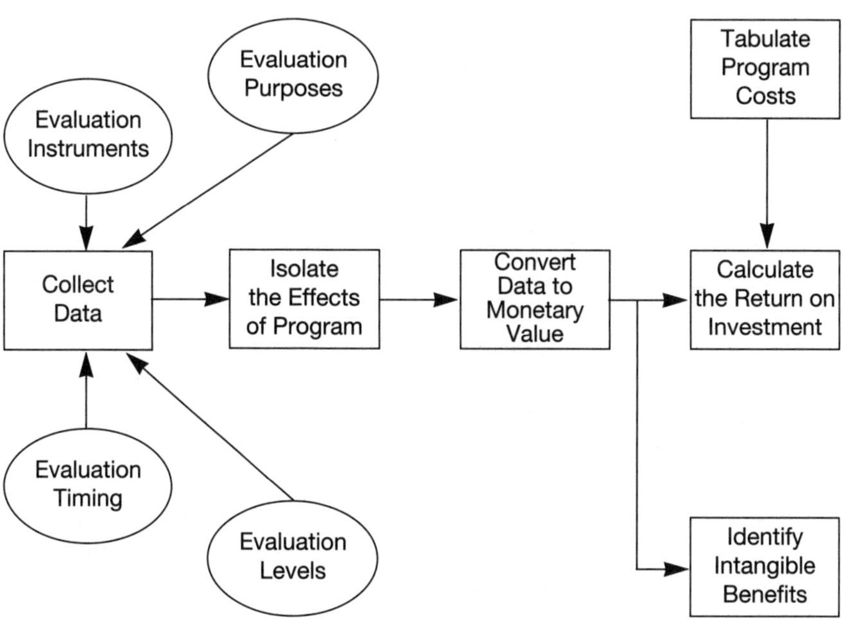

Figure 9-1. *ROI Process Model.*

Planning Data Collection

Four specific elements of the evaluation process must be understood when developing the plan for an ROI calculation. These are enclosed in the circles in Figure 9-1.

Examine the purposes for the evaluation. This often determines the scope of the evaluation, the types of instruments needed, the type of data collected, and the data collection methodology. For example, when an ROI calculation is planned, one of the purposes is to compare the cost and benefits of the program. This purpose has implications for the type of data collected (hard data), the data collection method (performance monitoring), the type of analysis (thorough), and the communication medium for results (formal evaluation report). For most programs, multiple evaluation purposes are pursued.

Consider the instrument selection. The instruments most familiar to the culture of the organization and appropriate for the setting and evaluation requirements should be used in the data collection process.

Determine the levels of evaluation. Training programs are evaluated at five different levels, as illustrated earlier. Data should be collected at Level 1, Level 2, Level 3, and Level 4 if an ROI analysis is planned. This approach ensures that the chain of impact occurs as participants learn the skills, apply them on the job, and obtain business results.

Determine the timing of the data collection. A final part of the evaluation plan is the data collection timing. In some cases, pre-program measurements are taken to compare with post-program measurements. In other cases, multiple measures are taken throughout the program. When pre-program measurements are not available, follow-up measurements are still taken afterward. It is important to determine the appropriate timing for the follow-up evaluation.

These four elements—evaluation purposes, instruments, levels, and timing—are all considerations in selecting data collection methods and developing a data collection plan.

Collecting Data

Data collection is central to the ROI process. Post-program data are collected and compared with pre-program situations, control group differences, and expectations. Both hard data (representing output, quality, cost, and time) and soft data (including work habits, work climate, and attitudes) are collected. Data are collected using various methods suitable for ROI calculations:

- Follow-up **questionnaires** are administered to uncover specific applications of training. Participants provide responses to a variety of open-ended and forced-response questions.
- Post-program **interviews** are conducted with participants to determine the extent to which they have utilized learning on the job. Interviews allow for probing to uncover specific applications and results.
- **Program assignments** are useful for simple short-term projects. Participants complete the assignments on the job, utilizing skills or knowledge learned in the program.
- **Action plans** developed in training programs are implemented on the job after the program is completed. A follow-up of action plans provides evidence of training program success.
- **Performance contracts** are developed when the participant, the participant's supervisor, and the instructor all agree on specific outcomes from training, prior to the program.
- **Performance monitoring** is sometimes used when various performance records and operational data are examined for improvement.

The importance of this step is to select the data collection method or methods appropriate for the setting and program within the time and budget constraints of the organization.

Isolating the Effects of Training

An issue often overlooked in most evaluation processes is the isolation of the effects of training programs. In this step, specific strategies are explored that determine the amount of performance directly related to the program. This step is essential because of the number of factors that will influence performance data after training. The specific strategies of this step will pinpoint the amount of improvement directly related to the training program. The result is increased accuracy and credibility of the ROI calculation. Many organizations have used the following strategies.[17]

- A **control group** arrangement is used to isolate training impact. With this strategy, one group receives training while a similar group does not. The difference in the performances of the two groups is attributed to the training program. When properly set up and implemented, control group management is the most effective way to isolate the effects of training.
- **Trend lines** are used to project the value-specific output variables if training had not been undertaken. The projection is compared with the actual data after training, and the difference represents the estimate of the impact of training. This strategy can be an accurate way to isolate the impact of training when two conditions exist: The pre-program trend is likely to continue during the evaluation period if the program was not implemented and no new influences entered the process during the evaluation period.
- A **forecasting model** is used when mathematical relationships between input and output variables are known. With this approach, the output variable is predicted using the forecasting model with the assumption that no training is conducted. The actual performance of the variable after the training takes place is then compared with the forecasted value to estimate the impact of training.
- **Participants estimate** the amount of improvement related to training. In this approach, participants are provided with the total amount of improvement, on a pre- and post-program basis, and are asked to indicate the percent of the improvement that actually relates to the training program.
- **Supervisors of participants** estimate the impact of training on the output variables. With this approach, supervisors of participants are presented with the total amount of improvement and are asked to indicate the percent related to training.

- **Senior managers** estimate the impact of training. In these cases, managers provide an estimate, or "adjustment," to reflect the portion of the improvement related to the training program. Although the estimates are perhaps inaccurate, some advantages to having senior management involved in this process do exist.
- **Experts provide estimates** of the impact of training on the performance variable. Because the estimates are based on previous experience, the experts must be familiar with the type of training and the specific situation.
- In supervisory and management training, **the subordinates of participants identify changes** in the work climate that could influence the output variables. In this approach, the subordinates of the supervisors receiving training determine if other variables that could have influenced output performance changed in the work climate.
- When feasible, **other influencing factors are identified** and the impact estimated or calculated, leaving the remaining unexplained improvement attributed to training. In this case, the influences of all the other factors are developed, and training remains the one variable not accounted for in the analysis. The unexplained portion of the output is then attributed to training.
- In some situations, **customers provide input** about the extent to which training influenced their decisions to use a product or service. Although this strategy has limited applications, it can be quite useful in customer service and sales training.

Collectively, these ten strategies provide a comprehensive set of tools to tackle the important and critical issue of isolating the effects of training.

Converting Data to Monetary Values

To calculate the return on investment, data collected in a Level 4 evaluation are converted to monetary values to compare program benefits to program costs. This requires a value to be placed on each unit of data connected with the program. Ten strategies are available to convert data to monetary values, and the specific strategy selected usually depends upon the type of data and the situation.[18]

- **Output data are converted to either profit contribution or cost savings.** In this strategy, output increases are converted to monetary values based on their unit contribution to profit or to cost reduction. These values are readily available in most organizations.
- The **cost of quality is calculated,** and quality improvements are directly converted to cost savings. This cost is available in many organizations as a standard value.
- **Participant wages and benefits are used for the value of time** for programs in which employee time is saved. Because a variety of programs focus on improving the time required to complete projects, processes, or daily activities, the value of time becomes an important and necessary issue.
- **Historical costs are used** when they are available for a specific variable. In this case, organizational cost data are utilized to establish the specific value of an improvement.
- When available, **internal and external experts estimate** a value for an improvement. In this situation, the credibility of the estimate hinges on the expertise and reputation of the individual.
- **External data bases are sometimes available** to estimate the value or cost of data items. Research, government, and industry data bases can provide important information for these values. The difficulty often lies in finding a specific data base related to the situation.
- **Participants estimate the value** of the data item. For this approach to be effective, participants must be capable of providing a value for the improvement.
- **Supervisors of participants provide estimates** when the supervisors are both willing and capable of assigning values to the improvement. This approach is especially useful when participants are not fully capable of providing this input or in situations where a supervisor needs to confirm or adjust the participant's estimate.
- **Senior managers provide estimates** of the value of an improvement when they are willing to offer estimates. This approach is particularly helpful to establish values for performance measures that are important to senior management.
- **Staff estimates** may be used to determine a value of an output data item. In these cases the estimates must be provided on an unbiased basis.

This step in the ROI model is important and absolutely necessary to determine the monetary benefits from a program. The process is challenging, particularly with soft data, but can be methodically accomplished using one or more of the above strategies.

Tabulating Program Costs

The other part of the equation on a cost benefit analysis is the cost of the program. Tabulating the costs involves monitoring or developing all the related costs of the program targeted for the ROI calculation. Among the cost components that should be included are:

- The cost to design and develop the program, possibly prorated over the expected life of the program
- The cost of all program materials provided to each participant
- The cost of the instructor/facilitator including preparation time, as well as delivery time
- The cost of the facilities for the training program
- The cost of travel, lodging, and meals for the participants, if applicable
- The cost of salaries plus employee benefits of the participants attending training
- Administrative and overhead costs of the training function allocated in some convenient way to the training program.

In addition, specific costs related to the needs assessment and evaluation should be included, if appropriate. The conservative approach is to include all possible costs so that the total takes into account every potentiality and is, therefore, fully loaded.

Calculating the ROI

The return on investment is calculated using the program benefits and costs. The benefit-cost ratio is the program benefits divided by cost. In formula form, it is:

$$\text{BCR} = \frac{\text{Program Benefits}}{\text{Program Costs}}$$

The return on investment uses the net benefits divided by program costs. The net benefits are the program benefits minus the costs. In formula form, the ROI becomes:

$$\text{ROI}(\%) = \frac{\text{Net Program Benefits}}{\text{Program Costs}} \times 100$$

This is the same basic formula used to evaluate other investments in which the ROI is traditionally reported as earnings divided by investment. The ROI from many training programs is quite high. For example, in sales training, supervisory training, and managerial training, the ROI can be large, frequently more than 100 percent, while the ROI value for technical and operator training may be lower.

For short-term programs, all the program costs could be included in the analysis along with one year of benefits, requiring the project to produce a payoff in one year. However, for most programs, the costs are significant, and implementation may span several months or years. Consequently, the costs and benefits must be captured during an appropriate time period to reflect the proper return on investment. The actual timing for capturing the benefits is a difficult issue. The longer the time frame, the more difficult it is to capture the benefits and isolate the effects of the program from other influences. In addition, a longer time frame delays the information concerning the ultimate success of the program. Thus, a shorter time frame is actually desired. Several issues determine the specific time:

- The time it takes for the program to have the desired effects and for the impact to be sustained for an appropriate evaluation period
- The time requirements recommended by the finance and accounting staff regarding the evaluation for this type of investment
- The actual length of time for the overall project development and implementation (For example, a project that takes only one month to implement may be evaluated in a shorter time frame than a project that takes two years to implement.)
- The desire of senior management to have an evaluation and payback developed from this effort

These issues, along with others, may drive the specific timing. The important point is to use proration or allocation to derive the appropriate time frame to evaluate the return on investment. The conservative approach is always recommended as it enhances the credibility of the process.

Identifying Intangible Benefits

Most training programs have both tangible, monetary benefits and intangible, non-monetary benefits. The ROI calculation is based on converting both hard and soft data to monetary values. Other data items are identified that are not converted to monetary values. These intangible benefits include items such as:

- Increased job satisfaction
- Increased organizational commitment
- Improved teamwork
- Improved customer service
- Reduced complaints
- Reduced conflicts

During data analysis, every attempt is made to convert all data to monetary values. All hard data, such as output, quality, and time, are converted to monetary values. The conversion of soft data is attempted for each data item. However, if the process used for conversion is too subjective or inaccurate, and if the resulting values lose credibility in the process, then the measure is listed as an intangible benefit with the appropriate explanation. For some programs, intangible, non-monetary benefits are extremely valuable, often carrying as much influence as the hard data items.

Implementation Issues

A variety of issues influences the success of ROI impact studies and the implementation of a comprehensive measurement and evaluation system. These must be addressed early to ensure that the ROI process succeeds. Specific issues include:

- Staffing and resource allocation for measurement and evaluation
- Policy statements concerning the measurement and evaluation

- Procedures and guidelines for different elements of measurement and evaluation
- Meetings and formal training sessions to develop skills for measurement and evaluation
- Strategies to improve management commitment and support for measurement and evaluation
- Mechanisms to provide technical support for evaluation
- Specific strategies to place more attention on results

Although success or failure often depends on these implementation issues, coverage of these topics is beyond the scope of this chapter. Chapter 8 covered these issues.

Planning of ROI

An important ingredient to the success of the ROI analysis is to properly plan for the ROI early in the process. Appropriate up-front attention will save much time later when data are actually collected and analyzed, thus improving the accuracy and reducing the cost of the ROI process. It also avoids any confusion surrounding what will be accomplished, by whom, and at what time. Two planning documents are the keys to the up-front analysis and should be completed before the program is designed or developed. The following sections describe both documents.

Data Collection Plan

As shown in Figure 9-2, the data collection form captures the major elements and issues regarding collecting data for the four evaluation levels. Broad areas for objectives are appropriate for planning. Specific, detailed objectives are developed later, before the program is implemented. The objectives for Level 1 usually include positive reactions to the program. Data collection is usually accomplished with a standard questionnaire administered during the program by the facilitator.

The specific objectives for Level 2 include those areas in which individuals involved in the program are expected to change knowledge, skills, or attitudes. The data collection method is the specific way in which learning is assessed, whether through a test, simulation, skill practice, or facilitator assessment. The timing for Level 2 evalua-

Level	Objective(s)	Data Collection	Timing	Responsibilities
I. Reaction				
II. Learning				
III. Implementation				
IV. Business Impact				

Figure 9-2. Data Collection Plan.

tion is usually during or at the end of learning activities, and the responsibility rests with the facilitator.

For Level 3 evaluations, the objectives represent broad areas of program implementation, including significant on-the-job activities. The evaluation method includes one of the data collection methods described earlier and usually is conducted a matter of weeks or months after program implementation. Because several groups often share responsibilities, it is important to clarify the responsibility issue early in the process.

Level 4 evaluation objectives focus on business-impact measures influenced by the program. The objectives may include the way in which each item is measured. For example, if one of the objectives is to improve quality, a specific measure would indicate how quality is actually measured, such as errors per thousand transactions. Although the preferred evaluation method is performance monitoring, other methods such as action planning may be appropriate. The timing depends on how quickly the program can generate a sustained business impact—usually a matter of months after implementation. The responsibility usually rests with the program evaluator.

The data collection plan is an important part of the evaluation strategy and should be completed prior to moving forward with the impact study. The plan provides a clear direction of what type of data will be collected, how the data will be collected, when the data will be collected, and who will collect them.

ROI Analysis Plan

Figure 9-3 shows an ROI analysis plan, which is a continuation of the data collection plan presented in Figure 9-2. This document captures information about several key items that are necessary to develop the actual ROI calculation. The first column lists significant data items, usually Level 4 data items. These measures will be used in the ROI analysis. The method to isolate the effects of the program is listed next to each data item in the second column. For most cases the method will be the same for each data item, but variations could occur. For example, if no historical data are available for one data item, then trend line analysis is not possible for that item although it may be appropriate for others.

Project: ____________ Responsibility: ____________ Date: ____________

Data Items (Typically Level 4 Measures)	Methods of Isolating the Effects of the Program	Methods of Converting Data	Program Cost Categories	Intangible Benefits	Other Influences/ Issues	Communication Targets

Figure 9-3. ROI Analysis Plan.

The methods of converting data to monetary values are included in the third column, using the strategies outlined earlier. The cost categories from the program are outlined in the fourth column. Instructions about how certain costs should be prorated would be noted here. Usually the cost categories remain consistent from one program to another. However, a specific cost unique to the program would also be noted here. The intangible benefits expected from the program are outlined in the fifth column. This list is generated from discussions about the program with sponsors, specialists, and experts.

Other issues or events that might influence program implementation and success are highlighted in the sixth column. Typical items include the staff capabilities, access to data sources, and unique data analysis issues. Finally, communication targets are outlined in the last column. Although there could be many groups that should receive the ROI analysis information, the following target groups are recommended:

- Senior management group
- Supervisors and managers who work in the area where the program is implemented
- Individual employees directly involved in program implementation
- HR staff
- Principal clients

All these groups need to know about the results of ROI analysis.

The ROI analysis plan and the data collection plan provide detailed information about calculating the ROI, illustrating how the process will develop from beginning to end. When thoroughly completed, these two plans provide the direction necessary for ROI evaluation.

Trend Consequences

Impact

Although much progress has been made, the ROI process is not without its share of problems and drawbacks. The mere presence of the process creates a dilemma for many organizations. When an organization embraces the concept and implements the process, the management team usually anxiously awaits results, only to be disappointed when the results are not quantifiable. For an ROI process to be useful, it must balance many issues, such as feasibility, simplicity, credibility, and soundness. More specifically, three major audiences must be pleased with the ROI process to accept and use it. These audiences are as follows:

HRD Practitioners. For years, training and development practitioners assumed that ROI could not be measured. When they examined a typical process, they found long formulas, complicated equations, and complex models that made the ROI process appear too confusing. With this perceived complexity, training and development managers could visualize tremendous effort required for data collection and analysis and, more importantly, increased cost necessary to make the process work. Because of these concerns, practitioners are seeking an ROI process that is straightforward and easy to understand so that they can easily implement the steps and strategies. Also, they need a process that does not require an excessive time frame to perform and will not consume too much valuable staff time. Finally, practitioners need an affordable process. With competition for financial resources, they need a process that will not command a significant portion of the budget. In summary, the ROI process, from the perspective of the practitioner, must be user friendly, not very demanding of the practitioner's time, and cost-efficient.

Senior Managers/Sponsors/Clients. Managers who must approve training and development budgets, request programs, or live with the results of programs have a strong interest in developing the ROI in training. They want a process that provides quantifiable results, using a method similar to the ROI formula applied to other types of investments. Senior managers have a never-ending desire to have it all come down to an ROI calculation reflected as a percentage. Along with practitioners, they want a process that is simple and easy to understand. The assumptions made in the calculations and the methodology used in the process should reflect their point of reference, background, and level of understanding. They do not want, or need, a string of formulas, charts, or complicated models. Instead, they need a process they can explain to others. More importantly, they need a process with which they can identify, one that is sound and realistic enough to earn their confidence.

Researchers. Finally, researchers will only support a process that measures up to their scrutiny and close examination. Researchers usually insist that models, formulas, assumptions, and theories are sound and based on commonly accepted practices. They also want a process that produces accurate values and consistent outcomes. If estimates are necessary, researchers want a process that provides the most accuracy within the constraints of the situation, recognizing that adjustments need to be made when there is uncertainty in the process. The challenge is to develop acceptable requirements for an ROI process that will satisfy researchers and, at the same time, please practitioners and senior managers. Sound impossible? Maybe not.

Criteria for an Effective ROI Process

To satisfy the needs of the three critical groups, the ROI process must meet several requirements. Ten essential criteria for an effective ROI process are outlined below. These criteria were developed in focus groups made up of managers and specialists in training and development.

- The ROI process must be **simple,** void of complex formulas, lengthy equations, and complicated methodologies. Most ROI attempts have failed with this requirement. In an attempt to obtain statistical perfection and use too many theories, several ROI models and processes have become too complex to understand and use. Consequently, they have not been implemented.
- The ROI process must be **economical** with the ability to be implemented easily. The process should have the capability to become a routine part of HR without requiring significant additional resources. Sampling for ROI calculations and early planning for ROI are often necessary to make progress without adding new staff.
- The assumptions, methodology, and outcomes must be **credible.** Logical, methodical steps are needed to earn the respect of practitioners, senior managers, and researchers. This requires a practical approach to the process.
- From a research perspective, the ROI process must be **theoretically sound** and based on generally accepted practices. Unfortunately, this requirement can lead to an extensive, complicated process.

Ideally, the process must strike a balance between maintaining a practical and sensible approach *and* a sound and theoretical basis for the procedures. This is perhaps one of the greatest challenges to those who develop models for the ROI process.

- An ROI process must **account for other factors** that have influenced output variables. One of the most often overlooked issues, isolating the influence of a program, is necessary to build credibility and accuracy within the process. The ROI process should pinpoint the contribution of the program when compared with the other influences.
- The ROI process must be **appropriate with a variety of programs.** Some models apply to only a small number of programs, such as productivity improvement. Ideally, the process must be applicable to all types of education and training programs, such as career development, organization development, and major change initiatives.
- The ROI process must have the **flexibility** to be applied on a pre-program basis, as well as on a post-program basis. In some situations, an estimate of the ROI is required before the actual program is developed. Ideally, the process should be able to adjust to a range of potential time frames for calculating the ROI.
- The ROI process must be **applicable with all types of data,** including hard data (which are typically represented as output, quality, costs, and time) *and* soft data (which include job satisfaction, customer satisfaction, absenteeism, turnover, grievances, and complaints).
- The ROI process must **include the cost of the program.** The ultimate level of evaluation compares the benefits with costs. Although the term ROI has been loosely used to express any benefit of education or training, an acceptable ROI formula must include costs. Omitting or understating costs only destroys the credibility of the ROI values.
- Finally, the ROI process must have a **successful track record** in a variety of applications. In far too many situations, models are created but never successfully applied. An effective ROI process should withstand the wear and tear of implementation and prove valuable to users.

Table 9-2
Criteria for an Effective ROI Process

Simple	Appropriate with a Variety of Programs
Economical	Flexibile
Credible	Computable with All Types of Data
Theoretically Sound	Includes the Cost of the Program
Accounts for Other Factors	Has a Successful Track Record

In practice, finding a process that can meet all of these criteria is difficult. The model presented earlier does meet these criteria, and hundreds of major organizations throughout the world have adopted it.

Key Questions

To determine if the ROI process is appropriate, the following key questions should be considered:

Key Questions

1. To what extent is this trend occurring in my organization?
2. How important is this trend?
3. How much progress has been made to develop ROI in our organization?
4. Does the training and development staff support the ROI process?
5. Is the training and development staff prepared for the ROI process?
6. What are the specific drivers within my organization?
7. What barriers exist for implementing the ROI process?
8. What happens if I do nothing?
9. To what extent does management support this process?
10. How much encouragement/pressure am I receiving now to implement the ROI process?

Outlook

From all indications, the ROI trend is here to stay. This conclusion rests on several assumptions. The drivers for the ROI process have been developing for years and will continue to intensify in the future. Evaluation data developed at the ultimate level will always be needed as long as there are training expenditures.

The ROI is a formula that has weathered the test of time. For many years, businesses have used the concept to measure the economic payoff for investment in buildings, equipment, and even companies. In recent years, it has been used to calculate the return on other types of investments, including training and development.

The ROI process is simple and converts evaluation into a quantifiable value. In addition, when used properly, it provides a string of other types of information that helps provide an overall assessment. Thus, it provides an ultimate level of evaluation of the effectiveness of a program.

Developing the ROI for a select number of programs is a challenging but necessary process. The ROI issue can no longer be ignored, and it must be implemented with a rational approach that is acceptable to the many stakeholders involved in the process. The challenge is to integrate the process into the organization gradually and with the support of various stakeholders.

References

1. Bartel, Ann P. "Return on Investments," in *What Works: Assessment Development and Measurement.* Alexandria, Va.: American Society for Training and Development, 1997.
2. Phillips, Jack J. (Ed.) *In Action: Measuring Return on Investment, Vol 1.* Alexandria, Va.: American Society for Training and Development, 1994.
3. Phillips, Jack J. (Ed.) *In Action: Measuring Return on Investment, Vol. 2.* Alexandria, Va.: American Society for Training and Development, 1997.
4. "Industry Report." *Training,* Oct. 1996.
5. Phillips, Jack J. "Corporate Training: Does It Pay Off?" *William and Mary Business Review,* Summer 1995.

6. Phillips, Jack J. "Measuring Training's ROI: It Can Be Done!" *William and Mary Business Review,* Summer 1995, pp. 6–10.
7. Chase, Nancy. "Raise Your Training ROI." *Quality,* Sept. 1997, pp. 28–41.
8. "Industry Report." *Training,* Oct. 1997.
9. Hronec, Steven M. *Vital Signs: Using Quality Timing Cost Performance Measures to Chart Your Company's Future.* New York: Amacom, 1993.
10. Robbins, Harvey and Findley, Michael. *Why Change Doesn't Work: Why Initiatives Go Wrong and How They Can Try Again and Succeed.* London: Orion Publishing Group, 1997.
11. Schaffer, R. H. "Consulting Begins With Results: The Key to Success." *The Journal for Quality and Participation,* Sept. 1997, pp. 56–62.
12. Gallagan, P. A. "IBM Gets Its Arms Around Education." *Training & Development,* 1989, pp. 37 and 43.
13. Fuchsberg, G. "Taking Control." *Wall Street Journal,* Sept. 10, 1993.
14. Phillips, Jack J. "ROI: The Search for Best Practices." *Training & Development,* Vol. 50, No. 2, Feb. 1996, pp. 42–47.
15. Friedlove, George T. and Plewa, Franklin J., Jr. *Understanding Return on Investments.* New York: John Wiley and Sons, 1996.
16. Phillips, Jack J. (Ed.) *In Action: Measuring Return on Investment, Vol. 1.* Alexandria, Va.: American Society for Training and Development, 1994, p. 7.
17. Phillips, Jack J. "Was It the Training?" *Training & Development,* Vol. 50, No. 3, Mar. 1996, pp. 28–32.
18. Phillips, Jack J. "How Much Is the Training Worth?" *Training & Development,* Vol. 50, No. 4, 1996, pp. 20–24.

10

TRAINING COSTS

Trend Definition and Validation

Brief Definition of Trend

The cost of providing training and development is increasing—there is more pressure for training and development managers to know how and why money is spent. The "fully loaded" cost of training is reported, which means that the cost profile goes beyond the direct costs and includes the cost of the time participants are involved in training and other appropriate overhead items. For years, management has realized many indirect costs of training exist, and now it is asking for an accountability of those costs. Cost information is used to manage resources, develop standards, measure efficiencies, and examine alternative delivery processes. In addition, program costs can be used to measure the actual return on investment.

Case Study: State Government in the United States

A large state government agency in the United States was audited by the state auditor's department. Although the audit was a management controls audit, a portion of the audit focused on training costs. Paraphrased comments taken from the auditor's report include the following:

> Costs tracked at the program level focus on direct, or "hard," costs and largely ignore the monetary value of time spent participating in or supporting training. The costs of participant time to prepare for and attend training are not tracked. For one series of programs, the inclusion of such expenses raised the total training cost dramatically. The agency stated that total two-year costs for the specific program were $608,834. This figure generally includes only direct costs and, as such, is substantially below the monetary value of time spent by staff in preparing for and attending the program. When accounting for pre-work and attendance, the figure comes to a total of $1.39 million. If the statewide average of 45.5 percent for fringe benefits is considered, the total indirect cost of staff time to prepare for and attend the program becomes $2,032,543. Finally, if the agency's direct costs of $608,834 are added to the $2.03 million indirect costs, the total becomes $2,641,377. Among other factors that would drive actual total costs higher still are:
>
> - Cost of travel, meals, and lodging for training participants
> - Allocated salaries and fringes of staff providing administrative and logistic support
> - Opportunity costs of productivity lost by staff in doing pre-work and attending training
>
> Failure to fully consider indirect, or "soft," costs may expose the agency to non-compliance with the Fair Labor Standards Act (FLSA), particularly as training spreads through rank-and-file staff. Because FLSA requires that such staff be directly compensated for overtime, it will no longer be appropriate for the agency to ask employees to complete training pre-work on their

own time. Continuing to handle such overtime work this way may also encourage false overtime reporting, skew overtime data, and/or increase the amount of uncompensated overtime.

Numerous barriers exist to agency efforts at determining how much training costs:

- Cost systems tend to hide administrative, support, internal, and other indirect, or "soft," costs.
- Costs are generally monitored at the division level rather than at the level of individual programs or activities.
- Cost information required by activity-based cost systems is not being generated.

As this case vividly demonstrates, the cost of training is much more than direct expenditures, and training and development departments are expected to report fully loaded costs in their reports. As a result of this audit, the agency began capturing costs in different categories and reporting both direct and indirect costs in its reporting mechanisms.

Evidence of Trend

Several important studies show evidence of increased attention to cost monitoring and cost reporting. The practitioner survey of global trends revealed a level of agreement regarding the trend's existence of 3.92 out of 5 (see Appendix 1). The importance of the trend was rated 4.83 out of 5, making it the most important trend of the sixteen. Practitioners are focusing more attention on cost control and cost monitoring.

The most recent *Human Resources Effectiveness Report,* an annual global survey developed by the Saratoga Institute, reported with increased accuracy and completeness than it had in previous years more data about the training and development costs.[1]

Collecting and monitoring costs has become an integral part of managing the training process and making improvements in systems processes and procedures.[2] As training functions are restructured, training costs play an important role in making restructuring decisions and process changes.

The American Society for Training and Development conducted a study of 300 HRD executives and managers concerning important trends in training. Many of these executives represented multinational companies with global operations. Two of the important trends identified were:

- Increased pressure to develop a business case for HRD interventions
- Increased pressure to demonstrate a return on investment

These trends will be even more pronounced in the next few years leading up to the new millennium.[3] Tabulating and monitoring accurate costs are an essential part of developing a business case, as well as demonstrating return on investment. Some studies show that as much as 5 to 10 percent of programs in organizations have been evaluated at the ROI level. For this to occur, costs must be compared with benefits, and the costs must be accurate and conservative to keep the process credible.[4]

Another study underscored the importance of comparing the cost effectiveness of different performance problem solutions and comparing the costs of different delivery methods for training solutions. Accurate, reliable, and complete cost data are a critical part of these comparisons.[5]

Finally, a major trend of outsourcing is occurring throughout the world as more and more firms contract out various training services, including training delivery.[6] Accurate, reliable, and thorough cost data are required to make an adequate outsourcing decision. In some cases, reporting fully loaded costs of training has led to the outsourcing decision as key executives realize the actual cost of a particular program or training service.

Causes and Drivers

Many influences caused the increased attention to monitoring training costs accurately and thoroughly. Some of the more important ones are listed here:

- Every organization should know approximately how much money it spends on training and development. Many organizations calculate this expenditure and make comparisons with that of other organizations, although comparisons are difficult to make because of the different bases for cost calculations.

- Some organizations calculate training and development (T&D) costs as a percentage of payroll costs and set targets for increased investment. For example, Motorola budgets 3.6 percent of its payroll for employee education.[7] Other organizations calculate training and development costs as a percentage of revenue, or they develop T&D costs on a per-employee basis. Arthur Andersen & Company spends about 9.5 percent of revenue on training. Total costs for training and development may exceed the overall budget for the training and development department as additional costs such as participants' salaries, travel expenses, replacement costs, facilities expenses, and general overhead are included. An effective system of cost monitoring enables an organization to calculate the magnitude of total training expenditures. Collecting this information also helps top management answer two important questions:

  1. How much do we spend on training compared with other organizations?
  2. How much should we spend on training?

- The training and development staff should know the relative cost effectiveness of programs. Monitoring costs by program allows the staff to evaluate the relative contribution of a program and determine how those costs are changing. If a program's cost rises, it might be appropriate to reevaluate its impact and overall success. It may be useful to compare specific components of costs with those of other programs or organizations. For example, the cost per participant for one program could be compared with the cost per participant for a similar program. Large differences may signal a problem. Also, costs associated with design, development, or delivery could be compared with those of other programs within the organization and used to develop cost standards.
- Accurate costs are necessary to predict future costs. Historical costs for a program provide the basis for predicting future costs of a similar program. Sophisticated cost models provide the capability to estimate or predict costs with reasonable accuracy.
- When a return on investment or cost benefit analysis is needed for a specific program, costs must be developed. One of the most

significant reasons for collecting costs is to obtain data for use in a benefits-versus-costs comparison. In this comparison, cost data are equally important as the program's economic benefits.

- To improve the efficiency of the training and development function, controlling costs is necessary. Competitive pressures place increased attention on efficiencies. Most training and development departments have monthly budgets with cost projections listed by various accounts and, in some cases, by program. Cost monitoring is an excellent tool for identifying problem areas and taking corrective action. From a practical and classical management sense, the accumulation of cost data is a necessity.
- Costs are necessary to evaluate alternatives to a proposed HRD program. Realistic cost data provide management with the true cost of a proposed program, which can be used to evaluate the cost effectiveness of alternatives. For example, the servicing division of a major credit card company decided to computerize its data management systems and relocate to a different area of the country. It faced the need to train a large number of employees immediately and expected its needs for training to continue into the future. These conditions suggested some type of mix of computer-based instruction and classic classroom training. To compare the two approaches, cost data had to be developed for each approach.
- Cost data are needed for the human resource information system. Training and development cost data must be integrated into existing data bases for other human resource functions, such as compensation, benefits, and selection information. Aligning training-cost information with these data bases provides information about training's relative contribution to human resource costs. Some sophisticated human resource information systems electronically track and monitor costs.
- Detailed costs are needed to plan and budget for future operations. A final driver for tracking costs is the preparation of next year's operating budget. The operating budget usually includes all the expenditures within the training and development department and may also include other costs such as participants' salaries and associated travel expenses. In recent years, the budgeting process has come under close scrutiny, and the practice of applying a percentage increase to last year's budget is no longer accept-

able for most organizations. An increasing number of organizations are adopting zero-based budgets, in which each activity must be justified and no expenses are carried over from the previous year. An accurate accounting of expenditures enables the training and development manager to defend proposed programs in a line-item review with management.

Trend Description

Capturing costs is challenging because they must be accurate, reliable, and realistic. Although most organizations can develop costs with more ease than the economic value of the benefits of training, the true cost of training is often an elusive figure, even in some of the best organizations. Although the total training and development budget can be developed easily, it is more difficult to determine specific costs of programs or components, especially when considering indirect costs. A systematic process is needed.

Cost Classification Systems

Training and development costs can be classified in two basic ways. One way is by describing the expenditure using words such as *labor, materials, supplies, travel,* and so on. These are expense account classifications. The other way is by establishing categories in the training process or function, such as program development, delivery, and evaluation. An effective system monitors costs by account categories but also includes a method for accumulating costs by the process/functional category. Although grouping by account categories is sufficient to give the total cost of the program, it does not allow for a useful comparison with other programs or indicate areas where costs might be excessive by relative comparisons. Therefore, the two above-mentioned basic classifications are recommended to develop a complete costing system.

Developing a Classification System

When developing a classification system, the following steps can help ensure that the system provides the information needed:

- **Define which costs will be collected.** A system of cost classification may be subject to several interpretations, so relevant costs must be identified. Cost accounts should be clearly defined to reduce possible classification errors, leaving little room for doubt as to how an item should be charged (for example, office supplies or duplication). Also, the various process/functional categories need to be clearly defined so those items can be properly grouped in those accounts.
- **Assign responsibility for developing the system.** Because the implementation of a costing system involves input from many people, each individual's or department's responsibilities should be detailed and consensus reached to reduce delays in implementation and errors in the final product.
- **Determine the process/functional categories.** Cost categories, such as administrative and developmental costs, should be determined early. Recommended categories are presented in the next section.
- **Determine the expense account classification descriptions.** Each of the account categories should be developed to be consistent with the organization's current chart of accounts and in a manner that will ease the application and use of the system. The classifications should be practical and describe the types of costs that make up each account.
- **Use standard cost data when appropriate.** Many situations exist in which standard cost data can be useful. Usually developed internally, standard costs can save time and can improve the accuracy of total cost calculations. An example of standard cost data is the fixed percentage of payroll allocated for employee benefits when calculating the total compensation of participants. Another example is the average per diem cost for participants attending an out-of-town program.
- **Carefully select data sources.** Selecting the most accurate data source is critical to the costing system. The source must be readily available, ideally from an existing system, and it should be consistent with other reports of the same data. Typical data sources include payroll records, budget reports, standard cost reports, travel expense records, purchase orders, and petty cash vouchers.
- **Consider a separate computerized system.** Although the cost-accounting system may be capable of tracking costs, it may be

appropriate to utilize a separate system using a PC-based arrangement. With local area network (LAN) capabilities and low costs, this approach is feasible.

Addressing these issues appropriately makes the development of a costing system easier and helps ensure that the system is implemented on schedule.

Process/Functional Classifications

Table 10-1 shows the process/functional categories for costs in four different ways. Column A has only two categories: (1) operating costs and (2) support costs. Operating costs include all expenses involved in conducting the program; support costs include all administrative, overhead, development, and reassessment expenses, as well as any other expenditure not directly related to conducting the program. Although it is simple to separate these two categories, it does not provide enough detail to analyze costs on a functional basis. Column B adds a third category and provides a little more detail but does not provide information on program development costs, which is useful data to have. Column C provides for development costs as a separate item, but it still falls short of an ideal situation. It offers no way to track evaluation costs, which are becoming a significant part of the total process. Column D represents an appropriate cost breakdown: assessment, development, delivery, and evaluation. The administrative costs are allocated to each of these areas.

Table 10-1
Process/Functional Categories for Cost

A	B	C	D
Operating Costs	Classroom Costs	Program Development Costs	Assessment Costs
Support Costs	Administrative Costs	Administrative Costs	Development Costs
	Participant Compensation and Facility Costs	Classroom Costs	Delivery Costs
		Participant Costs	Evaluation Costs

Needs assessment costs usually fall in the range of 15 to 20 percent of the training and development budget. Development costs run in the 30 to 35 percent range, while delivery consumes 40 to 45 percent of the budget. Evaluation is usually less than 5 percent.[8] The actual breakdown of costs depends on how costs are accumulated in the organization and varies considerably with each program, particularly in the development and delivery components. If a program is developed from one already in operation, development costs should be low. Similarly, for a lengthy program involving a large amount of participant time, the delivery costs may be much higher.

Expense Account Classifications

The most time-consuming step of developing a cost system is defining and classifying the various expenses. Many of the expense accounts, such as office supplies and travel expenses, are already a part of the existing accounting system. However, expenses exist that are unique to the training and development department, and these must be added to the system. The system design depends on the organization, the type of programs developed and conducted, and the limits imposed on the current cost-accounting system, if any. Also, to a certain extent, the expense account classifications depend on how the process/functional categories were developed, as discussed in the previous section. Table 10-2 illustrates the expense account system in one organization with more than 8,000 employees. Each account is assigned an account number and is clearly defined. Additional accounts could make the system more precise and avoid misallocation of expenses, but from a practical standpoint, this classification seems to be adequate for most training cost analyses.

Table 10-2
**Human Resource Development Costs—
Expense Account Classifications**

00	—	*Salaries and Benefits—Training and Development Staff* This account includes the salaries and employee benefit costs for training and development staff, both supervisory and non-supervisory.
01	—	*Salaries and Benefits—Other Employees* This account includes the salaries and employee benefit costs for other company personnel, both supervisory and non-supervisory.

Table 10-2 (continued)
Human Resource Development Costs—Expense Account Classifications

02 — *Salaries and Benefits—Participants*
This account includes the salaries and employee benefit costs for participants, both supervisory and non-supervisory.

03 — *Meals, Travel, and Incidental Expenses—Training and Development Staff*
This account includes meals, travel, and incidental expenses of employees of the corporate training and development department.

04 — *Meals, Travel, and Accommodations—Participants*
This account includes meals, travel accommodations, and incidental expenses for participants attending programs.

05 — *Office Supplies and Expenses*
This account includes expenses incurred for stationery, office supplies and services, subscriptions, postage, and telephone and telegraph services.

06 — *Program Materials and Supplies*
This account includes the cost of materials and supplies purchased for specific programs and includes such items as videos, binders, handout materials, and purchased programs.

07 — *Printing and Reproduction*
This account includes expenses incurred for printing and reproduction of all material.

08 — *Outside Services*
This account includes the costs incurred for fees and expenses of outside corporations, firms, institutions, or individuals other than company employees who perform special services, such as management consultants and facilitators.

09 — *Equipment Expense Allocation*
This account includes that portion of original equipment cost allocated to specific programs, including computers.

10 — *Equipment—Rental*
This account includes rental payments for equipment used in administrative work and programs.

11 — *Equipment—Maintenance*
This account includes expenses incurred in repairing and servicing company-owned equipment and furniture.

(table continued on page 200)

Table 10-2 (continued)
Human Resource Development Costs—
Expense Account Classifications

12 —	*Registration Fees* This account includes employee registration fees and tuitions for seminars and conferences paid for by the company.
13 —	*Facilities Expense Allocation* This account includes an expense allocation for use of a company-owned facility for conducting a program.
14 —	*Facilities Rental* This account includes rental payments for facilities used in connection with a program.
15 —	*General Training Overhead Allocation* This account includes general training and development overhead expenses prorated to each program.
16 —	*Other Miscellaneous Expenses* This account includes miscellaneous expenses not provided for elsewhere.

Cost Accumulation and Estimation

Cost Classification Matrix

The previous sections presented two ways of classifying costs: process/functional classifications and expense account classifications. Costs accumulate under both classifications, as the two are related. The final step in the process is to define which kinds of costs in the account classification system normally apply to the process/functional categories. Table 10-3 presents a matrix for the categories that are necessary to accumulate all training-related costs in the organization. Those costs, each of which is usually a part of one of the process/functional categories, are checked in the matrix. Each member of the training and development staff should know how to charge expenses properly. For example, when equipment is rented for use in the development and delivery of a program, should the cost be charged to development? Or to delivery? Usually, the cost is allocated to each in proportion to the extent the item was used for each category.

Table 10-3
Cost Classification Matrix

Expense Account Classification	Process/Functional Categories			
	Assessment	**Development**	**Delivery**	**Evaluation**
00 Salaries and Benefits—Training and Development Staff	X	X	X	X
01 Salaries and Benefits—Other Employees		X	X	
02 Salaries and Benefits—Participants			X	X
03 Meals, Travel, and Incidental Expenses—Training and Development Staff	X	X	X	X
04 Meals, Travel, and Accommodations—Participants			X	
05 Office Supplies and Expenses	X	X		X
06 Program Materials and Supplies		X	X	
07 Printing and Reproduction	X	X	X	X
08 Outside Services	X	X	X	X
09 Equipment Expense Allocation	X	X	X	X
10 Equipment—Rental		X	X	
11 Equipment—Maintenance			X	
12 Registration Fees	X			
13 Facilities Expense Allocation			X	
14 Facilities Rental			X	
15 General Training Overhead Allocation	X	X	X	X
16 Other Miscellaneous Expenses	X	X	X	X

Cost Accumulation

With expense account classifications clearly defined and the process/functional categories determined, it is an easy task to track costs for individual programs. This can be accomplished through the use of special account numbers and project numbers. An example illustrates the use of these numbers.

A project number is a three-digit number representing a specific HRD program. For example:

New employee orientation	112
Team leader training program	215
"Valuing Diversity" workshop	418
"Interviewing Skills" workshop	791

Numbers also are assigned to the process/functional breakdowns. Using the categorization presented earlier, the following numbers are assigned:

Assessment	1
Development	2
Delivery	3
Evaluation	4

Using the two-digit numbers assigned to the expense account classifications (see Tables 10-2 and 10-3), an accounting system is complete unless there are other requirements from the existing system. For example, if participant workbooks are reproduced for the "Valuing Diversity" workshop, the appropriate charge number for printing the workbooks is 07-3-418. The first two digits denote the account classification, the next digit represents the process/functional category, and the last three digits give the project number. This system enhances accumulation and monitoring of costs. Total costs can be presented:

- By program ("Valuing Diversity" workshop)
- By process/functional categories (delivery)
- By expense account classification (printing and reproduction)

Cost Monitoring and Reporting Issues

The most important task is to define which specific costs are included in a tabulation of program costs. This task involves decisions that the training and development staff makes and usually must be approved by management. If appropriate, the finance and accounting staff may need to approve the list. Table 10-4 shows the recommended cost categories to report for a fully loaded, conservative approach to estimating costs. These issues and categories go beyond the basic process/functional categories described earlier. Each category is described below.

Table 10-4
Training Program Cost Categories

Cost Item	Prorated	Expensed
Needs Assessment and Analysis	✓	
Design and Development	✓	
Acquisition	✓	
Delivery		✓
◆ Salaries/Benefits—Facilitator Time		✓
◆ Salaries/Benefits—Coordination Time		✓
◆ Program Materials and Fees		✓
◆ Travel/Lodging/Meals		✓
◆ Facilities		✓
◆ Salaries/Benefits—Participant Time		✓
Evaluation	✓	
Overhead/Training and Development	✓	

Prorated vs. Expensed Costs

All costs related to a program are usually captured and expensed to that program. Most are charged to each session individually. However, three categories are frequently prorated over some or all of the sessions of the same program. Needs assessment and analysis, design and development, and acquisition are all significant costs that should be prorated over the shelf life of the program. Some organizations will conservatively estimate one year of operation for the program; others may estimate two or three years. If there is some question about the time period, the finance and accounting staff should be consulted for the specific amount of time to use in the proration formula.

Evaluation costs may be prorated if the costs are significant and are not the same for each session. Training and development overhead is usually allocated to each program in some conventional and logical way.

Employee Benefits Factor

When presenting the salaries of participants and staff associated with programs, the employee benefits factor should be included. This number is usually a standard value in the organization and is used in other costing formulas. It represents the cost of all employee benefits expressed as a percentage of base salaries. In some organizations, this value is as high as 50 to 60 percent, while that value in other organizations may be as low as 25 to 30 percent. The average employee benefits factor in the United States is 38 percent.[9]

Needs Assessment and Analysis

Perhaps one of the often-overlooked items is the cost of conducting a needs assessment and analysis. In some programs this cost is zero because the program is conducted without a needs assessment. However, as organizations place increased emphasis on needs assessment, this item will become a more significant cost. All costs associated with the needs assessment and analysis should be captured to the fullest extent possible, including the time it takes staff members to conduct the assessment, direct fees and expenses for external consultants, and internal services and supplies used in the analysis. The total costs are usually prorated over the life of the program. Depending on the type and nature of the program, the shelf life should be kept to a reasonable number, usually in the one- to two-year time frame. Of course, expensive programs that are not expected to change significantly for several years are an exception.

Design and Development Costs

One of the most significant costs is that of designing and developing the program. These costs include internal staff time in both design and development, the use of consultants, and the purchase of supplies, videos, CD-ROMs, and other materials directly related to the program. Design and development costs are usually prorated, generally using the same time frame as the needs assessment and analysis. One to two years is normal unless the program is not expected to change for many years.

Acquisition Costs

In lieu of development costs, many organizations purchase packaged programs to use directly or in a modified format. Acquisition costs include the purchase prices of instructor materials, train-the-trainer sessions, licensing agreements, and other costs associated with the right to deliver the program. These acquisition costs should be prorated using the same rationale as above; one to two years should be sufficient. If the program requires modification or additional development, these costs should be included as development costs. In practice, many programs have both acquisition and development costs.

Delivery Costs

The largest segment of training costs usually comprises those associated with delivery. Five major categories are included.

- **Facilitators' and Coordinators' Salaries.** The salaries of facilitators and program coordinators should be included. If a coordinator is involved in more than one program, the portion of time required for that program should be allocated to the specific program under review. If external facilitators are used, all charges should be included for the session. The important issue is to capture all the direct time of internal employees or external consultants who work directly with the program. The employee benefits factor should be included each time direct labor costs are involved. This factor is usually a standard value generated by the finance and accounting staff and is usually in the range of 30 to 40 percent.
- **Program Materials and Fees.** Specific program materials, such as notebooks, textbooks, case studies, exercises, and participant

workbooks, should be included in the delivery costs, along with user fees and royalty payments. Pens, paper, certificates, and calculators are also included in this category.

- **Travel, Lodging, and Meals.** Direct travel costs for participants, facilitators, and coordinators are included. Lodging, meals, and refreshments are included for participants during travel, as well as meals during their stay for the program.
- **Facilities.** The direct cost of facilities for the training should be included. For external programs, this is the direct charge from the conference center, hotel, or motel. If the program is conducted in-house, the cost of the internal conference room should be estimated and included, even if it is not the practice to include facilities' cost in other reports.
- **Participants' Salaries and Benefits.** Participants' salaries and employee benefits for the time involved in the program represent an expense that should be included. If the program has already been conducted, these costs can be estimated using average or midpoint values for salaries in typical job classifications. When a program is targeted for a comprehensive evaluation, participants can provide information about their own salaries in a confidential manner.

Evaluation

To compute the fully loaded cost of a program, the total cost of the evaluation must be included. Evaluation costs include developing the evaluation strategy, designing instruments, collecting data, analyzing data, and preparing and distributing reports. Cost categories include time, materials, purchased instruments, and surveys. A case can be made to prorate the evaluation costs over several sessions instead of charging the total amount to any one session as an expense. For example, let's assume twenty-five sessions of a program are conducted in a three-year period and one session is selected for an ROI calculation. The evaluation costs could logically be prorated over the twenty-five sessions because the results of the ROI analysis should reflect the other sessions' successes and will perhaps result in changes that will influence the other sessions as well.

Overhead

A final charge is overhead—additional costs in the training function not directly related to a particular program. The overhead category represents any training department cost not considered in the above calculations. Typical items include the cost of clerical support, departmental office expenses, salaries of training managers, and other fixed costs. In some organizations, the total is divided by the number of program participant days for the year to obtain an estimate for allocation. This becomes a standard value to use in calculations.

Fully Loaded Costs

Training costs should be fully loaded whenever possible. In this conservative approach, all costs that can be identified and linked to a particular program are included. The philosophy is simple: If it is questionable whether or not a cost should be included, it is recommended that it be included. Cost reporting should withstand even the closest scrutiny of its accuracy and credibility. The only way to meet this test is to ensure that all costs are represented. Of course, from a realistic viewpoint, if the controller or chief financial officer insists on not using certain costs, then it is best to leave them out.

Trend Consequences

Impact

This trend is long overdue. Monitoring costs accurately provides an excellent management tool to make key decisions regarding specific programs or resources within the training and development department. It is difficult to imagine a professional training and development department without an effective cost classification and accumulation system.

Unfortunately, in many organizations the training and development function grew rapidly, and costs were not a major consideration in the early stages of development of the department. Implementing a cost accumulation system later in the process is more difficult and time consuming. An organization should consider its implementation as early as possible, while it can be done with a moderate amount of effort and expense. Sometimes it is best to scrap the current system and develop a new system. Usually a PC-based system is appropriate for networking to the different department offices. If a new system is developed, it should be developed with the input and concerns of the training and development staff. Also, each staff member must be fully aware of the process and accounts so that charges can be accurately accumulated and reported.

It is dangerous to communicate the costs of training without presenting benefits, but many organizations have fallen into this trap for years. Because costs can easily be collected, they are presented to management in all types of ingenious ways, such as the cost of the program, cost per employee, and cost per program development hour. Although these may be helpful for efficiency comparisons, presenting them without presenting benefits can be troublesome.

When most executives review training costs, a logical question comes to mind: What benefit was received from the program? This is a typical management reaction, particularly when costs are perceived as high. For example, in one organization, all costs associated with executive leadership programs were tabulated and reported to senior management. The total figure exceeded the estimates from the executive group, and senior management immediately requested a summary of the program's benefits. This reaction caused a review of all leaders and programs, with the ultimate conclusion that they offered few, if any, economic benefits. Consequently, the programs were drastically reduced. Although this may be an extreme example, it shows the danger of presenting only half of the equation. Some organizations have developed a policy of not communicating training cost data unless the benefits can be captured and presented along with the costs. Benefits data are included with the cost data, even if they are subjective and intangible, to help balance the two issues.

Key Questions

The following key questions must be addressed when exploring the development of additional cost data.

Key Questions

1. To what extent is this trend developing in my organization?
2. How important is this trend to me?
3. How much progress has been made in developing reliable and accurate cost control systems?
4. How much cost and effort would be involved in developing acceptable and accurate processes?
5. What resources will be required to develop the appropriate system?
6. What barriers will I encounter in trying to implement this system?
7. What will happen if I do nothing?
8. Will the staff resist this effort?
9. Is senior management asking for cost data?
10. What are the dangers of implementing a system?

Outlook

This trend will continue and accelerate. This logical, practical trend has been developing for years. It provides data that are essential for the management of the department, as well as for other managers and executives who must make decisions about training and development. The increased emphasis on evaluation of training programs supports the trend to monitor costs. Although training will always be viewed as an important part of a company's overall competitive strategy, only those programs in which the cost is outweighed by the benefits will survive.

References

1. Fitz-Enz, Jac. "The Human Resources Effectiveness Report." Saratoga, Ca.: Saratoga Institute, 1997.
2. Shandler, Donald. *Reengineering the Training Function: How to Align Training with the New Corporate Agenda.* Delray Beach, Fla.: St. Lucie Press, 1996.

3. Van Buren, Mark. *National HRD Executive Survey*. Alexandria, Va.: American Society for Training and Development, 1997.
4. Phillips, Jack J. (Ed.) *In Action: Measuring Return on Investment, Vol 2*. Alexandria, Va.: American Society for Training and Development, 1997.
5. Bramley, Peter. *Evaluation Training Effectiveness,* 2nd ed. London: McGraw-Hill, 1996.
6. Bassi, Laurie J., Gallagher, Anne L., and Schroer, Ed. *The ASTD Training Data Book*. Alexandria, Va.: American Society for Training and Development, 1996.
7. Henkoff, R. "Companies That Train Best." *Fortune,* Mar. 22, 1993, pp. 62–75.
8. Phillips.
9. "Annual Employee Benefits Report." *Nations Business,* Jan. 1996, p. 28.

11

PROFIT CENTERS

Trend Definition and Validation

Brief Definition of Trend

Organizations are converting the operation of the training and development department to that of a profit center rather than a cost center. Under the profit center arrangement, the department charges for products and services, using a competitive fee schedule. Its clients, the managers in the organization, have the option of purchasing programs and services from the training and development department or from external suppliers. Revenues generated from program fees offset operating expenses. Revenue that exceeds the operating cost results in profit for the organization.

Case Studies: IBM and Toronto Dominion Bank

IBM. During IBM's recent reorganization to regain market position, the decision was made that the company's education function must completely stand on its own. The education division of IBM, once a much-admired training entity that spent $2 billion on worldwide training each year, refashioned itself into a different kind of training function.[1]

In brief, the company:

- Split its education division into two separate subsidiaries, Skill Dynamics and Workforce Solutions. These two organizations are expected to keep balance sheets and submit profit-and-loss statements to IBM corporate headquarters, as do other IBM operating units.
- Told the two entities they must sink or swim. In other words, if Workforce Solutions and Skill Dynamics cannot persuade anyone inside or outside the parent company to buy training products and services from them, they will go out of business. IBM headquarters provides no subsidy.
- Allowed its education subsidiaries the opportunity to sell training products and services, including custom-designed training, to external companies. During 1993, Skill Dynamics earned an estimated $130 million from sales to outside firms.

By undertaking such significant changes in the way the company delivers training, IBM officials tacitly acknowledged that their old approach to education and development did not suit the kind of organization IBM wants to become in the future.

Toronto Dominion Bank. Toronto Dominion Bank sees the profit center concept as an important way for the training and organizational development function to add value. This large bank based in Toronto, Canada, has been undergoing radical change in markets and delivery processes, along with most North American banks. In response to market forces and competitive pressures, senior management gave the Education Centre two years to convert its current operating framework to a profit center.[2] The Education Centre and consulting services will then charge clients competitive fees. The bank's managers will have the option of using Education Centre services or those of other suppliers. The Education Centre staff at Toronto Dominion Bank laid the foundation to move from the current operating framework to that of the profit center concept. The Education Centre considers this approach a welcome challenge, and senior management perceives it as a necessity.

Evidence of Trend

The two cases above show different ways in which the profit center concept has been introduced. One is for purposes of survival, and the other is for the purpose of effecting an operational change so the training and development department will be more acceptable to senior management. The trend of moving to the profit center concept has developed slowly. Some publications in the early '80s suggested that by now the concept would be enjoying widespread use.[3] However, the difficulty of achieving success with the process hindered its development to a slow and gradual pace. Some argue that the demise of several training departments could have been prevented if the organizations had turned to the profit center concept.[4] Still others see this approach as a distant goal.

The 1997 National HRD Executive Survey indicates that the fee-for-services approach to training will continue to increase through the year 2000.[5] The results of the survey revealed an average rating of 3.04 out of 5 regarding shifting toward fee-for-services approach in training. With regard to this shift continuing during the next three years, the average rating was 3.43 out of 5.

The practitioner survey of global trends (see Appendix 1) reported on the extent of agreement with the existence of the trend. The rating was 3.8 out of 5. In regard to the importance of the trend, respondents rated the profit center concept 4.11 out of 5.

Causes and Drivers

Several drivers exist for the implementation of the profit center concept.

- The profit center concept is perceived to be the ultimate level of accountability as far as evaluation is concerned, as shown in Figure 11-1. The profit center concept allows the training and development department to operate as if it were a privately owned business, with profits showing the true measure of economic success. Its customers have complete autonomy to use the internal services or shop externally. As Figure 11-1 implies, the other levels of evaluation must be firmly in place and thoroughly understood by clients before a profit center can succeed. In essence, managers need to understand that the programs and services offered by the training and development department provide an excellent return on investment before they will pay the prices demanded under the profit center concept.

- With the emphasis on adding stakeholder value, the profit center is an easy way to meet this challenge. The economic value-added concept can easily be applied when the department is operating on an income versus expense basis. Also, the concept usually meets internal pressures to show shareholder value.[6]
- The third driver shifting training operations to the profit center concept is the challenge to provide products and services on a competitive basis. Some managers and practitioners are convinced they can offer superior programs for the same price as others. Converting to a profit center is perceived to be a challenge taken by some of the most progressive and innovative education and training functions. The idea attracts entrepreneurs who want to show the value of the services of the organization.

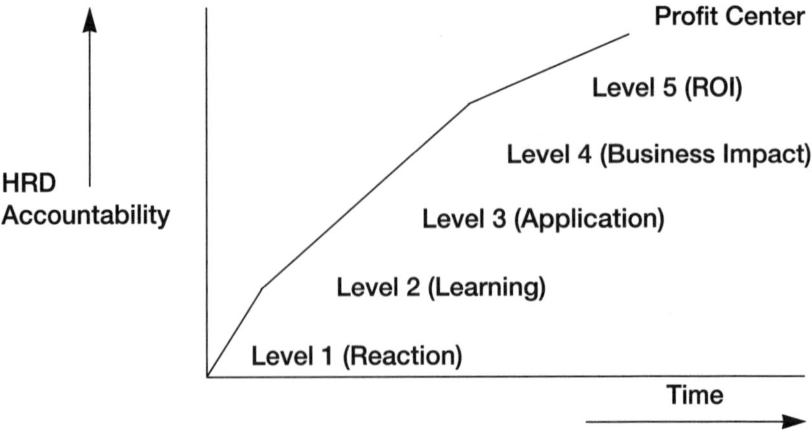

Figure 11-1. Levels of Evaluation.

- Another driver toward the profit center concept is the perception that the HRD department is excess cost to the organization. Many outside the department see training and development as a financial burden to the organization. Those references create frustrating conditions for many HRD professionals. One way to move to a self-sufficient posture is to convert the HRD department to a profit center.[7]
- Although there will always be a need to evaluate the costs versus benefits of certain programs, the profit center concept lessens the need to calculate the ROI for individual programs because the profit generated from revenues reflects the overall return for the department. Non-profitable programs will either be subsidized by profitable programs or will disappear.
- Some professionals perceive the profit center concept as being the same as an independent HRD/consulting firm. Hundreds of firms provide consulting services and HRD programs as their sole source of revenue. They develop and customize in-house programs to meet their clients' needs, with the need to make a profit.[8] The internal HRD department should be able to provide the same programs or services, also at a profit.
- In some cases, the management team demands this type of arrangement. Key operating managers want the freedom to use any services they wish and want to not be required to always "buy" the services from the in-house training and education function. These client pressures force some organizations to gradually move to a profit center concept, giving managers more autonomy to buy services externally.[9]
- Successful cases have sparked enthusiasm among training and development practitioners and senior executives. They perceive the profit center concept as a valuable way to address issues such as management support, increased funding, and concern about results. Published success stories have encouraged others to experiment with the process.[10]

Trend Description

If the profit center concept is effective, the HRD department must establish fees and prices for parts of or all of their efforts. Several types of profit center concepts exist, and many issues must be considered before making this conversion. This section addresses these issues and provides coverage about the true profit center.

Sources of Revenue

A typical HRD department has several sources of revenue, usually divided into the following categories:

- **Consulting and professional services.** User departments pay for services, including professional staff time devoted to conflict resolution, problem solving, needs analysis, or other activities aimed at developing employees in the organization. Service fees may also be collected for program development.
- **Program fees.** Internal clients pay fees for seminars, workshops, or other HRD programs. Fees cover the costs of delivering an HRD program, as well as overhead, analysis, development, and evaluation.
- **Products.** Product sales include self-contained packaged programs for departments or divisions within the organization. For example, a self-sufficient, computer-based instruction program that does not necessarily require support from the HRD staff is sold at a fixed price.
- **Administrative services.** User departments are charged fees for routine services provided by the HRD staff. Examples include processing tuition refund requests, coordinating outside seminar participation, and maintaining a human resources planning system.

A few organizations also receive income from sales of services and programs to other organizations. DuPont, Disney, General Motors, Ford, Xerox, and Westinghouse are only a few of the many organizations now selling their programs to the public.[11]

Fee/Price Determination

The determination of fees, charges, or prices for revenue items is critical to the success of a conversion. Prices must be high enough to generate the desired profit, yet low enough to be competitive. Three basic approaches are available for setting fees:

- **Fee negotiation.** The HRD staff and the client organization, whether a department, division, or section, can negotiate a fair and equitable fee for the services offered. This approach is particularly useful when determining the fee to charge for professional assistance. Some consideration might be given to using a rate similar to those set by external HRD consulting firms providing the same or similar services.
- **Competitive pricing.** Another possibility is to price the program or service equal to or less than the market price for the same or similar items. This is probably the best approach with a product such as a packaged HRD program or a workshop similar to one offered publicly. The prices must compete with those that are commercially available and, ideally, should be lower than those the organization can obtain externally. Of course, the enhanced quality and custom tailoring should be a definite plus. However, this approach is difficult when a program is needed and no programs are commercially available for comparison. In this situation, programs similar in terms of length, content, and difficulty may be used for comparison purposes.
- **Administrative service charges.** A third approach is to establish a charge for providing a service to the organization. This charge, determined internally with input from finance and accounting personnel, should be fair and equitable. An example is a 10 percent service charge (of tuition paid) for processing all tuition refund applications.

Variations of the Profit Center Concept

The concept described above reflects a true profit center. With fixed or negotiated fees and prices, the revenue offsets expenses, and additional funds represent profit generated by the HRD department. The ROI is the departmental earnings divided by the investment in resources to deliver the products and services. Although this concept may represent utopia, it is in the distant future for most organizations. Variations short of the true profit center may be appropriate for some organizations on an interim basis:

Protected profit center. When a profit center is subsidized to ensure the availability of resources, it is called a protected profit center. This approach involves pricing some services and products and subsidizing other programs and essential services. This approach assumes that it is difficult to establish prices for some necessary services. Departments may not use the HRD department to supply those services, and the result may cause inefficiencies. For example, if a department is unwilling to pay a 10 percent administrative services charge for the tuition refund program and insists on processing its own tuition refunds, it could jeopardize the program's standards. An easy way to avoid this problem is to subsidize the department to provide funds necessary to administer those programs.

Cost center. Another approach involves estimating the cost of various services and products delivered and then charging the client for those costs. All department costs are allocated in some way to user departments. This approach requires detailed and accurate cost forecasts and cost accumulation. Also, when parts of the organization refuse to use programs or services, the cost for providing those products and services to other parts of the organization may increase. Suppose ten departments normally share the cost of an HRD program, and then two of those ten departments decide not to participate. All costs, including prorated development and delivery costs, must be spread over eight departments instead of ten, raising the overall cost for those eight departments. This approach provides little incentive for HRD departments to minimize costs, and no opportunity for a profit exists.

Break-even center. This variation is similar to the cost center concept except that fees and prices are established to enable the department to reach a break-even point at the year's end. Higher prices are established for popular or frequently offered programs to offset losses on programs or services that are difficult to price or that represent a loss. With this approach, users may pay more for some programs and less for others although they should cost approximately the same. The major problem is the lack of opportunity for profit in the HRD department.

Considerations for Conversion

Several critical factors should be considered when converting to the profit center concept.[12] The strength or weakness of these factors may determine if such a move is feasible.

A conversion from an expense-based department to a profit center requires gradual change. Management may have concerns about the concept of paying for these services. One organization approached the conversion with the following ten sequential steps:

1. Establish HRD accounts in each department.
2. Allocate all costs or outside programs/seminars to user departments.
3. Allocate the costs of special, non-routine HRD programs.
4. Charge each user department for tuition refunds of their employees.
5. Charge a fee for participation in major programs.
6. Set prices for all formal HRD programs.
7. Charge all management trainee salaries to the sponsoring department.
8. Negotiate fees for new program development.
9. Negotiate fees for consulting work.
10. Charge an administration fee for all regular support services.

This organization took approximately five years to move from a centralized, budget-based department to a self-sufficient profit center.

Products and services provided by the organization must be effective and viewed as worthwhile investments. The HRD department must have an excellent reputation for success with previous programs; otherwise, such a conversion could be disastrous.

A successful conversion requires good management support and commitment at all levels. Management must see the need for effective HRD and be willing to pay for it, investing today for a return tomorrow. Also, managers must be willing to let employees participate in programs and become more involved in the development and implementation of new programs.

Commitment to the conversion to a profit center must include the entire HRD staff. Too often, a major change is implemented at the initiation of one key individual in the HRD department. A successful conversion requires the commitment and involvement of all staff members. Otherwise, the function could cease to exist.

Revenue items must be competitively priced. Charging more than the competition on the premise of providing a better product may not influence profit-minded executives. Operating department managers are seeking results, and they must be convinced they will receive a superior product at a fair price.

Simple and equitable methods for charging departments must be devised. One problem that may surface is duplicate charging. In many organizations, the HRD department is funded through direct charges or allocations to all operating departments, regardless of their participation in programs. If a department is charged an additional fee for employee participation in an HRD program, there is a double charge. This perception causes some conversion efforts to fail. A more realistic approach is to credit a predetermined amount to all departments and charge only if the fees or prices of the products and services used become greater than the allocated amount. This approach encourages use of the products and services of the HRD department. For example, a department may have a $15,000 cost allocation for the HRD department. When the department sends a participant to a program or uses a department service, the predetermined price is credited to the department's account. If the department uses more than its $15,000 allocation, the excess amount is charged against the department. A manager interested in HRD will certainly use the total allocation for the department, assuring that $15,000 worth of HRD products and services are utilized.

The impact of the profit center concept on the organization must be considered. This analysis includes the types of courses delivered, services provided, reaction of the management group, and reaction of the HRD staff.

Some courses, particularly those perceived as unnecessary, will die a natural death because no one will pay for them. This may be cause for concern. Suppose all team leaders, supervisors, and managers are required to participate in a valuing diversity workshop. The company feels that all leaders should understand various laws and the company's commitment to diversity. If some managers do not perceive the program as essential and worthwhile, they may feel reluctant to send participants. These issues must be addressed before conversion.

Some insight into impact may be gained by surveying management to determine its willingness to use the HRD department's services if the managers must pay directly for them. This survey can help determine process feasibility. Negative attitudes might signal problems ahead or pinpoint areas where attention is needed before implementing a conversion plan.

It is important to examine the philosophy and structure of the organization before implementing the profit center concept. This concept is not as effective if training is decentralized to the lowest level in the organization because it is difficult to pinpoint precise costs to charge to the user organization. In essence, a highly centralized approach moves the cost of training to the user organization, which makes this action a step toward the concept of paying for services provided.

Overall, the profit center approach is a legitimate, viable alternative for many organizations.[13] It should be pursued only if HRD is respected and already considered a contributing force in the organization. A conversion that succeeds can be rewarding to the HRD department; however, a failure can be disastrous.

Trend Consequences

Impact

This trend could be good news or bad news for training and HRD, depending on the readiness of the department to move toward becoming a profit center. The important point is to determine the impact on the organization and future utilization of the trend.

The profit center concept is not for every training and development function or even most functions. This unique trend generates more interest in itself than actual success with its application. This situation reflects the difficulties of implementing the process and making it work in an effective and productive way.

One of the most critical steps toward making the profit center concept work is to examine the impact of the process on current programs. This can be forecasted by reviewing each product and service and estimating the actual value or price for the service if purchased on a competitive market. Total revenue from those products and services is compared with the expenses of the training and development function. If the analysis yields a significant deficit, then the profit center concept may be difficult to implement, at least in the short term. If this initial analysis shows a profit, then the profit center may be easy to implement and may warrant serious consideration.

The most significant obstacle for implementation involves resistance from the training and development staff. Staff members may not see the need for the process and will fear that the programs in which they are involved will not be purchased and thus will eventually disappear. Also, they will fear what will happen to not only the program but the function if the management team does not buy their services. These fears can turn into realities if the programs are not delivering results at the present time.

To ensure that current programs produce results, most organizations implement the profit center after evaluation at Levels 4 and 5 has been applied in a comprehensive and effective way. When the management team sees the value of the programs, in terms of business impact and return on investment, it will purchase internal programs. Managers will go where they have seen proven results. Thus, evaluation at Levels 4 and 5 is considered a prerequisite for the implementation of the profit center concept.

As with any significant change, the profit center will be accepted if the employees are informed and prepared for the change. When they see what is involved in the profit center process, when they see why it is needed, and when they are allowed to provide input, they may accept the process and provide their best efforts to make it successful.

Key Questions

The following questions are important in considering conversion to a profit center:

Key Questions

1. Do I agree with this trend?
2. How important is the profit center concept to my organization?
3. Are internal and external forces causing the profit center concept to be developed?

Key Questions (continued)

4. How much progress has been made to implement the profit center concept?
5. Does the current structure support or inhibit the profit center concept?
6. Does the HRD staff support this process?
7. What must be done to move toward the profit center concept?
8. What will happen if I do nothing?
9. Will top management support the process?
10. How long will it take my organization to fully implement this process?
11. What will be required to develop this concept in the near future in my organization?
12. Which product or service will be offered initially?
13. What types of pricing structures will be used?
14. How will this concept be communicated?

Outlook

Although this trend has developed slowly, it is becoming a goal or viable option for many organizations. It may be more appropriate for HRD organizations that are perceived to be providing optional programs. For example, a leadership center whose sole purpose is to provide leadership training may be forced to move to a profit center concept to compete with suppliers for the same type of services. The profit center may not be appropriate for a full-service HRD department in a very large organization, particularly one with a variety of mandatory programs. Because of the required core courses, government-required programs, and services necessary to support other functions, the profit center concept may experience operational problems. On the positive side, the profit center may represent the best way to fully expand and grow the education and training function. Few executives argue with growth plans when those plans are funded with revenues that are freely funneled into the training and development department, through internal or external sources.

References

1. Geber, B. “A Clean Break for Education At IBM.” *Training,* Feb. 1994, pp. 33–36.
2. Howard, Brian. “Implementing the ROI Process at TD Bank,” in *Implementing Evaluation Systems and Process.* Alexandria, Va.: American Society for Training and Development, 1997.
3. Phillips, Jack J. *Handbook of Training Evaluation and Measurement Methods.* Houston, Tex.: Gulf Publishing, 1983.
4. Hale, Judith A. and Westgaard, Odin. *Achieving a Leadership Role for Training.* New York: Quality Resources, 1995.
5. *National HRD Executive Survey.* Alexandria, Va.: American Society for Training and Development, 3rd Qtr. 1997.
6. Donovan, John, Tully, Richard, and Wortman, Brent. *The Value Enterprise: Strategies for Building a Value-Based Organization.* Toronto, Canada: McGraw-Hill, 1998.
7. Mercer, Michael W. *Turning Your Human Resources Department into a Profit Center.* New York: Amacom, 1989.
8. Maister, David H. *Managing the Professional Services Firm.* New York: Free Press, 1997.
9. Rackham, Neil, Friedman, Lawrence, and Ruff, Richard. *Getting Partnering Right.* New York: McGraw-Hill, 1996.
10. Bleech, James M. and Mutchler, David G. *Let's Get Results, Not Excesses!* Hollywood, Fla.: Lifetime Books, 1995.
11. Pepitone, James S. *Future Training: A Roadmap to Restructuring the Training Function.* Dallas: AddVantage Learning Press, 1995.
12. Kaplan, Robert S. and Cooper, Robert. *Cost and Effect: Using Integrated Cost Systems to Drive Profitability and Performance.* Boston: Harvard Business School Press, 1998.
13. Keen, Peter G. W. *The Process Edge: Creating Value Where It Counts.* Boston: Harvard Business School Press, 1998.

12

BUDGETING

Trend Definition and Validation

Brief Definition of Trend

As organizations recognize the importance and necessity for training and development, budgets continue to increase annually by organization, industry, and country. In addition, the process to develop a budget for a training and development organization is becoming more structured and accurate as training becomes an essential function within the organization.

Case Studies: Arthur Andersen & Company and Westpac

Arthur Andersen & Company. When Arthur Andersen founded his famous accounting and consulting firm more than eighty years ago, he used part-time accountants to perform tax and audit work. However, he quickly became convinced that his employees would be more productive if they worked full time and participated in training programs. This commitment to job training and development helped make Arthur Andersen & Company one of the world's largest accounting and consulting firms. The investment in training and development has reached almost one half million dollars, which amounts to approximately 5.5 percent of revenues. The company devotes an average of 150 hours of training to each employee per year. This commitment reflects how Arthur Andersen & Company continued the corporate philosophy of its founder.

The main focus of the training and development activity at Arthur Andersen is its Center for Professional Education (CPE), located near Chicago. The CPE is responsible for a wide range of programs and services, including training design and development, curriculum planning, and training support. The CPE provides almost ten million hours of training each year in a variety of formats, including classroom training and multimedia programs delivered at computer workstations.[1]

Westpac. A financial services group headquartered in Sydney, Australia, with more than 50,000 employees, Westpac invests approximately 8 percent of its total payroll on training and development. Westpac's emphasis on training began with a comprehensive review of the effectiveness of training efforts. The review discovered a wide disparity in the quality of design and delivery of various training efforts, as well as inefficiencies in the training process. As a result, Westpac created a separate business entity called Westpac Training to manage the provision of training services to the company.

Westpac Training quickly developed a system for identifying training needs and determining training strategies for all units of Westpac. It required that training strategies be linked to overall human resource strategies, which in turn would link to corporate business objectives. Each unit now sets its own training strategies to support staff development.[2]

These two cases vividly illustrate the tremendous commitment to training and development in organizations today.

Evidence of Trend

The practitioner survey of global trends shows that an increased training budget is one of the most visible trends, with a response of 4.32 out of 5 for level of agreement (see Appendix 1). The importance of the trend was rated 4.07 out of 5. Strong agreement exists among practitioners that budgets continue to increase year after year and that this represents an important trend.

In one of the most comprehensive studies of training budgets, *Training* magazine's Industry Report from 1997 shows that training expenditures in the United States totaled $58.6 billion in 1997.[3] This represented a 5 percent increase from the previous year. The report has noted an increase each year that budgets have been monitored. In the last five years, budgets increased 26 percent. This amount does not include the cost of participants' salaries as they attend training, nor does it account for on-the-job informal training. When these two are added, a budget could easily approach $200 billion.

Although the studies by country vary in completeness and accuracy, for the most part, budgets increase annually. In the United Kingdom, the annual training budget is about twenty-five billion pounds per year. This amount is expected to increase and reach fifty billion in a few years.[4] A survey of members of the International Federation of Training and Development Organizations listed the increase in training budgets as a distinct trend, occurring in the vast majority of the thirty-five countries represented. A variety of studies pinpoint these expenditures, expressing them as a percentage of payroll.[5] For example, Australia spends 1.7 percent of payroll on training expenditures, as does Germany. The Netherlands spends 1.5 percent, while France spends 2.5 percent—a tremendous increase from earlier years. The United States spends about 1.8 percent of payroll on training.

In a Benchmarking Forum conducted by the American Society for Training and Development, total training expenditures measured 2.2 percent of payroll, up from 2.14 percent the year earlier. Forum members are large, multinational organizations with a progressive approach to training and development.[6]

A major study, conducted by a former secretary of labor, concluded that industrialized nations, such as the United States, would need to spend 4 to 5 percent of payroll on education and training to develop and maintain high-income, world-class economies.[7]

Causes and Drivers

Many influences have driven increases in the funding of training and in accuracy of the budgeting process.

- Many organizations, industries, and countries see training as an investment instead of a cost. Consequently, senior managers are willing to invest because they can anticipate a payoff for their investments. For example, organizations in England now view training as an investment instead of a cost.[8] These firms realize that training has an important influence on their success. Some companies set minimum targets for training. For example, Saturn Corporation, maker of Saturn automobiles, has been an outstanding success since its introduction in the late '80s. Saturn is a completely new type of company that has excelled at building top-quality, low-priced, efficient automobiles, as well as excellent customer satisfaction. One of the secrets to its success is a heavy investment in training. As a standard, Saturn requires one hundred hours of training per year for each employee, including the president. If the training requirements are not met by every employee, bonuses are reduced for all employees.[9]
- Training and development is perceived as an important change agent. Most organizations are undergoing tremendous, sometimes radical, changes in the name of total quality management, reengineering, transformation, and other change initiatives. At the heart of the process is training designed to change mind-sets, develop skills, and equip staff for implementing the changes. Training is a major ingredient required for successful implementation. In some organizations, training is the most important tool for implementation of change.[10]
- The technology revolution, dispensed worldwide, caused a tremendous increase in the amount of training. New technology requires new skills and upgrading of current skills. An increased investment in training is considered a necessity.[11]

- In developing countries, increased training is needed as new jobs are created and new plants and processes are established. Skill upgrading is necessary to develop core competencies needed to maintain a productive labor force. In some countries, the governments require minimum levels of funding for training to ensure that skills are developed. A formal budgeting process is considered one of the most important management tools for efficient and effective operation. Formal budgeting has moved into the training function so that training budgets are developed along with budgets for other major functions and entities, using the same budgeting guidelines and processes.
- As learning organizations continue to be implemented in many organizations, additional focus is put on learning and training. In addition, the concern about intellectual capital and human capital has created a desire to invest more heavily in learning activities and formal training.

Trend Description

Developing a Training and Development Budget for a Country—The USA Experience

Determining total training and development expenditures for an entire country is a difficult challenge. The toughest issues include deciding what type of data to collect, locating funding sources for the collection, deciding who to use as samples in the study, and assigning responsibility for data collection and reporting. Each of the thirty-five countries contacted in one of the studies for this book is attempting to estimate its total training expenditures. However, the amounts and procedures vary considerably, resulting in reliability and validity concerns. Although much progress has been made, much room for improvement exists. Perhaps one of the most accurate and reliable estimates of training and development expenditures comes from the United States. Three organizations estimate the magnitude of the training investment. The U.S. Department of Labor, through regular surveying and reporting processes, attempts to capture the training estimate in intricate intervals. The American Society for Training and Development estimates the training investment for its 50,000 members. The most reliable and credible data come from *Training* magazine's annual Industry Report. The magazine captures the total expenditures by a variety of categories.[12] The results from the 1997 report are presented below, in summary form, along with a few selected items and information about the process. The survey section illustrates the type of data needed and how the data were generated.

The Survey Process. *Training* magazine surveys a sample of all businesses with one hundred or more employees and extrapolates the results across all companies with one hundred or more employees. A sample of 1,559 usable responses reflected the total population of 136,605 organizations of this size. This sample size is adequate to make estimates with a variance of plus or minus 2.5 percent and a 95 percent confidence level. The data reflect the direct expenditures in training only. The data do not include salaries and employee benefits for participants during the time they are in training. Nor do they include the cost for informal on-the-job training.

1997 Budgets. According to the study, organizations in the United States with one hundred or more employees budgeted $58.6 billion for training in 1997, representing a 5 percent increase from the previous year. Of that total, $40.7 billion went toward training-staff salaries, representing 70 percent of the total. Facilities and overhead accounted for $4.3 billion, or 7 percent of the total. External seminars and conferences totaled $3.7 billion, as did hardware, with each representing 6 percent of the budget. Off-the-shelf materials amounted to $2.2 billion, or 4 percent of the total, and customized materials represented $2 billion, or 4 percent. Finally, almost $2 billion, or 3 percent, went to outside services. Consistent with the trend reported in this chapter, the budgets in this report showed an upward trend in the last five years. Budgets steadily increased by about 5 percent per year, totaling 26 percent. For 1997, the greatest increases in expenditures were realized in hardware, seminars/conferences, and outside materials. The survey also addressed predictions for 1998. Forty-seven percent of respondents, who were the T&D managers, predicted an increase in budgets for 1998, while 6 percent predicted smaller budgets. Forty-eight percent indicated budgets would remain about the same.

Types of Training. Another important issue addressed by the survey involves how the actual budget is spent according to types of training. The broad categories show $15 billion (26 percent) is spent on professionals while $14.5 billion (25 percent) is spent on managers. Twelve percent, or $7.1 billion, is spent on the sales staff, and all others receive the remaining $20.8 billion, representing 36 percent. The survey also estimates the number of individuals trained and the number of hours of training for several job groups, including administrative employees, production workers, customer service employees, first-level supervisors, sales support, middle managers, executives, and senior managers. First-level supervisors receive the greatest amount of training at thirty-four hours each. The report details expenditures for and participation in forty-one types of training, including training specific to organization and industry, as well as specific instructional methods and media.

Workplace Trends. The Industry Report focuses on several workplace trends and issues, such as the type and extent of remedial training (literacy training). It also explores other key issues, including benchmarking, engineering, total quality management, teams, downsizing, and partnering. Additional information about social issues and the extent of outsourcing is presented. In the United States, external contractors perform 38 percent of program design and development and 32 percent of delivery, underscoring an important trend.

Training Technology. A final section of the survey explores the amount of technology used in training and development. Specific issues covered include information technology training budgets, use of electronic performance support systems, use of online Internet services, and use of teleconferencing.

Status. The Industry Report compiled by *Training* magazine is a comprehensive and thorough study. It is respected as a consistent, reliable indicator of expenditures. If anything, it underestimates the actual expenditures in the industry. It serves as an important barometer for training and development departments to compare their current expenditures with those of others, and it indicates specific trends that are critical to the industry and suppliers.

The Budgeting Process

The budgeting process usually begins with delivery of the budget package, which contains specific guidelines, forms, procedures, and special instructions for developing the budget. It also contains the approval process, the philosophy, concerns, and other issues often communicated along with budget packages. The good news is that the training function is considered a mainstream activity in the organization, subject to the same kind of control and budgeting requirements. The department is required to participate in the budgeting process along with other functions. The process through which the budget is developed has become more formal, organized, and accurate. The bad news is that the budget by itself can be constraining, can take time, and may be inflexible in its administration.

The budget has become the most widely used tool of control for managers. Budgets allow the department to know where it stands, spot various trends, and control resources during the fiscal year. When the budget is approved, it should communicate three important things:

- The plans of the training and development department are outlined. This includes programs and services needed by operating and support departments to help them meet specific operational and strategic goals.
- Each program or service should add value to the organization, ultimately captured as either increased revenue for the same resources or the reduction of costs. In essence, almost all programs either increase productivity, improve quality, save time, reduce costs directly, or improve satisfaction for customers and employees.
- Each program or service has a specific unit cost associated with it. The total costs of all programs and services are included in the overall budget, while the cost per program and per participant are included in the detail attachments.

These three major statements characterize an ideal budget. Unfortunately, many budgets fall short of providing the appropriate information about all three. This represents an ideal situation, sought by many as the budget is developed each year.

Collecting Information. In addition to information about specific program needs, several types of information should be collected when developing the budget. These include:

- Operating plans of the organization
- Strategic plans or multi-year operating plan
- Capital expenditure budget
- Operating performance of the organization
- Financial performance of the organization
- Major operating issues and concerns
- Special audit and investigative reports that address concerns or problem areas
- Customer satisfaction data
- Work climate and attitude data from employees
- Management inventories and succession-planning documents
- Performance appraisals
- Specific projects in process

These items can supply information that may provide direction for implementation of the budget. New programs should be tied to specific needs, which are addressed later in the training and development process.

Types of Budgets. Although many different types of budgets unique to the organization can exist, three major categories often appear, and these are presented below. The specific application of these types can vary with the organization and its special issues and concerns.

1. *Fixed and Variable Budgets.* Sometimes the budgets divide into two major categories:

    - The fixed budget is those costs that will not directly vary with the amount of work to be conducted. Facilities for training and development, equipment, and overhead support staff all fit in this category.
    - The variable budget represents costs directly related to specific output, such as the number of programs or the number of participants attending programs. Program materials, travel expenses, and instructor time are examples of variable costs.

2. *Planning, Programming, and Budgeting System.* The budgeting system initially launched by the federal government is now used by many organizations. In this planning, programming, and budgeting system, the budget is developed around specific programs. Five basic steps should be followed when using this approach.

   - Specify and analyze basic objectives in each major area of activity.
   - Analyze the output of planned programs in light of the specified objectives.
   - Measure total cost of the programs for several years as a projection.
   - Analyze alternatives to the programs.
   - Make the approach an integral part of the actual budget.

3. *Zero-based Budgeting.* Some organizations are beginning to use a zero-based budget, which means the budget is developed from the ground up, with no holdover from the previous year. In this approach, every program or service is justified in the budgeting process. Zero-based budgets remove the temptation to add to the previous year's budget or develop a budget based on what was accomplished in the previous year. Starting from zero requires careful analysis of the cost of different programs, as well as the value added as various priorities are considered. With this approach, activities, programs, or services are developed into a format for decision making. Various activities or programs are evaluated and prioritized. Finally, the resources are allocated to those with the highest priority.

An organization-specific approach to budgeting could be a blend of all three of these types or a subset of one of these types.

Types of Programs

Selecting the specific types of programs is both a necessary and challenging process. It is necessary to plan adequately and accurately develop the budget. The detail summary of planned programs is essential. It is challenging because all the needs that will surface during the year may not be known. The needs assessment and analysis process sometimes does not coincide with the development of the budget. Basically, four types of programs and services exist.

- **Ongoing programs that are repeated each year.** For example, training for new first-level supervisors will be needed each year as new supervisors are chosen.
- **New programs based on perceived needs or actual needs assessments.** Customer services training for a particular job category, based on predetermined needs assessment, is an example of this.
- **Consulting services provided by the training and development staff to help the organization improve performance.** Although some consulting services can be predicted based on previous work, other consulting services will focus on perceived needs or actual needs as they develop.
- **Other services and support processes, including administrative functions such as tuition refund.** These services are often justified based on the level of activity or participation required.

Overall, determining specific types of programs may be the most difficult yet the most crucial part of the budgeting process. It must be completed using as much information as possible and based on legitimate needs analyses. Chapter 3 reflects on the trend of increased use of needs assessment and analysis.

Trend Consequences

Impact

Developing a training and development budget is an essential part of managing any function, activity, or process in an organization. The trend toward larger and more formal budgets is the result of many influences detailed earlier in this chapter. Budgets can be a welcome tool for the training and development staff because they can make it possible to coordinate work and measure progress against monetary goals. Budgets can also act as signaling devices to take corrective actions. When used properly, a budget can be helpful in learning from past practices. It also improves the allocation of resources within the department and communication of priorities. In some cases, budget performance can be an important ingredient in the performance appraisal process.

On the negative side, budgets can become a problem if not used properly. If the budget is not flexible, individuals may stick to the budget regardless of what needs to be done. Budgets are usually based on what has occurred previously, and a situation confronted during a certain year may be completely different from a situation that occurred the previous year. Budgets can become complex, confusing, and time consuming. Also, budgets can allow individuals to play games with the funding by anticipating budget cuts and spending all the money, whether it is necessary or not.

Key Questions

Some key questions must be asked when assessing this trend.

Key Questions

1. To what extent do I perceive this to be a trend?
2. How important is this trend to me?
3. What has been the experience with my budgets in the last few years?
4. Have budgets increased, decreased, or remained the same?
5. How organized and formal is the budgeting process?
6. Is the process consistent with other budgeting processes in the organization?
7. Do I need to formalize the process or improve budgeting in some way?
8. What problems or barriers will I encounter as I try to improve the budgeting process?
9. What happens if I do nothing?
10. Is it possible to increase the T&D budget each year?
11. What is necessary to accomplish the increase, and how can the increase be presented?
12. Does management support the budgeting process?

Outlook

Training and development budgets should continue to grow. In almost every major organization, training budgets should increase, resulting in budget increases for the entire industry and country. It appears that this trend will continue, based on the necessity and importance of the training process and the perceived payoff of the training investment. The budgeting process will continue to be more formal, developed with the same budgeting guidelines of other functions in the organization.

References

1. Harris, David M. and DeSimone, Randy L. *Human Resource Development.* Fort Worth, Tex.: Dryden Press, 1994.
2. Marquardt, Michael J. and Engel, Dean W. *Global Human Resource Development.* Englewood Cliffs, N.J.: Prentice Hall, 1993.
3. "Industry Report." *Training,* 1997.
4. Coulson-Thomas, Colin. *Creating the Global Company.* London: McGraw-Hill Book Company, 1992.
5. Bassi, Laurie J. *The ASTD Training Data Book.* Alexandria, Va.: American Society for Training and Development, 1997.
6. Bassi, Laurie J. and Cheney, Scott. "Benchmarking the Best." *Training & Development,* Nov. 1997.
7. Marshall, Ray. "America's Choice—High Skills and Low Wages." *Labor Relations Today,* Oct. 1990.
8. Williams, Teresa and Green, Adrian. *A Business Approach to Training.* London: Gower, 1997.
9. Sherman, Joe. *In the Rings of Saturn.* Oxford, England: Oxford University Press, 1994.
10. Robbins, Harvey and Findley, Michael. *Why Change Doesn't Work: Why Initiatives Go Wrong and How They Can Try Again and Succeed.* London: Orion Publishing Group, 1997.
11. Burrus, Daniel. *Techno Trends.* New York: Harper Business, 1995.
12. "Industry Report." *Training,* Oct. 1997.

13

LEARNING ORGANIZATIONS

Trend Definition and Validation

Brief Definition of Trend

The interest in the learning organization continues to grow. In today's changing and complex business environment, organizations must create a learning environment and transfer learning into improved performance. Competitive pressures require organizations to develop a work force of continuous learners who enhance knowledge and skills and their ability to learn. Learning is no longer an isolated event but an integral part of daily work in an organization.

Case Studies: Land O'Lakes and Polaroid Corporation

Land O'Lakes. Land O'Lakes has approximately 6,000 employees and generates almost $3 billion in sales. The company grew in most recent years because of acquisitions and joint ventures. As with most organizations, Land O'Lakes experienced pressure to increase profitability. In an effort to do so, the company reduced costs by enhancing inventory management, improving technology, and reducing the work force.

In an effort to provide needed training in light of the organizational changes, the company developed a core curriculum of courses. Along with the development of the core curriculum, one division introduced the concept of total quality management (TQM), a comprehensive continuous-improvement process. Inspired by this division's pursuit of learning and process improvement, executive management decided to incorporate TQM throughout the organization. The purpose of this commitment was to find systems and behaviors inconsistent with quality principles and to consider them for redesign or exclusion. One of the first targets for reform was the company's approach to training.

A cross-functional task force was created to evaluate the current training system. The team members developed what they believed to be the attributes of a learning organization. The attributes included the following:

- Learning is considered a lifelong continuous process.
- The environment is one in which people want know how to learn and are encouraged to learn.
- There is critical examination of operating assumptions, theories, and facts.
- Learning is sought in every situation.
- Appropriate talent is matched with appropriate tasks.
- Learning is shared and applied on the job.
- The improvement effort is continually examined and evaluated.

Since the implementation of the TQM process within the Land O'Lakes organization, one of the main thrusts has been the encouragement of employees to take responsibility for their own learning. The company encourages each employee to develop an individual learning plan compatible with his or her group's learning direction or his or her personal learning needs. Employees and management appreciate the value of building a learning infrastructure and more clearly understand the importance of learning.[1]

Polaroid Corporation. Polaroid's efforts to create a learning organization led the organization to develop a system with which the company can leverage its intellectual capital. A knowledge management system was developed for the training department in an effort to make learning available anywhere at anytime.[2] The system is a combination of Lotus Notes and Domino programs, used to link the data base to the Internet and intranet.

Polaroid recognized the economic gains when it first pursued the development of its knowledge management system. Using this system, a cross-functional group of employees (professionals from the sales, marketing, finance, human resources, information technology, and communication departments) can communicate, solve problems, and share learning. By having information readily available and easy to transfer, employees can compare the successes and failures of different training tools. Also, information about customers, as well as competitor information, can be shared quickly for immediate response.

Polaroid is seeing improvement in performance because of the implementation of the knowledge management system. Cycle times in its sales and marketing departments (that is, the amount of time it takes a salesperson to realize a sale) have diminished since the implementation of the system. The organization plans to implement the knowledge management system on a global basis.

Evidence of Trend

Clear evidence supports the continued acceptance of the learning organization concept. More organizations are emphasizing the need to strategically manage training efforts to improve performance and enhance competitive positioning. Corporations are emphasizing the need to manage intellectual capital. Many organizations are putting a more formal emphasis on learning by assigning executive management to oversee learning and human capital efforts.

The practitioner survey of global trends shows the adoption of the learning organization concept as a visible and important trend (see Appendix 1). Practitioners demonstrated their agreement with the existence of this trend with a rating of 4.09 out of 5. The level of importance of this trend is rated 4.47 out of 5, the seventh most important trend.

A National HRD Executive Survey conducted by the American Society for Training and Development (ASTD) addresses the issue of building a learning organization. The results of the survey indicate that 91 percent of the respondents believe that building a learning organization is important while only 9 percent believe the concept is not important.[3] This supports the practitioner survey results previously mentioned, indicating a trend toward the learning organization concept. Other issues covered in the survey, with regard to the learning organization concept, include:

- Technologies used to support the learning organization
- Practices through which companies use learning to become more effective
- Issues, behaviors, and activities through which companies encourage employees
- Characteristics of a learning organization

Additional evidence of this trend includes the emphasis being placed on individual disciplines of the learning organization concept. For example, systems thinking is an important element of learning organization principles. The March 1997 *Info-line,* published by the American Society for Training and Development, addresses the discipline of systems thinking, exclusively.[4]

Learning organization principles and concepts are also being taught and implemented in the formal education setting. The Rio Salado Community College department of student services implemented the learning organization concepts in an effort to focus on departmental growth.[5] The doctoral program in human resource development at Vanderbilt University in Nashville, Tennessee, requires students to participate in a course about learning organizations.

Along with survey results, other evidence of this trend is shown by the popularity of many new books focused on the learning organization. At last count, more than twenty of these books existed. These books support the idea that continuous learning is key to the success of any organization.

Causes and Drivers

Several influences drive increased acceptance of learning organizations. The more important ones are listed below:

- **Increasingly globalized marketplace.** The globalization of the economy has increased the abundance of energy sources, increased the competitiveness of corporations, and enhanced telecommunication.[6] Globalization is bringing together cultures and values that, at one time, were isolated to specific regions and countries. Therefore, organizations are being forced to change the way they operate. These changes include fostering employees' abilities to think in global terms, allowing them to understand the degree to which decisions can impact an organization from a worldview. It also requires employees to understand the impact of change within the global economy, as well as in their own organizations.
- **The need to have closer ties with customers and suppliers and to know more about competitors.** The need to understand processes, technologies, and information about customers, competitors, and suppliers has caused organizations to rethink their training efforts and to focus more on developing continuous learning opportunities. Organizations are learning to manage their intellectual capital by understanding how to align it with the organization's strategic direction and how to place it within the organization so that employees can increase their skills and abilities, thus improving products and services.[7]
- **Changes within the organization.** The speed at which changes take place and information is disseminated creates the necessity for employees to learn faster. Increased technological advancement has given rise to changes in how information is disseminated. Interactive television, computer-based training, Web-based training, and digital video have all changed the way employees learn.[8]
- **Organization structure and staffing.** Virtual offices have distanced employees from central learning facilities, encouraging independent, autonomous learning. Increased diversity in work organizations has increased the need for employees to understand and value differences in thinking, culture, and values.
- **The total quality management movement.** The last two decades saw a proliferation of total quality management programs in all types of

organizations. The need and desire for zero defects required learning to focus on processes and systems thinking.[9] Most TQM programs include a variety of learning activities and formats.

- **The organization's need to obtain and maintain knowledge assets.** More organizations are aware of the need to protect intellectual capital and to grow, maintain, and retain the knowledge employees bring to the organization. "Knowledge employees" are in high demand in most organizations, with no let-up in sight. Knowledge employees are more educated and highly skilled than in the past. Therefore, organizations now must find ways to attract those high-intellect employees and provide them opportunities to grow, be creative, and be motivated so the organization can retain them and their knowledge. Knowledge employees expect their work environment to provide personal fulfillment and to offer opportunity to spread their talents and abilities.
- **Changes in customer expectations.** Customers require companies to understand their needs, as well as learn innovative ways to meet their expectations. Customers place high standards on service, competitive pricing, and availability of products and services. These high expectations require companies to encourage employees at all levels to make quick decisions in response to customers. This pushing down of decision making has caused companies to change the way they offer learning to employees.

Trend Description

The premise behind the learning organization is that the organization learns not just as individuals but as teams with a common goal. This continuous, systematic process of learning and the degree of learning within the organization determines the ability of that organization to transition to the demand of constant change. No universal characteristics to describe a learning organization exist. Rather, an organization can direct its learning by key fundamental principles. The learning organization concept is not directed solely at management. This concept is directed at the organization as a whole. In a learning organization, all employees are encouraged to capture, share, and use knowledge so the organization continuously meets all current and future challenges.

Disciplines of the Learning Organization

Although no blueprint is available by which to design a learning organization, there are five key disciplines, as identified by Peter Senge.[10]

- An organization must be committed to lifelong learning in order to develop the skills and expertise necessary to the organization. This **personal mastery** brings together both individual learning and organizational learning.
- Individuals have deeply ingrained images of how they understand the world. **Mental models** direct responses to events and situations. Until individuals recognize these models, they are inhibited from making progress in learning.
- When individual vision and goals are tied to the vision and goals of the organization, the **shared vision** creates a committed organization. In organizations today, teams, rather than individuals, are the learning units.

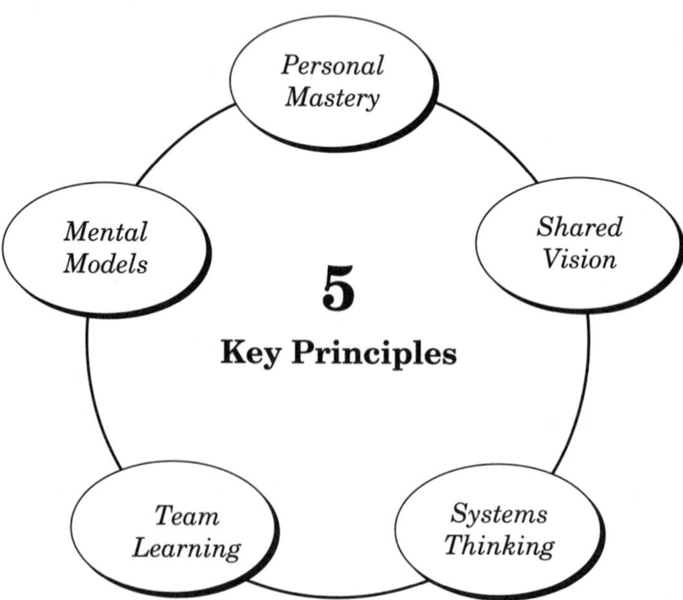

Figure 13-1. *Summary of the Five Key Principles of the Learning Organization.*

- When teams are free of inhibitions, genuine dialogue can begin. This **team learning** allows members to create the learning with which to accomplish the desired results.
- The final discipline, **systems thinking,** brings together the previous four disciplines to create a whole. Systems thinking brings the entire perspective into view. Systems thinking is the cornerstone principle of the learning organization.

Building on Senge's five key disciplines of the learning organization are activities through which learning organizations are developed.[11]

Learning from history is a way organizations can anticipate results if behavior on the job remains constant. Organizations can review past successes and failures, assess them systematically, and record lessons learned. By utilizing data bases, case studies, post-project reviews, and other sources, organizations can bring in new perspectives of ways to conduct business.

Learning from others can enlighten management as to new techniques and processes. Although they may come from different fields, an organization still can learn the way work gets done in another organization. Benchmarking is one way in which organizations can learn from each other. Other ways include feedback via surveys and questionnaires, and callbacks regarding services and products.

Transferring learning is the key to any learning initiative. A training or learning activity is an isolated event until it is disseminated throughout the organization or applied on the job. Learning can be passed to others in the organization through oral reports, written communication, site visits, job rotation programs, videotapes, or audiotapes.

Characteristics of the Learning Organization

Along with these five key disciplines, current learning organizations have many different characteristics.[12] These characteristics include:

- **Opportunities for continuous learning.** This includes a plan for approaches to learning. These approaches can include work assignments, formal training, mentoring, and individual self-development. Managers have the responsibility of recognizing what learners need to know and assessing their desire to learn.
- **Interaction between individuals and change.** Although the flow of information is available to all members of an organization, indi-

viduals are encouraged to question and challenge information, as well as share personal viewpoints. The climate required to allow such dialogue is one in which mistakes and failures are rewarded, and individuals must be encouraged to use their mistakes as developmental opportunities. This climate offers opportunities for candid communication.

- **Responsiveness to organization members.** Information must be readily available and accessible to members of the organization while transferred knowledge must be expedited from one part of the organization to another.
- **Investment in training and development for all employees.** Employees and customers consider learning to be an investment in the future credibility of the organization, the future integrity of the organization, and future satisfaction in the stability of the organization. To ensure these things, learning opportunities should be available to everyone, regardless of position or level within an organization.
- **Shared vision of the future with all employees.** The culture allows employees the right to say how the vision will develop.
- **Integration of work and learning.** Both work and learning share the same objectives, and all employees are encouraged to achieve those objectives. Learning organizations invite employees to enhance their knowledge in whatever their preferred learning styles. Some employees enjoy traditional classroom learning while others enjoy the autonomy of individual learning. Learning organizations enable people to choose their learning styles and the speed at which they learn. Learning organizations use current, new technologies of delivery. These delivery techniques are made available to individuals throughout the organization.
- **Encouragement to continuously learn.** The learning organization encourages employees to think and contribute, whether through classrooms, book groups, or candid conversations.

Learning Organization Model

Learning takes place at different levels in an organization (including the individual level), through groups and teams, large business units and networks, and the network of customers, suppliers, and other groups. The learning organization offers a highly social learning environment. Employees learn as they work together in achieving goals, and they help other employees learn. Figure 13-2 is a model of learning organization imperatives.[13] As illustrated in the figure, learning within organizations is a complex system. The relationships between the organization and the individuals within that system have an immediate impact on how and what the organizations learn. Most learning organizations evolve because the organization is seeking some kind of change within its infrastructure. By transforming themselves into new environments, organizations can overcome many of the problems currently facing them. Fundamental shifts of employees' understanding of how learning impacts work are required before an organization can develop into a learning organization. A pre-condition of the creation of a learning organization is the assessment of current capabilities. Once the current situation is assessed, the organization then decides which strategies to implement.

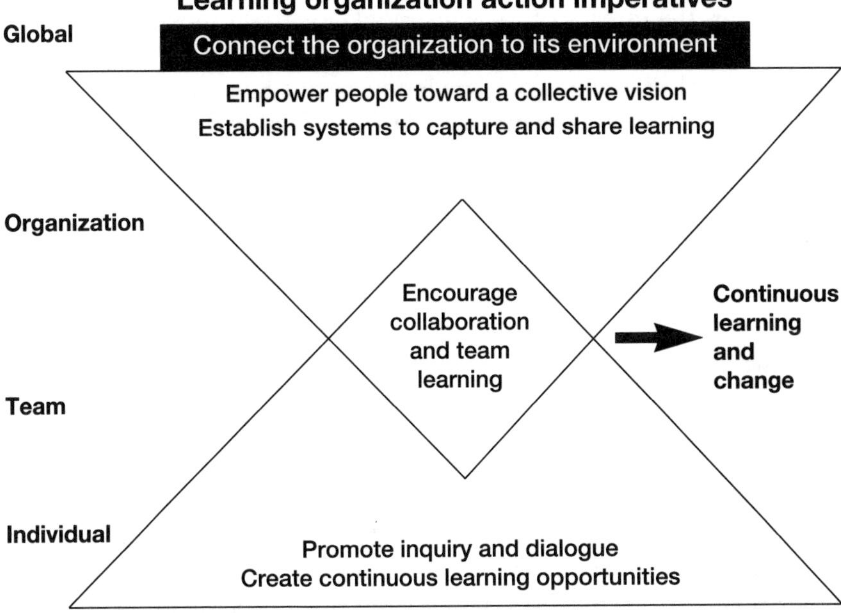

Figure 13-2. Model of the Learning Organization. (Source: Watkins, Karen E., Marsick, Victoria J. (Eds.), and Phillips, Jack J. (Series Ed.) *In Action: Creating the Learning Organization.* Alexandria, Va.: American Society for Training and Development, 1996, p. 5.)

As illustrated in Figure 13-2, beginning with the individual level, the infrastructure creates a continuous learning opportunity. Learning should be strategic and should come from the employees' work.

At the individual level, dialogue should be promoted. There should be a culture of questioning and experimentation within the organization. The team level encourages collaboration. At this level the focus is not necessarily on teamwork but on learning as a team. The center level is the organization level, where learning is captured in policies, procedures, guidelines, and strategies. The final level is the global level. Learning at this level extends beyond organizational and global boundaries. At this level, large global organizations must learn to think of themselves as one single organization.

Many models are used in creating and developing learning organizations. For the most part, those models share several characteristics. The learning organization must focus on transformation. Infrastructure must be created to ensure knowledge is captured and shared. All levels of employees and management must learn to think systematically about the impact of their decisions. Learning must become part of daily work. A greater impact of learning is seen when a greater percentage of the employee population participates. Policies and systems within the organization must be structured to support and reward learning for individuals, teams, and the organization. Systems must be in place to measure the change in learning.

As this section highlights, key differences exist between the traditional training environment and the learning organization environment. Table 13-1 compares differences between the two environments.[14] The table underscores and summarizes the key principles of the learning organization.

Managing Knowledge

With the creation of the learning organization, an increased capacity of intellectual capital is realized. Studies are routinely conducted to estimate the value of employee know-how, patents, brand names, and other forms of knowledge. These studies show a steady rise in the value of knowledge from 38 percent of corporate assets in 1982 to 62 percent in 1992. In 1997, knowledge accounted for 80 percent of all corporate assets.[15] It is a major responsibility of the organization to

Table 13-1
Differences Between Traditional Training and the Learning Organization Environment

Traditional Training Environment	Learning Organization Environment
◆ Instructor-driven learning	◆ Self-directed learning
◆ Scheduled/prescriptive approach	◆ Self-serve approach
◆ Classroom-based delivery	◆ Multi-delivery modes
◆ Programs as main currency	◆ Competencies as main currency
◆ Attendance as determinant of capability	◆ Competency demonstration as determinant of capability
◆ Offered as one size fits all	◆ Only targets gap between current and required capability
◆ Based on generic training needs analysis	◆ Based on individual competency assessment

Adapted from: Greenwood, Tracy, Wasson, Avtar, and Giles, Robbie. "The Learning Organization: Concepts, Processes, and Questions." Performance & Instruction, *Apr. 1993, p. 8.*

monitor and manage the knowledge of the individuals within the organization. McKinsey & Company focuses on spending approximately 10 percent of its revenues to manage intellectual capital.[16] The proactive management of knowledge helps the organization as a whole.

Although many organizations feel knowledge management is expensive, knowledge can prove even more expensive if unmanaged. To effectively manage knowledge, organizations must use a combination of its people and technology. Individuals provide clarification, interpretation, and understanding of a context, while computers and technology capture and distribute rapidly changing structured knowledge. Organizations must create an environment in which their people and technology are used cooperatively to manage knowledge. The degree of power and the influence of that knowledge sometimes determine the value of knowledge within an organization.

Knowledge management can be a political process. Oftentimes managers perceive the politics in managing knowledge to be a deterrent while other managers value the political influence and use it to more effectively utilize knowledge within the organization. Many organizations are creating groups whose primary function is to manage knowledge. The purpose of these knowledge managers is to facilitate the distribution and use of knowledge within an organization. These knowledge managers face an ever-changing process that influences the accuracy of assessment of current knowledge. Knowledge managers must find new ways to disseminate and utilize knowledge while remaining flexible enough to address new information as it arises.

Many organizations view knowledge managers and knowledge employees as intellectual capital of the organization. With more information pursued and made available to members of an organization, intellectual property becomes one of the most valuable assets of the organization.

Learning organizations promote the increase of employee knowledge. Yet, one challenge is to effectively grow, maintain, and retain the knowledge. Many organizations combine the knowledge of employees into knowledge data bases. These data bases are strategic endeavors to help executives change the direction of the organization. Examples of these knowledge data bases include:

- Andersen Consulting—Knowledge Xchange
- Booz • Allen & Hamilton—KOL (Knowledge On Line)
- Ernst & Young—Center for Business Knowledge
- PricewaterhouseCoopers—Knowledgeview

Why would organizations stock knowledge into these data bases? One reason is the financial reward for investing in technology to manage knowledge. Andersen Consulting saves millions of dollars in shipping costs by using data bases. A second reason is that it is much easier to tap into another employee's knowledge by tapping into a data base. A third reason is that data bases help share information globally. A final reason is to track information such as turnover.[17]

Measuring Learning

Continuous learning and improvement are at the core of the learning organization concept. To ensure that learning is actually producing improved performance, it must be measured. Simply measuring learning against specified objectives, however, is not enough. Learning must be measured in terms of organizational changes, ultimate outcomes, or business results.[18]

There are three phases of individual learning.[19] The first phase is cognitive. Here, members of the organization are exposed to new ideas, expand their knowledge, and begin to think differently. The second phase is behavioral, where employees internalize their new insights and begin to alter their behavior. The third phase is performance improvement. During this phase, changes in behavior lead to noted and measurable improvements in results, such as superior quality, better delivery, increased market share, increased customer satisfaction, or intangible benefits.

Many reasons exist for measuring learning. This book identified many of these reasons in previous chapters. However, listed below are several other purposes for measuring learning.[20]

- **To identify opportunities for training.** This is so that a direct linkage between learning goals, business goals, and strategic objectives can be projected.
- **To determine deficits in knowledge, skills, and attitudes.** The gap between where employees are and where they need to be is determined.
- **To enhance the learning process.** To continuously improve any process, the process must be continuously measured.
- **To provide accountability for the use of resources.** The training department must be accountable for the use of its resources. Continuously assessing the use of time, money, and materials will help hold the organization accountable for resource utilization.
- **To determine the business impact of learning.** This leads to the ultimate goal of any learning intervention—the return on investment. The organization must determine if the learning intervention is actually producing bottom-line results and if there is evidence of improved performance based on the new knowledge, skills, and attitudes acquired from the learning event.

Measuring learning ensures that training interventions produce results for the organization and that performance continuously improves. A key aspect of measuring learning is the transfer of the new knowledge to the employees and their on-the-job performance. The following section addresses this issue.

Transferring Learning

The results of any learning intervention are determined by the change in on-the-job performance and business impact. Learning new skills or gaining new knowledge is not enough to improve performance. Individuals must have the support, resources, capabilities, and incentives to transfer their skills and knowledge to the workplace.

Unfortunately, high levels of transfer are unusual in the absence of conscious collaborative efforts by major stakeholders to support the transfer.[21] The focus on performance, and its requirement for transfer of learning, means that a shift in perspectives is necessary for organizational stakeholders—top decision makers, managers, team leaders and members, learning professionals, strategic planners, union officials, quality specialists, financial and budgetary experts, customers, suppliers, and others. They must consider learning activities as the input to the learning process that results in transfer to performance as the desired outcome. Table 13-2 identifies the learner and work-environment characteristics that enhance the probability of learning transfer.[22]

Table 13-2
Learner and Work-Environment Characteristics Supporting the Transfer of Learning

Learner Characteristics	Environment Characteristics
◆ Ability	◆ Supportive organizational climate
◆ Aptitude	◆ Preliminary discussion with supervisor
◆ Personality	◆ Opportunities to use new learning
◆ Need for achievement	◆ Goal setting and feedback following training
◆ Internal locus of control	
◆ Motivation	
◆ Confidence	
◆ Desire for success	
◆ Voluntary attendance at training	
◆ Job involvement	
◆ Belief in training's value	
◆ High self-expectations	

Source: Baldwin, T. T. and Ford, J. K. "Transfer of Training: A Review and Directions for Future Research." Personnel Psychology, *Vol. 41, 1988, pp. 63–105.*

Managers who have high-priority learning requirements are realizing that their visible involvement throughout the learning process is essential in attaining the work-force performance they need. Learners are gaining new status as partners in planning and implementing their learning activities and in becoming responsible for strategies to support their learning achievements. Training professionals are moving into partnership roles with managers, learners, and other stakeholders to manage the transfer process. Transfer of learning is an integral part of the learning organization concept.

Building a Learning Organization

A learning organization represents an advance in the way employees think within the workplace. The learning organization provides an environment for new thinking. Organizations will encourage individuals to learn through specially constructed units of the organization. To flourish as learning organizations, companies need to reconfigure themselves based on four dimensions of the organizational subsystem: vision, culture, strategy, and structure. The vision gives the individuals of the organization the sense of future and the guidance to move forward. Building a shared vision around learning is the foundation of becoming a learning organization. This shared vision provides focus and helps to develop goals for individuals. The vision fosters risk taking and experimentation.[23] Culture determines the nature of learning within an organization. For the most part, culture has been one of non-learning; therefore, to become a learning organization, cultural values that have been instilled in the cultural organization must change. These cultural changes include developing a climate in which learning is rewarded and that places the responsibility of learning on all individuals in the organization. Learning organizations reward individuals for risk taking and innovative new ideas, and commit significant funding to encourage learning and to support quality.

The third part of the subsystem, strategy, sets forth the plan to become the learning organization. Strategic goals, job behaviors, and skills should be mapped out for individuals, along with business objectives. Learning activities incorporated into the business processes should also be included. Learning should be a part of all processes within the organization. Fundamental thought processes will have to change in order to integrate learning into the work environment.

Recently, it has been recognized that up to 95 percent of learning occurs while an individual is on the job. Organizations must leverage that to ensure that maximum learning is taking place.

The final component of the learning subsystem is the structure. The structure determines a level of control, monitoring and performance, and lines of communication. Restricted boundaries and bureaucratic processes prohibit learning from taking place. Therefore, to become a learning organization, these boundaries must move. The organization must be open and flexible. The structure of the organization is designed around the need to learn. Generally, a flatter organization is more conducive to the flow of information and to learning. The new structure should allow for collaboration, sharing of information, and networking among the individuals.

Before the creation of a learning organization, an assessment of the organization's belief in the value of learning is necessary to transform the abstract concept of a learning organization into specific initiatives. Some people find it easy to envision a learning organization and relish the opportunities it provides. Others find it more difficult to accept the concept and suspect it is yet another fad. Figure 13-3 is a checklist that will help determine the beliefs of an organization with regard to developing a learning organization.[24]

(text continued on page 257)

To establish how easy or difficult you will find it to create your own learning organization, run down the following statements, checking the ones you agree with and putting an X beside the ones you disagree with. Please respond to each statement with either a checkmark or an X, however marginal the difference.

Learning Organization Beliefs

1. ❑ I believe that most of what people learn "just happens" as a natural consequence of doing things and keeping busy.
2. ❑ I believe you cannot make people learn, only make it more likely that they will.
3. ❑ I believe learning has to be left to discretion (i.e., it cannot be made mandatory).

Learning Organization Beliefs (continued)

4. ❑ I believe that once people form their attitudes they rarely change them.
5. ❑ I believe that learning and continuous development are too important to leave to chance.
6. ❑ I believe that the experiences I learn most from are the experiences others will learn most from.
7. ❑ I believe most people in most organizations rarely do more than they believe they have to/are "allowed" to.
8. ❑ I believe that complacency is the biggest enemy of continuous improvement/development.
9. ❑ I believe it is more important to learn from mistakes than to learn from successes.
10. ❑ I believe the "culture" of most organizations unintentionally reinforces many unwanted behaviors (i.e., deference, caution, blaming, covering up mistakes).
11. ❑ I believe learning from experience mostly happens intuitively (i.e., it isn't necessary to do it deliberately or consciously).
12. ❑ I believe people learn, not organizations.
13. ❑ I believe that developing people is a prime responsibility of any manager.
14. ❑ I believe the more senior you are, the less you need to learn.
15. ❑ I believe that "learning is our business and we sell the by-product of that learning."
16. ❑ I believe that inside every mistake there are lessons waiting to get out.
17. ❑ I believe the learning organization is doomed unless it is done top-down.
18. ❑ I believe learning is the only sustainable competitive advantage.
19. ❑ I believe learning has occurred when people can demonstrate that they know something they didn't know before and/or can do something they couldn't do before.
20. ❑ I believe learning is best done through courses, conferences, seminars, and workshops.

(figure continued on page 256)

Learning Organization Beliefs (continued)

Score Key

Simply move your checkmarks and Xs into the boxes below (pay close attention to the numbering of the boxes) and award yourself 5 points for each check and 0 for each X.

	✓ or X	Score		✓ or X	Score
1.	☐	☐	2.	☐	☐
3.	☐	☐	5.	☐	☐
4.	☐	☐	7.	☐	☐
6.	☐	☐	8.	☐	☐
9.	☐	☐	10.	☐	☐
11.	☐	☐	12.	☐	☐
13.	☐	☐	15.	☐	☐
14.	☐	☐	16.	☐	☐
17.	☐	☐	18.	☐	☐
20.	☐	☐	19.	☐	☐

Total your scores for each column.

☐	☐
Beliefs that hinder	Beliefs that help

Finally, subtract the left-hand total (for beliefs that hinder) from the right-hand total (for beliefs that help) and write the answer in this box. (It is possible to have a negative score.) ☐

Learning Organization Beliefs (continued)

Interpretation

Score Ranges	
+35 to +50	Excellent. You already hold beliefs that are entirely compatible with the learning organization "philosophy."
+15 to +30	Fine. You hold many beliefs that will make it relatively easy for you to accept the learning organization "philosophy."
−5 to +10	You hold some beliefs that you will need to overhaul before you can fully accept the learning organization "philosophy."
−50 to −10	Unfortunately you hold lots of beliefs that will hinder your acceptance of the notion of a learning organization. But all is not lost. Your first step is to look again at the beliefs that help (the right-hand column on the score key) and see if you can persuade yourself to change your mind about some of those.

Figure 13-3. *Learning Organization Beliefs Check.* (Adapted from: A handout distributed by Peter Honey, United Kingdom, at a conference about the learning organization. Kuala Lumpur, Malaysia: Jan. 1995.)

(text continued from page 254)

Once the status of the organization's belief in learning is determined, it is necessary to create a climate that encourages learning, which involves thinking and challenging the status quo. Many managers are intimidated by employees who think independently. They feel the threat of losing their authority. Many times managers are afraid to allow employees to participate in programs for fear their work will go undone. Many employees are afraid to think on their own for fear they will be punished for it or be viewed as not being a team player. For these reasons, the right environment must be created on the front end of the process.

A second step in building a learning organization is to address issues about why traditional training in the organization may not have worked in the past. Some reasons include:[25]

- Training was not linked to strategic business needs of the organization.
- Training was offered on a broad basis—one size fits all.
- Managers sometimes resisted training and prohibited its implementation.
- Participants were often left with a lack of understanding of how to apply learning to the job.
- Lack of accountability inhibited interest in applying learning.
- Managers who were genuinely interested in getting the most out of training did not receive support for its implementation.

The next step in developing a learning organization is to map out the vision of the organization. Executives, managers, and employees throughout the organization must share the vision. Members of the organization should understand its vision and where the company and its industry is going. They should understand the importance of training, not only from the position of profitability and efficiency, but also from the point of view of the customers, stockholders, and suppliers.

The final step is putting the vision into action. Systems and processes should be in place to allow organization members to learn, grow, and flourish. Learning should be encouraged and supported. Technology should be used that will provide information easily and quickly throughout the entire organization. Programs should be offered that contribute to employee growth, performance improvement, and bottom-line results. Measures should be in place to monitor the effectiveness of the learning organization so that adjustments can be made for continuous improvement.

Trend Consequences

Impact

Although no two learning organizations are exactly alike, organizations—and more specifically, training and development functions—will realize similar results because of the global impact of this trend. Change from a traditional organization to one that embraces continuous learning, risk taking, free flow of information, and collaboration will cause organizations to embrace continuous learning strategically tied to the future of the organization, rather than learning offered on the basis of what is popular at the time. The learning organization will support and encourage development of employees at all levels of the organization, rather than providing opportunities based on time, grade, and position of the employee. The learning organization will encourage self-development, as well as team development, and will reward teams for their results. Employees will be responsible for their own learning and will work closely with the training department and their supervisors to develop personal learning plans.

There are three major benefits of becoming a learning organization:

- **Builds long-term capacity.** The increase in knowledge of managers and employees will help the organization grow and prosper. It will also increase the value of the organization's human capital. Learning that focuses on business results also increases job performance. The improved performance is then measured to ensure that it is based on learning and not on some outside influence, such as system or procedure changes. In this way it can be demonstrated that learning contributed to one of the most valuable outputs in an organization—the bottom line.
- **Enables people to change mind-sets.** The learning organization encourages new ways of thinking and provides the tools necessary to enhance the ability of employees to think systematically. It also freely offers information so that employees can more clearly understand changes in their work environment.
- **Creates the ability to think and work systematically.** The learning organization is a process. Systematic thinking is the cornerstone

of a learning organization. The systems and processes in place will assist employees in their ability to think and work in effective and efficient ways.

The training and development group will experience a definite impact from this trend. To achieve the benefits of the learning organization, the training and development department must redefine its roles, processes, and procedures. Training must foster individual learning, as well as group and organizational learning. Consequently, special attention must be paid to how the learning organization concept will influence and impact the training and development function. Some staff members will welcome moving to the learning organization. For others, the change will create uncertainties they may not want to address.

The learning organization expands the role of the traditional training department, often causing the function to take on a new title, such as the Learning Institute or the Learning Center. It effectively creates additional services and products to expand and push learning out to many parts of the organization. The training staff shifts some control of the design, development, and delivery of the learning processes to operating managers and specialists. Although this can be unsettling, when the training and development staff understands the need for the learning organization concept and what it can mean for the whole organization, resistance will often diminish.

The training and development staff will now be responsible for embedding continuous learning strategies into training programs. These will include learning groups, reading groups, labs with self-learning materials, and online learning. The staff will be responsible for teaching people how to learn from experience and how to think systematically.[26]

In essence, the learning organization concept transforms the traditional training and development staff from a doing role to more of a supporting role for learning intervention. Training and development staff members often lose the direct responsibility for many of the programs and processes but become responsible for supporting them in a variety of ways. This support includes education, information, involvement, communication, and measurement to ensure that the learning is moving the organization. The training and development department must be prepared for the learning organization concept and understand how the department supports it throughout implementation. Most importantly, the staff should be involved in measuring the success of the overall process to ensure collective learning and improvement throughout the organization.

Key Questions

In looking at this trend and how it relates to an organization, some key questions to ask are as follows:

Key Questions

1. Do I agree with this trend?
2. How important is this trend to my department and me?
3. What characteristics of a learning organization exist in my company?
4. How much progress has been made to develop a learning organization?
5. Does the training and development staff support this trend?
6. If not, what must be done to prepare them for this trend?
7. What will happen if I do nothing?
8. What specific resources will be necessary to change the culture in my organization to that of a learning organization?
9. Are the resources available?
10. Does the management group support this process?
11. How can we prevent this from being a fad?
12. How will the success of the learning organization be measured?

Outlook

Globalization of the marketplace, changes in customer expectations, and changes in employee expectations and work environments are causing organizations to rethink their strategies of organizational learning and the management of worker knowledge. The economic environment will continue to diminish, and changes will take place more rapidly, causing a continuous need for perpetual learning, adaptability, flexibility, innovation, and creativity. *Workforce* magazine commissioned a special six-month study to determine the direction of the human resource profession during the next ten years.[27] With regard to work-force development, predictions for 2008 include lifelong learning as a requirement. Human capital development and organizational productivity will be a key focus of organizational strategic planning. The outlook for learning organizations is bright.

References

1. Driscoll, Mike and Preskill, Hallie. "The Journey Toward Becoming a Learning Organization: Are We Almost There?" in *In Action: Creating the Learning Organization.* Karen E. Watkins, Victoria J. Marsick (Eds.), and Jack J. Phillips (Series Ed.), Alexandria, Va.: American Society for Training and Development, 1996, p. 71.
2. "Creating and Leveraging Intellectual Capital." *HR Executive Review: Leveraging Intellectual Capital,* Vol. 5, No. 3, 1997.
3. *National HRD Executive Survey.* Alexandria, Va.: American Society for Training and Development, 1996.
4. Zulauf, Carol Ann. "Systems Thinking." *Info-line,* Mar. 1997.
5. Murphy, Sheila E. "Implementing Learning Organization Principles and Quality Assurance: A Practical Model." *Performance Improvement,* Vol. 36, No. 9, Oct. 1997, pp. 33–36.
6. DeVito, James D. "The Learning Organization," in *The ASTD Handbook of Training and Development.* Alexandria, Va.: American Society for Training and Development, 1996, p. 81.
7. Marquardt, Michael J. *Building the Learning Organization.* New York: McGraw-Hill, 1996, p. 13.
8. Marquardt, p. 8.
9. Marquardt, p. 11.
10. DeVito, p. 83.
11. Garvin, David A. "Building a Learning Organization." *Harvard Business Review,* July–Aug. 1993.
12. Longworth, Norman and Davies, W. Keith. *Lifelong Learning.* London: Kogan Page Limited, 1996.

13. Watkins, Karen E., Marsick, Victoria J. (Eds.), and Phillips, Jack J. (Series Ed.) *In Action: Creating the Learning Organization.* Alexandria, Va.: American Society for Training and Development, 1996, p. 5.

14. Greenwood, Tracy, Wasson, Avtar, and Giles, Robbie. "The Learning Organization: Concepts, Processes, and Questions." *Performance & Instruction,* Apr. 1993, p. 8.

15. Halal, William E. "Organizational Intelligence: What Is It, and How Can Managers Use It?" *Strategy & Business,* 4th Qtr. 1997, p. 11.

16. Davenport, Thomas H. "Some Principles of Knowledge Management," in *The ASTD Training and Performance Yearbook.* Alexandria, Va.: American Society for Training and Development, 1997, p. 465.

17. Stewart, Thomas A. *Intellectual Capital: The New Wealth of Organizations.* New York: Doubleday, 1997, pp. 111–115.

18. Phillips, Jack J. *Handbook of Training Evaluation and Measurement Methods,* 3rd ed. Houston, Tex.: Gulf Publishing, 1997.

19. Garvin.

20. Brinkerhoff, Robert O. and Gill, Stephen, J. *The Learning Alliance: Systems Thinking in Human Resource Development.* San Francisco: Jossey-Bass, 1994.

21. Broad, Mary L. "Challenges for Organizational Performance," in *In Action: Transferring Learning to the Workplace.* Jack J. Phillips (Series Ed.), Alexandria, Va.: American Society for Training and Development, 1997.

22. Baldwin, T. T. and Ford, J. K. "Transfer of Training: A Review and Directions for Future Research." *Personnel Psychology,* Vol. 41, 1988, pp. 63–105.

23. Marquardt, p. 69.

24. Adapted from a handout distributed by Peter Honey, United Kingdom, at a conference about the learning organization. Kuala Lumpur, Malaysia: Jan. 1995.

25. Kline, Peter, and Saunders, Bernard. *Ten Steps to a Learning Organization.* Arlington, Va.: Great Ocean Publishers, 1993.

26. Watkins, Karen E. and Marsick, Victoria J. "Building the Learning Organization: A New Role for Human Resource Developers." *Studies in Continuing Education,* Vol. 14, No. 2, 1992, pp. 115–129.

27. *Workforce,* Jan. 1998, p. 51.

14

MANAGEMENT PARTNERSHIPS

Trend Definition and Validation

Brief Definition of Trend

The training and development staff members, and particularly those in leadership roles, are developing productive relationships with key managers in their organizations. With emphasis on working with line managers, these relationships are developed to reach common goals and improve performance as employees participate in programs and utilize resources from the training and development department. Building this relationship involves direct actions to improve management commitment and support, enhance reinforcement to participants, secure active involvement in the process, and maintain productive partnerships.

Case Study: First Union National Bank

The Wholesale Banking College of First University is responsible for the training and development activities of the Wholesale Banking Division of the First Union National Bank. The college, headed by Doug Steele, has partnered with key managers in the Wholesale Banking Division throughout the organizations' twelve-state banking area.[1] An important element of the partnership relationship is the advisory board, which provides direction to the college. Most of the members of the advisory board are operating executives, including the president of the Wholesale Banking Division. The advisory board provides direction, guidance, support, and a review of the Wholesale Banking College activities. In addition to board input, other executives are involved in determining the specific training and development needs for commercial bankers, reviewing program content, and assisting in follow-up evaluations. In many of the programs, key executives either teach or coordinate parts of the program and provide one-on-one coaching and support for those who participate in the program. This productive partnership enhances the utilization of the resources of the college.

Evidence of Trend

In the global study of practitioners, this issue received an overall rating of 3.95 out of 5 for agreement with the existence of the trend (see Appendix 1). For importance of trend, the rating was 4.57 out of 5, underscoring the significance and progress for this issue in training and development departments.

This trend is part of a larger trend of developing partnership relationships between several different groups. While organizations are developing partnerships with customers, suppliers, employees, and managers in cross-functional areas, in recent years the training and development staff has made much progress with developing effective partnerships with key managers.

A recent study conducted by the conference board identifies ten critical trends for the next ten years. Developing partnership relationships among the management groups is identified as one of those important trends.[2]

Some experts view the partnership trend as an extension of previous important interventions that have dominated the business landscape. Building an effective partnership relationship is seen as an extension of reengineering, total quality management, and lean production.[3]

A study from England about the changing world of training concludes that training is much more effective when conducted through management at the work site. In essence, management becomes an essential partner in delivering and evaluating training.[4] Another study of the benefits of partnering shows that its principle power is in problem solving and decision making, with a focus on creatively managing organizational challenges, such as implementing successful training and development programs.[5]

Causes and Drivers

- Several influences drive this trend. Some consider the trend to be logical, rational, and long overdue. It is an old idea whose time has come. Partnering and collaborating have been ongoing practices in many Asian countries for years. Only recently have they spread significantly to other countries and nations.[6] As information about management practices continues to proliferate and the successes of effective techniques are publicized, effective management practices are adopted by a wide variety of cultures. Partnerships now represent an important tool for the training and development staff.
- Developing a productive relationship with line management is a win-win relationship. It creates value by helping the line manager achieve goals while providing direction and guidance for the training and development staff. When the relationship is operating effectively, there are no losers in this process.
- An effective collaborative relationship with management is the best route to success in developing and implementing training and development programs.[7] Input from the management team is an important and integral part of the process at every step. Management involvement is sometimes critical to the implementation of a program. An effective relationship can help guarantee success with quality input and helpful cooperation.
- The partnership relationship is an outgrowth of the learning organization movement. Most major organizations have trans-

formed (or are in the process of transforming) to learning organizations. In the classic definition of the learning organization, the management team takes a more active role in the learning process and partners with learning providers to ensure that employees acquire the skills and knowledge necessary for success.[8] In essence, management becomes a willing partner in the process.

- Finally, many success stories of partnering relationships have been publicized causing others to pay more attention to this process. Many organizations deliberately planned and organized attempts to build the relationship to a productive level. These success stories created additional interest, causing others to pursue the process.

Trend Description

Management's actions and attitudes significantly affect the impact and success of an organization's training and development programs. This trend explores this influence and the environment outside program development and delivery. Although the training and development staff members may have no direct control over some of these factors, they can exert a tremendous amount of influence on them.

Several terms need additional explanation. *Management commitment, management support, management involvement, reinforcement, maintenance of behavior,* and *transfer of training* are overlapping terms and are sometimes confusing. *Management commitment* usually refers to the top-management group and includes its pledge or promise to allocate resources and support to the training and development effort. *Management support* refers to the actions of the entire management group, which reflects its attitude toward the training and development process and staff. The major emphasis is on middle and first-line management. Their supportive actions can tremendously impact the success of programs. *Management involvement* refers to the extent to which managers and other professionals outside the training and development department are actively engaged in the learning process in addition to participating in programs. Because *management commitment, support,* and *involvement* have similar meanings, they are used interchangeably in current literature.

Reinforcement, maintenance of behavior, and *transfer of training* also have similar meanings. *Reinforcement* refers to actions designed to reward or encourage a desired behavior. The goal is to increase the probability of the behavior occurring after a participant attends a program. *Maintenance of behavior* refers to the organization's actions to maintain a change in behavior on the job after the program is completed. *Transfer of training* refers to the extent to which the learned behavior from the program is used on the job. The term *line managers* is used to represent key managers involved in producing, selling, or delivering the products and services.

Increasing Commitment

Commitment is necessary to secure the resources for a viable training and development effort. Table 14-1 shows the ten general areas of

Table 14-1
The Ten Commitments of Top Management

For strong top-management training and development commitment, the chief executive officer should:

1. Develop or approve a mission for the training and development function.
2. Allocate the necessary funds for successful training and development programs.
3. Allow employees time to participate in training and development programs.
4. Get actively involved in training and development programs and require others to do the same.
5. Support the training and development effort and ask other managers to do the same.
6. Position the training and development function in a visible and high-level place on the organization chart.
7. Require that each training and development program be evaluated in some way.
8. Insist that training and development programs be cost-effective and require supporting data.
9. Set an example for self-development.
10. Create an atmosphere of open communication with the training and development manager.

emphasis for strong top-management commitment. These ten areas need little additional explanation and are necessary for a successful training effort.[9]

Now for the big question. How can top-management commitment increase? Quite often the extent of commitment is fixed in the organization before the training and development manager becomes involved with the function. The amount of commitment varies with the size or nature of the organization. It usually depends on how the function evolved, the top-management group's attitude and philosophy toward training and development, and how the function is administered. The key to the question of increasing commitment lies in how the effort is administered. The staff can have a significant effect on future top-management commitment for the department and the function. The following six areas represent items that can increase commitment to training and development in an organization.

Results. Top-management commitment usually increases when programs obtain desired results. This is a vicious cycle because commitment is necessary to build effective programs with which results can be obtained. And when results are obtained, commitment increases. Nothing is more convincing to a group of top executives than programs with measurable results they can understand. When a program is proposed, additional funding is usually based solely on the results the program is expected to produce.

Management Involvement. Commitment increases when all levels of management are extensively involved. This involvement, which can occur in almost every phase of the learning process, shows a strong cooperative effort toward developing employee potential within the organization. Chief executives want their managers to make a concerted effort to increase their staffs' and departments' skills and knowledge. Specific techniques for increasing involvement are covered later in the chapter.

Professionalism. A highly professional training and development group can influence the commitment from top management. Achieving excellence is the goal of many professional groups and should be the mandate of the training and development department. The department must be perceived as professional in all actions, including welcoming criticism, adjusting to the changing needs of the organization, maintaining productive relationships with other staff, setting examples throughout the company, and practicing what its programs teach. Professionalism shows up in the attention paid to detail in every program—detail that non-professionals often overlook.

Communicating Needs. The training and development department must be able to communicate development needs to top-management members and make them realize that training is an integral part of the organization. This communication may be in the form of proposals or review sessions with the top-management group. When chief executives accept the need, they will respond through additional commitment.

Resourcefulness. The department should not be a narrowly focused function. Too often the department is regarded as capable in technical training, team development, or management development, but not in problem solving. When the department is viewed as versatile, flexible, and resourceful, it is used to help solve organizational performance problems and not confined just to formal development activity. The result: Additional commitment on the part of management.

Practical Approach. The training and development department must be oriented toward the practical. A department that focuses too much on theories and philosophical efforts may be regarded as a non-contributor in the organization. Although there is a place for theoretical processes, learning solutions should be followed by practical application. Programs should be how-to in nature and must be taught by experienced people who understand the program content, as well as the business. This practical approach will help ensure additional commitment.

Increasing Management Support

Support Ideal. Middle- and first-level managers are important to program success. Before discussing the techniques involved in improving the support for programs, it is appropriate to present the concept of ideal management support. Ideal support occurs when a manager reacts in the following ways to a participant's involvement in a training and development program:

- Encourages participants to be involved in programs
- Volunteers personal services or resources to assist with training and development
- Outlines expectations with the participant before the participant attends the program, detailing what changes should take place or what tasks the participant should accomplish after completing the program
- Reinforces the behavior change resulting from the program; this reinforcement may be demonstrated in a variety of ways
- Conducts a follow-up of the results achieved from the program
- Rewards participants who achieve outstanding accomplishments as a result of attending the program

This kind of support for a program represents utopia for the training and development department. Support is necessary before and after the program is conducted. Effective actions prior to a program can significantly impact learning from the program and application on the job.

Degree of Support. A key area of support involves post-program activities. In this context the terms *support* and *reinforcement* are almost synonymous because when support is exhibited, it reinforces what the participants learned. Before pursuing specific techniques for improving post-program support and reinforcement, it is useful to classify managers into four different types according to their degree of support. The term *manager* is primarily used to represent the supervisor of a participant in a program. The same classification scheme can apply to other managers above that level. A label has been attached to each type of manager that best describes the attitude and actions of each type toward training and development.

- **Supportive.** This manager is a strong, active supporter of all learning efforts who wants to be involved in programs and wants his or her employees to take advantage of every appropriate opportunity. He or she vigorously reinforces the material presented in programs and requires participants to apply it successfully. He or she publicly voices approval of training and development, gives positive feedback to the department, and frequently calls on the department for assistance, advice, and counsel. This manager is an ally and a valuable asset.

- **Responsive.** This manager supports training and development but not as strongly as the supportive manager. He or she allows employees to participate in training and development programs and encourages them to get the most out of the activities. This manager usually voices support for programs, realizing that it is part of his or her responsibility, but does not usually go out of his or her way to aggressively promote the training and development department or its activities. This manager reinforces the material presented in the program, probably at the prodding of the HRD staff.
- **Non-supportive.** This manager privately voices displeasure with formal learning programs. He or she reluctantly sends participants to programs, doing so only because everyone else does or because the organization requires it. This manager thinks the organization spends too much time with training and development and does not hesitate to mention how he or she achieved success without formal training. When participants return from a program, they get little, if any, reinforcement from this manager. This manager's actions may destroy the value of the program. A typical comment after a program will be, "Now that the program is out of the way, let's get back to work."
- **Unresponsive.** This manager works actively to keep participants from attending training and development programs. He or she openly criticizes the department and its programs. This manager believes that all training and development should be accomplished on the job. When participants return from a program, the manager usually gives negative reinforcement with typical comments such as, "Forget what was discussed in that program and get back to work." Fortunately, this type of manager is rare in today's setting; however, there may be enough of these individuals to cause some concern.

Improving Support. The degree to which management supports programs is based on the value it places on training, the function and role of training, and in some cases the actions of staff members. To improve management support, the department should carefully analyze each situation and work to improve relationships with individual managers or the management group. This requires a series of critical steps, outlined here.

1. Identify key managers whose support is necessary. They may be the decision makers, the entire middle management group, or all of senior management.
2. Analyze and classify the degree of support, following the descriptions in the previous section. Input from the entire staff may help classify all key managers.
3. Analyze reasons for support or non-support. Managers usually show support (or non-support) for training and development based on a series of facts, beliefs, and values related to training and development.
4. Select the best approach. The strategy for improving a relationship with a particular manager depends on his or her degree of support. A section later in this chapter, Developing Partnerships with Managers, explores specific strategies to improve support.
5. Adjust the approach if necessary. Managers are individuals, and what works for one may not work for another. If an attempt to change a manager's behavior does not work, possibly another approach will succeed.

Improving Reinforcement

With results-based training, an effective relationship must exist between the facilitator, the participant, and the participant's supervisor. This relationship can be viewed as part of a three-legged stool, with the legs representing the major stakeholders. One leg of the stool is the discussion leader, who conducts the program. The next leg is the participant, who experiences the program. The third leg is the participant's supervisor, who reinforces what is being taught. If any leg is missing, the application of training collapses.

The importance of involving the participant's supervisor as an integral part of the process cannot be overstated. Too often participants return from a program to find roadblocks to successfully applying what they learned. Faced with these obstacles, even some of the best participants revert to old habits and forget most of what they learned in the program. In fact, regardless of how well the skill training is conducted in the classroom, unless it is reinforced on the job, most of the effectiveness is lost.[10]

The reason for this painful finding lies in the nature of learning. In learning a skill, participants go through a frustrating period when the skill does not feel natural and is not producing the desired results. This period represents a results decline and is difficult for most participants. However, those who persist gain the expected reward from the new behavior. If the participant continues the new behavior or skill, it eventually feels more natural, and performance improves. However, without proper reinforcement, particularly during the time when results decline, participants may abandon the acquired skills. They may revert to the familiar old ways of behavior with no change.

Although self-reinforcement and peer reinforcement are helpful, participants' immediate managers are the primary focus for reinforcement efforts.[11] An immediate manager can exert significant influence on the participant's post-program behavior by providing reinforcement in the following ways:

- Helping the participant diagnose problems to determine if new skills are needed
- Discussing possible alternatives for handling specific situations; acting as a coach to help the participant apply the skills
- Encouraging the participant to use the skills frequently
- Serving as a role model for the proper use of the skills
- Giving positive rewards to the participant when the skills are successfully used

Each of these activities reinforces what has been taught and can tremendously impact participants.

Improving Management Involvement

Management involvement in training and development is not a new process. Organizations have practiced it successfully for many years. Although almost as many opportunities exist for management's involvement in the training and development process as there are steps in a training design model, management input and active participation generally only occur in the most significant situations. Line management should be involved in most of the key decisions of the training and development department. The primary vehicles for obtaining or soliciting management involvement are presented here.

Program Leaders. The key to involving management and professional personnel is to use them as course leaders or instructors. This presents some unique challenges to the training and development department. Not everyone has the flair for leading discussions in a development program. The extent to which managers are involved in programs can vary considerably. In some efforts the training and development staff conducts the entire program. At the other extreme, some programs are conducted entirely by line management. The right combination depends on these factors:

- The professional ability of the training and development staff
- The capabilities of line management and other professional personnel
- The value placed on having line management and other professional staff identified with the program
- The size and budget of the training and development staff
- The physical location of the program as compared with the location of line management personnel

There may be other factors for the specific organization. The use of managers in training programs creates a strong atmosphere of teamwork and is sometimes necessary to make the program effective.

Advisory Committees. Many organizations develop committees to enhance line management involvement in the training and development process. These committees, which act in an advisory capacity to the department, may have other names, such as councils or people development boards. As shown in Table 14-2, committees can be developed for individual programs, specific functions, or multiple functions. They can be one-time committees or standing committees, depending on the duration of the program. Committees can be used in many stages of the process, from needs analysis to communicating program results. The training and development staff benefits from management input and from its commitment as well, once the committee buys into a particular program. Managers find it difficult to criticize something of which they are a part.

Table 14-2
Types of Committees

Responsible for:	Examples:
Individual Program	New Supervisors' Development Program Committee Account Executives' Training Program Committee Product Knowledge Course Committee Apprenticeship Training Committee
Specific Function	Sales Training Committee Nurse Development Committee Quality Control Training Committee Underwriting Training Committee
Multi-functions	Management Development Committee Faculty Development Committee Skills Training Committee Government Compliance Training Committee

Training and Development Task Forces. Another potential area for management involvement is through the use of a task force. The task force consists of a group of employees, usually management, who are charged with the responsibility for developing a training and development program. Task forces are particularly useful for programs beyond the scope of training and development staff capability. Also, a task force can considerably reduce the time required to develop a program.

A major difference in the function of a task force and the function of a committee is that the task force is required to produce something. It must devote a considerable amount of time to developing the program. The time required may vary from a two-week assignment to a six-month, full-time project. This time span, of course, depends on the nature of the program being developed and the availability of assistance for the task force.

The task force approach is economical. It relieves the training and development staff of time-consuming program development that may be impossibile in a subject unfamiliar to the staff. It not only is the proper way to go but also, in some cases, is necessary to achieve the desired results. Additional involvement on the part of management and professional personnel can improve the program's credibility and enhance the results.

Managers As Participants. Managerial participation can range from attending the full program to auditing a portion to examine its content. However, participation may not be feasible for all types of programs, such as specialized courses designed for only a few individuals. It works best when one or more of these conditions exist:

- A high percentage of the manager's subordinates will attend the program.
- Support and reinforcement from the manager are essential to the program's success.
- It is essential for the manager to have the same knowledge or skills that the subordinates will learn from program attendance.

Involving Managers in Training Evaluation. A final major area in which managers can be involved in the training and development process is in the evaluation of programs. Although management is involved to a certain extent in assessing the ultimate outcome of training programs, this process focuses directly on evaluation through a team or committee approach. One approach requires managers to examine collectively the application and business impact of training. Six steps are used:

1. Invite clients to participate in focus groups.
2. Ask clients to collect data regarding the training's application and impact.
3. Ask participants to share positive results of training.
4. Ask participants to share negative or unachieved results.
5. Reconvene the entire group to share overall results.
6. Consolidate lists and agree on actions.

In addition, by involving managers and executives and showing them how evaluation can work, increased commitment and support should follow.

New Roles for Managers. The approaches described above are primary ways to involve managers in the training and development process when the focus is on achieving results. However, many other ways abound in which managers can be involved. In essence, these types of management involvement define new training roles for managers in an organization.[12] In these roles, managers:

- Coordinate/organize training
- Participate in needs assessment
- Train employees
- Serve as subject-matter experts
- Reinforce training
- Evaluate training application and impact

It is imperative that managers assume these key roles, and the staff must communicate frequently about the program's results. Collectively, this process will increase support and commitment, as well as enhance input from each training role.

Benefits of Management Involvement. In summary, using management and professionals in the training and development process produces six major benefits.

1. It adds more credibility to the program than the program might otherwise have.
2. The program belongs to the management group because that group has been involved in the process of developing, conducting, or evaluating it.
3. Program participants and training staff interact more with other management, which makes for a stronger working relationship.
4. It enhances the skills of those managers involved in the process.
5. It is more economical to use other managers and professional staff than to add staff to the training and development department.
6. It rewards good managers for their contributions to the effort.

All these advantages should encourage more organizations to use the skills and expertise of managers in the training and development process. The staff cannot afford to ignore the influence of the management group—in particular, key operating and support managers. Otherwise, the programs may not achieve desired results.

Developing Partnerships with Managers

As a conclusion, this section summarizes the actions needed to build a partnership with management, and in some situations, previous sections are repeated. Overall, this section represents the major steps needed to address this issue in a comprehensive way.

A partnership relationship can take on several different formats and descriptions. In some organizations, the relationship is informal, loosely defined, and ill-structured. By design, these organizations do not want to develop the relationship to a formal level but continue to refine it informally. In other organizations, the process is formalized to the extent that specific activities are planned with specific individuals, all for the purpose of improving relationships. The quality of the relationships is discussed, and assessments are typically taken to gauge progress. Still, in others, the process is very formal, where individuals are discretely identified and a written plan is developed for each individual. Sometimes a contract is developed with a particular manager. Assessments are routinely taken, and progress is reported formally. Although these three levels of formality are distinct, a training and development department can move through all these different levels as the partnering process matures and achieves success.

For relationship building to be effective, the training and development staff must take the initiative to organize, plan, and measure the process. The staff must want to develop the relationship. Rarely will line managers approach the training staff to nurture these relationships. In some organizations, line managers do not want to develop relationships or to be bothered with the time it may take to work through these issues. They may see no need for the relationship and may consider it a waste of time. This requires the training and development staff to properly assess the situation, plan the strategies, and take appropriate actions, routinely and consistently, to ensure that the process is working.

For this process to be effective, the executive/manager responsible for the training and development function must take the lead and involve others as appropriate and necessary. The direction must come from the top. Although this responsibility cannot be delegated, it can involve many other members of the training and development staff, if not all. Two critical issues are involved. The first, and perhaps most important, deals with the specific steps necessary to actually develop a partner relationship. Second, a set of principles must be followed when building and nurturing the relationship.

Steps to Develop a Partner Relationship

1. **Assess the current statuses of partnership relationships.** The first course of action is to determine the current condition. Table 14-3 shows some of the key issues involved in determining current status. It is recommended that the instrument be completed by the key staff members of training and development to determine present status and that it be used to plan specific issues and activities. In essence, this instrument provides information for planning and provides an opportunity to determine progress in the future. Some of the most important actions to enhance support follow:

    - Utilize pre-program agreements and commitments to determine specific goals and objectives for participants in the program.
    - Clearly define responsibilities of all stakeholders in the training and development process.
    - Prepare the participants for the program by providing clear instructions and expectations.
    - Encourage managers to attend programs designed for their subordinates.
    - Conduct follow-up discussions with participants to determine success with application of the skills and knowledge.
    - Encourage managers to provide advice and counsel to the training and development department about key issues and concerns.

    A total score of 20 or less on the Table 14-3 assessment indicates that a partnership is non-existent and the potential for a partnership developing is weak. If the score is in the 21–50 range, several problems exist with the partnership or anticipated partnership. Some progress can be made, but it will be difficult. If the score falls in the 51–60 range, the partnership is working effectively or has great potential for working. A score of 61 or better reflects an outstanding partnership relationship or a great potential for one. By providing the appropriate up-front attention, it may be possible to assess the potential before spending a significant amount of time on the relationship.[3]

Table 14-3
Assessment of Partnership Potential for Success

Scale
1 = definitely no
2 = more no than yes
3 = neither yes nor no
4 = more yes than no
5 = definitely yes

	Circle One				
1. **Choice of partners** (Is this a strategically valuable partner for training and development?)	1	2	3	4	5
2. **Willingness to become a partner** (Does this party desire to become your partner?)	1	2	3	4	5
3. **Trust** (Is there an adequate level of trust or the possibility of achieving it?)	1	2	3	4	5
4. **Character and ethics** (Does this partner operate in an ethical manner?)	1	2	3	4	5
5. **Strategic intent** (Are the long-term aspirations of both partners compatible?)	1	2	3	4	5
6. **Culture fit** (Do the partners come from compatible cultures?)	1	2	3	4	5
7. **Common goals and interests** (Are the goals and interests of the partners shared fairly equally?)	1	2	3	4	5

(table continued on page 282)

Table 14-3 (continued)
Assessment of Partnership Potential for Success

8. **Information sharing** (Can both partners freely share information?)	1	2	3	4	5
9. **Risks shared fairly** (Are the risks to both partners fairly equal?)	1	2	3	4	5
10. **Rewards shared fairly** (Are the rewards and potential gains for both partners fairly equal?)	1	2	3	4	5
11. **Resources adequately matched** (Do both partners have adequate resources to support the relationship?)	1	2	3	4	5
12. **Duration mutually agreed upon as long term** (Do the partners agree on a long-term partnership?)	1	2	3	4	5
13. **Commitment to partnership by both** (Is there a fairly broad level of commitment by both partners?)	1	2	3	4	5
14. **Value given and received** (Do both partners have similar perceptions of the value the other brings to the partnership?)	1	2	3	4	5
15. **Rules, policies, and measures** (Do these key issues reinforce the desired partnership behavior?)	1	2	3	4	5
Total Score: ____________					

2. **Identify key individuals for a partnership relationship.** Building a partnership works best when it clearly focuses on a few individuals. Not every manager could or should be considered a partner, although training and development should have a productive relationship with every individual and associate. The key individuals who can make the most difference with their

involvement in the training and development function should be targeted for this activity. These potential partners may be key operating managers whose support or influence is well respected in the organization. Targeted managers are typically at the middle management level although this could fluctuate with the particular situation. There is no prescribed number, only a total amount that is reasonable in terms of the specific activities planned.

3. **Learn the business.** An effective partnership relationship cannot be developed unless the training and development staff member understands the operational and strategic issues of the organization. These staff members must devote time to understanding how the organization functions and the issues, concerns, and problems facing these key managers. In essence, the training and development staff should view the organization from the perspective of the manager, becoming aware of the issues facing the manager on a daily basis. Without this knowledge and understanding, effective communication is impossible.
4. **Consider a written plan.** The process is often more focused when it is written with specific details for each manager. In some organizations, the plan is tailored to a particular manager. Specific activities are undertaken depending on the perceptions, behavior, and influence of that manager. Having a written plan ensures that the process receives attention with proper coordination.
5. **Offer assistance to solve problems.** The training and development staff exists to support managers. An offer of assistance to help solve problems, enhance performance, remove impediments, and otherwise help the manager achieve departmental, division, and company goals is an important initiative to begin the relationship. Although early in the process managers may not accept the offers, eventually they will, providing an opportunity for training and development to deliver helpful assistance. This also provides an excellent opportunity to demonstrate that training and development can deliver results.
6. **Show results of programs.** When results are achieved, quick communication with managers is important to demonstrate to them how a program achieved success. In addition, the results achieved from other programs should be communicated to

these key managers. Communication should be rich with data, precise, conclusive, and not very disruptive or time consuming. Routine communication of results builds the type of support necessary for the manager to change perceptions of the training and development function.

7. **Publicize partners' accomplishments and successes.** Every opportunity to give proper credit to the accomplishments of the partner should be taken. Focusing attention on the partner's success, even if it was achieved with the assistance of the training and development function, helps build the relationship.
8. **Ask the partner to review needs.** Whenever a needs assessment is requested or undertaken as part of an overall macro-level assessment, the partner should be asked to review the information and confirm, or add to, the needs. This provides an opportunity to demonstrate the processes and techniques and to show the extent to which the training and development staff is attempting to focus on legitimate needs.
9. **Have partner serve on an advisory committee.** A helpful approach to provide guidance and direction to the training and development staff or a particular program is to establish an advisory committee. Having the partner serve on this committee provides an excellent chance to build the relationship and enhance the support from the manager. Although it can sometimes be time consuming, the advisory committee is one of the best ways to develop appropriate relationships and support from key managers.
10. **Shift responsibility to partner.** Although training and development has multiple responsibilities, the primary responsibility for training and developing employees must lie with the management group. Through the partnership relationship, the responsibility for the training and development should be gradually shifted to the partner. Although this may already be the partner's responsibility, these efforts are designed to get the partner to assume more responsibility and take a greater role in providing the direction and accountability for training and development.
11. **Invite input from the partner about key plans and programs.** Routinely, these key managers should be asked to provide

information about key issues, such as needs assessment, critical program issues, the implementation of new technology, program design and delivery, and follow-up evaluation. Topics may also include resource requirements and budgeting, and in some cases, they may involve details such as the timing of programs and reporting of information from the training and development staff.

12. **Ask partner to review program objectives, content, and delivery mechanisms.** As a routine activity, these managers should review the objectives, content, and planned delivery for each new program or major redesign in their individual areas. Not only does this develop the partnership relationship; it also provides important input necessary to make each program more successful.
13. **Help the partner solve a problem.** This step builds on earlier steps. As the relationship develops, offer to help with a problem, meet a particular need, or address a particular challenge confronting the manager. When this is completed, it shows the value and importance of the training and development function.
14. **Invite partner to conduct/coordinate a program.** If appropriate, the partner should be asked to help coordinate or conduct a part of a program. This action increases buy-in for the process, helps shift responsibility to the manager, and often results in a higher-quality program. Managers find it difficult to criticize a process of which they are a part. Significant involvement activities, such as conducting part of the program, may be one of the most helpful ways to build the partnership while enhancing the success of the program.
15. **Review progress and re-plan strategy.** Periodically the partnership process should be reviewed to check progress and readjust or re-plan the strategy. The assessment instrument can be taken again, or the staff can informally review the progress. This review should include a discussion of each partner and the progress that has been made.

Key Principles. As the specific steps listed above are undertaken, it is important to preserve the nature and quality of the relationship with a partner. Several essential principles serve as an operating framework to develop, nurture, and refine this critical relationship. Table 14-4 lists these key principles, which should be integrated into each step.

Table 14-4
Key Principles When Developing a Partnership Relationship

1. Have patience and persistence throughout the process.
2. Follow win-win opportunities for both parties.
3. Deal with problems and conflicts quickly.
4. Share information regularly and purposefully.
5. Always be honest and display the utmost integrity in all the transactions.
6. Keep high standards of professionalism in each interaction.
7. Give credit and recognition to the partner routinely.
8. Take every opportunity to explain, inform, and educate.
9. Involve managers in as many activities as possible.
10. Eventually, ensure that a balance of power and influence is realized between the two parties.

Trend Consequences

Impact

This trend can have a very positive impact on the organization if it is utilized properly and the appropriate emphasis is placed on it. Building effective relationships enhances the credibility of and respect for training and development while helping to ensure success. This trend is important because of the benefits that can be derived from it.

Some training and development staff members may be inhibited in their efforts to make progress, and a few will be intimidated because of the significant changes that must take place to develop these relationships. It will take time, priority, and focus and will require planning. This is sometimes an area where training and development staff members feel uncomfortable because of their lack of knowledge of operations. However, this trend is critical for a results-based training and development process.

Key Questions

The following questions should be considered as this trend is developed:

Key Questions

1. Is this trend important to me?
2. How much progress have I made with this issue?
3. What barriers exist for developing an appropriate working relationship with managers?
4. Are we prepared to involve management in this process?
5. What resources will be needed to make this work?
6. What will happen if I do nothing?
7. What will be the payoff for my department?
8. How formal should this process be?
9. What specific actions will be appropriate?
10. How will management react?

Outlook

The driving forces creating this trend should continue in the future. These drivers and influences should only strengthen as organizations explore ways to make all processes successful for all groups in the organization. Building partnerships between training and development and management is a desired objective for most organizations, as well as a natural evolution of organizations as they form coalitions, work groups, alliances, and new organizational structures.

References

1. Wallace, Debi. "The Results Based Approach of Evaluating Learning," in *In Action: Implementing Evaluation Systems and Processes.* Jack J. Phillips (Ed.), Alexandria, Va.: American Society for Training and Development, 1998.
2. Melohn, Tom. *The New Partnership.* Essex Junction, N.H.: Omneo, 1994.

3. Godfrey, A. Blanton. "Ten Clear Trends for the Next Ten Years," in *Profiting from Total Quality*. New York: The Conference Board, 1993, pp. 10–11.
4. Mariotti, John L. *The Power of Partnerships: The Next Step Beyond TQM, Reengineering and Lean Production.* Oxford, England: Basil Blackwell, 1996.
5. Williams, Teresa and Green, Adrian. *A Business Approach to Training.* London: Gower, 1997.
6. Sujansky, Joanne G. *The Power of Partnering: Vision, Commitment, and Action.* San Diego: Pfeiffer and Company, 1991.
7. Lasserre, Phillippe and Schutte, Hellmut. *Strategies for Asia Pacific.* London: MacMillan, 1995.
8. Shaw, Edward. *The Six Pillars of Reality-Based Training.* Amherst, Mass. HRD Press, 1997.
9. Phillips, Jack J. (Series Ed.) *In Action: Creating the Learning Organization.* Alexandria, Va.: American Society for Training and Development, 1996.
10. Phillips, Jack J. *Handbook of Training Evaluation and Measurement Methods,* 3rd ed. Houston, Tex.: Gulf Publishing, 1997.
11. Broad, Mary L. and Newstrom, John W. *Transfer of Training.* Reading, Mass.: Addison Wesley, 1992.
12. Bell, Chip R. *Managers As Mentors: Building Partnerships for Learning.* San Francisco: Berrett-Koehler Publishers, 1996.
13. Adapted from Mariotti, John L. *The Power of Partnerships: The Next Step Beyond TQM, Reengineering and Lean Production.* Oxford, England: Basil Blackwell, 1996.

15

TECHNOLOGY

Trend Definition and Validation

Brief Definition of Trend

The use of technology-based learning is rapidly increasing. The preferred term for any form of technology to deliver or support learning, *technology-based learning,* is being applied in a variety of ways. Much of the emphasis is on electronic delivery systems that provide information and facilitate learning. Learning technology incorporates presentation, as well as delivery method, using interactive multimedia, videoconferencing, virtual reality, GroupWare, and electronic performance support systems. The Internet/intranets, CD-ROMs, satellites, e-mail, and voicemail are common examples of technology used for learning applications.

Case Studies: American Express, Andersen Consulting, and Digital Equipment

American Express. For 250 client service representatives in the Minneapolis office of American Express Financial Services, training has been cut in half, and productivity has soared using the electronic performance support system (EPSS) designed by the director of training technology.[1] Customer service managers were afraid that designing an EPSS to help client representatives open new insurance accounts would take too long to learn and would cost too much. By moving the introduction of the application to videotape and building in more context sensitivity, the EPSS has proven successful.

The EPSS was evaluated based on three criteria:

- How much training employees needed
- How accurately employees entered data
- How long it took employees to enter each transaction

Using a control group of classroom-trained employees, American Express determined that accuracy went from 78 percent to 97 percent for the experimental group. Processing time was reduced from 17 minutes per transaction to 3.9 minutes. The control group needed 12 hours of training while the experimental group required only 1.75 hours for each task. This type of increased productivity and efficiency occurs frequently when using technological advances in training.

Andersen Consulting. Andersen Consulting was spending more than $200 million on training for 30,000 employees. Working with the Institute for Learning Sciences at Northwestern University, the company produced a series of multimedia modules for its Business Practice course. Rather than needing six weeks of traditional training, employees use a CD-ROM to train before each new assignment. This just-in-time training is a self-paced learning opportunity that replaces instructor-led training.

The interactive training course is available with subtitles for employees for whom English is a second language. Employees can gather information and develop hypothetical client interactions.

Andersen's senior consultants contributed to the CD-ROMs so new employees can benefit from their experiences. The new multimedia course reduced training time from 65 hours per employee to 40 hours and saves approximately $10 million annually in training and payroll expenses.[2]

Digital Equipment Corporation. To meet the demand for experienced professionals with current skills, Digital Equipment Corporation, a large computer manufacturer based in the United States, developed a work-force capability planning tool to use with its employees worldwide.[3] Work-force planning generally includes hiring new employees, providing career pathing for key jobs, and providing succession planning for key positions. Digital Equipment Corporation defines work-force planning as a process of managing the work force according to the number, alignment, and skill levels of employees needed to cover the quantity and complexity of the work force present today and in the future.

In response to these issues and key initiatives at Digital, the company launched a work-force capability planning tool on a pilot basis in 1996. This online tool, which employees can access from their offices through the World Wide Web, accomplishes work profiling and employee development planning. A complete data base of all possible work capabilities is the foundation of this tool. From this list, users create a work profile, assessment, and development plan. The system then stores the profiles in this data base and in a repository of individual records. The tool supports the following steps in performing the process:

- Create the work profile
- Assess competency
- Create a development plan based on skill gaps
- Implement the plan
- Measure performance progress against the plan

The tool and data base are accessible to both employees and their managers. The managers can use the tool to create work-force plans tied directly to business strategy. When managers need to know if they have the capability to deliver a particular service or project, the data base can provide the appropriate information. The new system, which costs approximately $500,000 to develop, will reduce the time needed to analyze individual skills against future needs. This will enable unit managers to spend less time behind their desks and more time with their customers and employees.

Evidence of Trend

No trend in training and development is more visible than the exploding application and use of technology. Based on responses to the global survey, practitioners are aware of and agree with this fact. Where the survey asked for input regarding the application and use of technology, practitioners' rating was 4.68 out of 5 as to their agreement with the trend's existence (see Appendix 1). When asked to rate the trend's importance, the respondents' rating was 4.32 out of a possible 5 points.

One of the most comprehensive assessments of technology in the learning environment comes from the annual Industry Report from *Training* magazine.[4] The 1997 report mirrors many of the changes reported in the preceding years and provides a glimpse of changes in the future. It also underscores the frustrations and difficulties of using technology. With the explosion of potential applications, technology is being used to deliver training and development but still at a much slower pace than anticipated. In essence, most of the projections for use of technology in the learning environment fall short of actual use. However, the rate of actual application is changing rapidly.

The 1997 report revealed one of the largest increases in the use of technological delivery of training, with 32 percent of programs delivered through multimedia compared with 68 percent through instructor-led courses. The use of technology in delivery of training has steadily increased in recent years, and the prospects continue for greater use in the future. The same report showed that two thirds of training and development departments use an Internet or intranet service regularly, but mostly for e-mail or research and information. The study reported that just 6 percent of organizations say they use this type of service to deliver training, although many indicate that number will change dramatically.

The study also revealed that, of all organizations, 12 percent have developed electronic performance support systems to provide employees with computerized coaching, training, job aids, or reference manuals. These systems are more likely to be developed in larger organizations with 10,000 or more employees. Of this size of organization, 28 percent have actually developed an EPSS system. The same study revealed that teleconferencing and audio/video data or multimedia have found a broad range of corporate applications. Teleconferencing is used in business meetings by 54 percent of the organizations, whereas 35 percent use it for distance learning and education; another 35 percent use it in professional development. Indeed, based on this annual study, technology applications are rapidly increasing. However, these applications are still far short of the possibilities in the training and development field.

Another helpful review of the application of technology in learning comes from the State of the Industry Report from the American Society for Training and Development.[5] Although the ASTD is an American-based organization, it reflects input from its members throughout the world. Many of the large organizations that belong to ASTD are multinational firms. In the State of the Industry Report, ASTD uses a comprehensive survey to compare the status of two other groups of organizations. One group is composed of what are considered leading-edge organizations, which means they are high-profile organizations generally regarded as the best places to work. These organizations are benchmarked regularly and well known throughout the world. The second comparison group is the Benchmarking Forum, a group of organizations participating in a comprehensive benchmark study sponsored by ASTD.

To highlight the difference in the two groups, it may help to examine their average total expenditures on training and development as a percent of payroll. The entire sample for the State of the Industry Report reported a 1.46 percent investment. The leading-edge organizations invested about 3.93 percent, whereas the Benchmarking Forum participants invested about 2.35 percent of payroll. Table 15-1 shows a comparison of their usage of delivery methods using technology.

Table 15-1
Comparing Use of Delivery Methods

	Entire Sampling	Leading Edge	Benchmarking Forum
Instructor-led as % of Training Time	84%	81%	70%
% of Organizations Using			
CBT (Computer-based Training)	35%	66%	84%
CD-ROM	30%	44%	N/A
Multimedia	22%	31%	81%
EPSS	7%	16%	37%
Intranet	3%	13%	N/A
% of Growth In Training Time by 2000			
CD-ROM	20%	23%	N/A
Intranet	17%	22%	N/A

Source: Bassi, Laurie J. and Van Buren, Mark. "The 1998 State of the Industry Report." Training & Development, *Jan. 1998, pp. 21–49.*

It becomes clear that the leading-edge organizations invest significantly more money in the application and use of various learning technologies to deliver training than the other two groups do. Even though the numbers suggest that the vast majority of training is still instructor-led, the important point is that the percentage of training delivered by technology is changing rapidly. For example, in 1997 the Benchmarking Forum reported 70 percent of programs as instructor-led, compared with 78 percent in 1996 and 84 percent in 1994. The changes occurring in the use of technology are significant.

Still another report on the status of the industry comes from a survey of human resource development executives conducted in 1997 by the American Society for Training and Development. The 275 panel members involved in the survey represent organizations throughout the world.[6] The survey reveals the extent to which organizations in 1997 used or expected to use electronic learning technology as delivery systems. Executives confirmed the significance and importance of learning technologies. Ninety-two percent of the HRD executives and 82 percent of top executives considered learning technologies to be of widespread importance. One of the most significant findings was the prediction of the use of learning technologies to replace instructor-led processes. Collectively, panel members predicted that by the year 2000, learning technology would deliver 35 percent of all training. The top three choices of these executives for learning technologies were computer-based training (CBT) on disk or hard drive, videoteleconferencing, and CBT on CD-ROM. The same executives predicted that by the year 2000 many organizations will enhance their use of distributive technologies, such as intranets, multimedia on local- or wide-area networks, and the Web—all of which are capable of digitally combining text, video, and audio.

According to researcher Elliott Masie, one of the world's premier minds on learning technology, online learning is becoming a corporate reality. More than 83 percent of *Fortune* 500 companies have an institutional objective of implementing online learning in the next year. Major projects are under way to add intranet-based training programs to the learning options list of almost every major organization. Now more than 275 vendors are building content programs for delivery via corporate networks.[7]

Masie's Technology & Learning ThinkTank (his research group) surveyed users to determine their desires for the application of technology to the training function. The following is a sampling of what they indicated they would like to see:

- A single Web site on the company intranet that would allow managers and employees to access all the learning resources in the organization
- The ability to enter a job or job family name of an employee and get a personalized view of the applicable programs available
- The ability to obtain detailed information about all formats of learning, including internally and externally instructor-led programs, online courses, fixed media coaching resources, books, and on-the-job training

- The capability to preview programs when possible using a sample media clip, learner previews of the program, or other input about the applicability, relevance, and quality of the program
- The ability to handle all aspects of the learning registration process online
- The ability to build and view a learning portfolio of accomplishments
- The ability to access advice about the best programs, including the capability for pre-testing online with assessment capabilities to guide the user to the appropriate selection of programs

Regardless of which way the technology applications are explored, the changes are dramatic. Although the applications have been slow to develop in terms of widespread use, particularly in countries outside the United States, overwhelming evidence exists that changes are occurring rapidly in terms of applications.

Causes and Drivers

The predominant influences driving the use of technology vary throughout the industry. Some influences are intuitively obvious while others are more subtle.

- One of the important influences for the development and application of technology for training is the need of those involved in the process to save time. First, and perhaps most importantly, these people need to save the time required to travel to a learning facility, whether it is in the next building or 200 miles away. Travel time is significant for traditional classroom training. Technology delivery near the work site virtually eliminates this element. The second timing issue is the need to reduce the time involved in actual learning. Technology-based learning can reap significant savings in the time required to reach certain levels of knowledge and skill acquisition. Typically, technology-based learning projects that are designed to replace instructor-led classroom learning will take a much shorter time frame to accomplish the same learning objectives. When Andersen Consulting replaced a six-week, instructor-led basic business course with multimedia training, the learning time for employees dropped approximately 40 percent.[8] Time considerations aside, this was caused in large part by the fact that technology-based learning tends to be more to the point, has fewer interruptions, and allows participants to learn at their own pace.

- The cost of training has driven the development of technology. As evidenced by the trends in this book, training costs continue to escalate. The cost of providing facilities, such as elaborate buildings in a corporate university setting, is tremendously expensive. As the demand for training continues to grow, organizations cannot afford to continue to provide classroom space. Thus, a learning delivery alternative is needed—one that places training at or near the work site. Also, the significant expenses of travel, including hotels and lodging, can be virtually eliminated as technology is used to deliver learning. The expense to develop training using technology is greater than traditional training development costs, but savings are found in their long-term use. Table 15-2 compares the cost of instructor-led training and Web-based training.[9] Suppose twenty-four hours of Web-based training costs $150,000 to develop while forty hours of instructor-led training costs approximately $50,000. Assuming all technical equipment and systems are in place, the initial cost to develop the Web-based training is significant. However, if out of a class of twenty participants, one half need to travel to receive the training, additional costs are incurred. Plus, the cost of the instructor's time must be considered. As Table 15-2 shows, the total cost for instructor-led training for twenty participants is $63,000. As shown in the table, every time the instructor-led training is offered, an additional $13,000 in costs is incurred. The break-even point for instructor-led training and Web-based training occurs at 140 participants. The cost of additional participants is eliminated when employees learn on the Web.

Table 15-2
Cost Comparison: Instructor-led Training vs. Web-based Training

		Costs Instructor-led Training	Costs Web-based Training
Course Development		$ 50,000	$ 150,000
Travel & Expenses per Off-Site Trainee		1,000	0
Training Materials per Trainee		50	0
Instructor Per Session		2,000	0
Total Cost to Train:	20	63,000	150,000
	40	76,000	↓
	60	99,000	
	...	...	
	140	151,000	
	500	375,000	
	1,000	700,000	150,000

Source: Touger, Hallie E. "Impact of Technology on Training Evaluation," in Evaluating Corporate Training: Models and Issues. *S. M. Brown and C. Sidner (Eds.), Norwall, Mass.: Kluner Academic Press, p. 285.*

- The work itself is becoming increasingly computer intensive. A significantly larger percentage of the work force uses the computer, and in some organizations every employee uses a personal computer (PC) or is networked. The availability of this important tool to each employee creates an appropriate setting to deliver training at the work site. Thus, computer-based or Web-based training is a natural application for these knowledge workers.
- Two important trends related to technology development are merging to create the right set of circumstances to develop technology in a cost-effective way. First, the cost of technology is decreasing significantly, making training applications more viable. A Web-based program can be developed more quickly and more inexpensively than was possible just a few short years ago. In addition, the trend of increasing the capacity and capability of hardware and software has made technology much more adaptable to training situations. The growth of software applications coupled with the growth of hardware and communication tech-

nology has made some training programs possible that were not feasible a few years ago. Some predict that it will be possible to present virtually all types of training in a simulated format in the future. Today, almost every type of environment can be simulated using the computer. Even personal skills can be developed in Web-based training applications.

- The need for just-in-time training has made technology a more viable option. Today employees need training quickly and need to acquire skills as soon as those skills are needed on the job. This situation renders traditional classroom training inefficient because a training and development department may have to wait until an adequate number of employees needs a certain type of training before providing it. With technology-based training, only the employees who need the training will receive it at the time it is needed.
- Employees today are often extremely busy and are sometimes virtually glued to their workplaces. Prying them away to attend a formal session is becoming increasingly difficult. This situation necessitates that more training be delivered at or near the work site, often in small increments to minimize the amount of disruption. This often drives the development of technology on the job so that employees can obtain learning in small increments even at the work site.
- Although total training expenditures seem to be growing, the actual head count of the training staff is diminishing. More functions of training are being outsourced, yet there is a requirement for more training to be delivered. This situation is highlighted in other trends presented in this book. This situation creates a dilemma for training and development to provide more training with less staff to a dramatically changing work force. In many situations technology is the only answer to this problem. With technology, more and more programs are being developed and placed on the Web, thus freeing up much-needed staff for other programs that must be delivered in the instructor-led mode.
- Finally, technology-based learning sometimes is the only, or most efficient, way to accomplish certain types of training. In certain critical situations involving safety and compliance, for example, computerized simulation is the only realistic approach to providing real-life training opportunities. Computerized flight simula-

tors are an obvious example of technology-based learning that cannot be provided on the job. In other situations the technology delivery is the most efficient way to develop and present the process. Consider the simple example of a brief training program about a new policy change. Preparing materials for a face-to-face meeting may be too expensive even from the materials and coordination standpoint, let alone the travel, classroom facilities, and coordination time. With technology, the process can be delivered based on the individual requirements and needs of the target audience members and without paper materials.

In summary, the training and development function is moving swiftly to more technology-based applications because of a wide variety of influences. This is extremely visible as evidenced by the No. 1 ranking provided by the participants in the global trends survey. Essentially, the vast majority of the respondents strongly agreed that this is a trend in training and development.

Trend Description

Technology-based learning is the preferred description for technology associated with training, education, and human resource development. This catch-all term includes the technology applied to learning situations. It can range from the most basic type of technologies, such as audiotapes, to sophisticated simulations employing a full range of technologies.

Even though this book has described the tremendous amount of change that has taken place in the training and development performance improvement process, the speed of change in the domain of information technology makes these changes look like a gradual evolution. Computers are increasingly becoming a necessity in modern life, and as a result, the power and speed of computers have grown exponentially. A parallel phenomenon is the major revolution in the design and development of software, which began in the 1970s and continues at an extraordinary pace. Not surprisingly, technology-based learning reflects the same dramatic changes although its application has been slower than the actual development of hardware and software.

Technology in training allows flexibility in learning locations, as well as training methods. Learners are able to choose a convenient time and place to train. This learning includes the use of the Internet and intranets, CD-ROMs, electronic mail, the World Wide Web, satellite TV, and other methods of distribution. Key issues driving technology-based learning include effectiveness, efficiency, and cost.

The challenge for training and HRD professionals is to attempt to address the technology issue on a rational and logical basis. Key actions that the training and development department must take include the following:

- Deciding if and when to use a specific technology application
- Using technology to meet learner-specific needs
- Using technology to meet the organization's needs
- Selecting appropriate staff methods and tools to supply the technology
- Applying basic design principles involved in technology applications
- Working effectively with program designers and software publishers

Fortunately, many excellent references are available to guide professionals through this maze.[10] This section attempts to provide a brief glimpse of some of the technology applications to build an appreciation for the almost endless possibilities that exist for the training and development field.

The Classroom of the Future

Perhaps one of the important starting points in examining technology is to explore the classroom of the future to illustrate the technology that is available and operational. Although technology-based learning is particularly useful in the job setting, it also has a dramatic effect on the classroom. An excellent example of the classroom of the future comes from the University of Houston's twenty-first century classroom, which has been dubbed a "smart classroom." This classroom, along with three others, a teleconferencing room, and a multimedia development lab, showcases the state of the art in technology training equipment and is located in downtown Houston, Texas.[11] The Technology Teaching and Learning Center (TTLC), as it is called, opened in September 1997 and uses a broad range of advanced training resources including the following:

- **Four classrooms.** Each classroom has thirty-eight high-performance PCs that are continually upgraded with the newest technology.
- **Remote-control cameras.** Three Canon VC-C1 cameras in each classroom capture the instructor's image, as well as those of students. Remote controllers turn the cameras to focus on an instructor or a student and project the images to in-room monitors or to distant classrooms.
- **AMX touch panels.** Instructors use the AMX Corporation flexible control system to adjust audio, room lighting, and camera views. For example, an instructor can press one button to start a videocassette recorder (VCR) and automatically dim the room lights.
- **Large-screen monitors.** Three Sony KV-32S20 32-inch color monitors in each classroom display screen images from an instructor's PC or from any student PC.
- **Voice-activated microphones.** Eighteen Audio-Tech AT845R ceiling microphones help students communicate within each room. The microphones activate when a student speaks but not when someone coughs or whispers.
- **ClassNet.** This image-projection system, from Minicom Advanced Learning, allows instructors to view student screens and even take over their PCs to demonstrate a software feature.
- **Local-area network.** A fiber-optic network runs throughout the TTLC building. Three Compaq servers power the network. One server houses instructional software for the classrooms. A second handles faculty and staff e-mail. The third server, a Compaq 2500, performs file- and printer-sharing chores.
- **Wide-area video network.** The compressed video network (CVN) connects TTLC training rooms with classrooms at distant sites. A codec (compressor/decompressor) squeezes data into compact packets that travel to Madge Networks, video network hub. Once across the T-1 line, the video goes to a multipoint communication unit that can thread calls into a single videoconference. Finally, a receiving-end codec unpacks the data on their way to a student's PC.

- **Main distribution facility (MDF).** The heart of the network and audio/video systems, the MDF contains a high-performance PC, the codec, and the network hub.
- **Multimedia production lab.** Students use the lab for making CD-ROMs and editing videos. The lab is equipped with a Media 100 Inc. non-linear broadcast video editing system, Sony CPD-200SF 17-inch monitors, a Sony PAC-D30/ST camcorder, Fostex 6301 studio-class speakers, and Boris Effects digital video effects software from Artelsoft.

The classroom, along with the others in the Technology Teaching and Learning Center, is fully functional, and each classroom costs approximately $900,000. This underscores the tremendous complexity and possibilities available to the classroom and the attendant technology costs. It also underscores several other key issues about the implementation of technology. As the University of Houston experienced, significant delays and integration hassles occur as the equipment is installed and networked to become fully functional. The significant cost brings up the concern about payback—if and when the technology investment will reap an appropriate return. Getting others to use the technology is also a challenge faced by the University of Houston and others who are installing similar types of future-oriented classrooms. It's one thing to have the technology; it is another altogether to use it regularly and appropriately.

Web-based Learning

Commonly referred to as the 'Net, the World Wide Web, or simply the Web, the Internet is the largest computer network in the world. It interlinks many thousands of smaller networks operated by universities, research centers, government departments, and nonprofit and commercial organizations worldwide.[12] More than twenty-five million host computers are on the 'Net, and the number of users is approaching 200 million. Several thousand Internet sites are created every day, with hundreds of new organizations and users joining hourly. It is exploding by leaps and bounds.

The Web makes it possible to communicate quickly, easily, and inexpensively anywhere in the world. In fact, distance becomes irrelevant, which makes it ideal for global learning solutions. A program can be sent simultaneously through the Web to Brussels, Sydney, Hong Kong, and Toronto with virtually no cost. The Web brings a range and quantity of information to users' fingertips that would be impossible to find through any other source. Millions of pages of text, graphics, sounds, video simulations and animations, and computer programs are available. All can be downloaded on a personal computer by the simple click of the mouse.

The Internet also provides a way to share information and to communicate, co-produce, and interact with a vast number of users. The Internet provides real-time information—its distribution is immediate. From a learning perspective, the Internet has almost limitless potential to provide lectures, forums, bulletin boards, publications, online help, simulations, file transfer, and even role-plays.

The intranet is a private version of the Internet and, essentially, is the Internet technology used within a group, organization, or company. Many large organizations now have their own intranets. The intranet offers the advantages of privacy within an internal network.

Of ASTD's Benchmarking Forum members, 81 percent anticipate an increase in the use of the Internet for training.[13] The Internet and intranets will eventually be the major tools for interactive, multimedia training.

One difference between the Internet and the intranet is the speed of delivery. The Internet is slower in delivery of information and training programs, while intranets are much faster because they are not tied to one supplier's standard and the individual company can determine its needed power and speed. The intranet market will eventually outperform the Internet because of the former's ability to streamline communication within the organization. Intranets are less costly and do not require printed materials, diskettes, or CD-ROMs.

Deciding if a program is appropriate to be placed on the Web requires some serious consideration. Although it is tempting to place all programs on the Web, careful consideration can prevent inappropriate programs from being placed on the Web. To address this issue fully, Table 15-3 shows a list of questions that, when addressed, will provide some answers.[14]

Table 15-3
Web Test

BASIC CONSIDERATIONS	Score
1. **If the audience is:**	
◆ All at the same location	0
◆ At multiple remote sites	5
◆ A field force at individual locations	10
2. **If the program:**	
◆ Will not change very often	5
◆ Will change frequently	10
3. **If the program requires:**	
◆ Full-motion video	–10
◆ Sound and limited video	0
◆ Text, graphics, and animation	10
4. **If the content has:**	
◆ Not been developed yet	0
◆ Been used successfully in a classroom	5
◆ Been used successfully in an interactive program	10
5. **If the content being presented:**	
◆ Stands alone	0
◆ Would benefit from links to other Web sites	10
6. **If the program:**	
◆ Features fully interactive learning with immediate feedback	5
◆ Has limited interactivity	10
7. **If learners prefer:**	
◆ Group learning	0
◆ Independent learning	10
8. **If it is more appropriate to:**	
◆ Set training schedules	3
◆ Allow learners to set schedules	10
9. **If learners:**	
◆ All have the same skill level	5
◆ Have widely varying skill levels	10
10. **If consistency is:**	
◆ Not important	0
◆ Somewhat important	5
◆ Very important	10
11. **If performance tracking across multiple courses or modules is:**	
◆ Not needed	0
◆ Desirable	5
◆ Required	10

(table continued on page 306)

Table 15-3 (continued)
Web Test

	BASIC CONSIDERATIONS	Score
12.	**If skills are:**	
	◆ Soft	0
	◆ Hard	5
	SUBTOTAL	
	CORPORATE CONSIDERATIONS	
13.	**If past experience with technology-based training was:**	
	◆ Not favorable	0
	◆ Neutral	5
	◆ Very favorable	10
14.	**If management views technology as:**	
	◆ Awful	0
	◆ A necessary evil	5
	◆ Great	10
15.	**If the target audience on a regular basis:**	
	◆ Uses neither e-mail nor the Web	0
	◆ Uses e-mail but not the Web	5
	◆ Uses the Web	10
16.	**If your company:**	
	◆ Has never implemented a multimedia training program	0
	◆ Has implemented stand-alone multimedia training programs	5
	◆ Has implemented networked multimedia training programs	10
17.	**If the significant number of the target audience currently:**	
	◆ Has no access to the Internet or corporate intranet	–20
	◆ Has dial-up access	0
	◆ Has real-time access	10
18.	**For cost comparisons, if development costs:**	
	◆ Are separated from delivery costs	0
	◆ Are included with delivery costs	10
19.	**If hardware at learner site is:**	
	◆ Not available at all	0
	◆ Available but has to be upgraded	5
	◆ Available	10
20.	**If person making recommendation:**	
	◆ Has a poor track record	–10
	◆ Has no track record	0
	◆ Has a great track record	10

Table 15-3 (continued)
Web Test

	CORPORATE CONSIDERATIONS	Score
21.	**If staff:**	
	◆ Cannot manage an Internet/intranet project	0
	◆ Can manage a project	10
22.	**If:**	
	◆ No one is available to administer the program	–5
	◆ The administrator does not have Internet experience	0
	◆ The administrator has Internet experience	5
23.	**If staff:**	
	◆ Does not know anything about authoring	0
	◆ Will contract with experienced designers and authors	10
	◆ Can design and author applications	10
24.	**If troubleshooters:**	
	◆ Cannot be made available	0
	◆ Can be made available	10
25.	**If existing trainers:**	
	◆ Will no longer be needed	0
	◆ Can be transferred to new positions	5
	◆ Can be used on Internet/intranet projects	10
	SUBTOTAL—CORPORATE CONSIDERATIONS	
	SUBTOTAL—BASIC CONSIDERATIONS	
	TOTAL	

SCORING

Less than 135	If the total score is less than 135, the Web-based training, either Internet- or intranet-based, should not be considered.	Do not consider
135–200	It is worth consideration but only after a second review of the issue.	Needs review
More than 200	The Internet may be an ideal vehicle for the training program.	Ideal

Source: Adams, Nina. "Web Test." Inside Technology Training, *Mar. 1997, pp. 32–33.*

CD-ROM

Although currently considered one of the best delivery systems for technology-based learning, CD-ROM has some disadvantages. Employees cannot update the CD-ROM, and they must have computers with the ability to read CD-ROMs to receive training. Many corporations want to hold onto computer equipment until it has little use remaining; therefore, some outdated equipment is inaccessible for CD-ROM capabilities.[15] As an alternative to purchasing new PCs, some companies are supplying stand-alone CD-ROM drives to enhance dated equipment.

A CD-ROM has vast storage capacity. The 12-centimeter (4.75-inch) compact disk can hold up to 270,000 pages, 15,000 black-and-white or color illustrations, 9 million words, 60 minutes of sound, and 65,000 dictionary entries. The storage capacity allows for reduced cost per unit of information, as well as increasing information management potential. A single CD-ROM with supporting materials equals hours of learning instruction.[16]

Interactive Communication

Interactive communication includes electronic mail, interactive TV, and teleconferencing. Through these vehicles, instructors, participants, and subject-matter experts can communicate with each other. E-mail is especially effective when communicating with others in different time zones around the world. The greater the interactivity, the more effective the training.

Video-teleconferencing uses standard video equipment and uplinks to a satellite with participation from various locations. Although video-teleconferencing can be used individually, it is usually utilized by groups of trainees. The development of the video-teleconferencing programs is a minor issue. Organized learning is not expected in these situations. Usually development includes maximum use of the video camera capabilities, telephone, fax, and computer.[17]

Computer conferencing, however, is geared to individual users in any location. Trainees link with the host computer, and the instructor begins addressing the topic. Trainees comment on the issues and can also create side discussions to elaborate on particular issues. In standard classroom training and video-teleconferencing, trainees can participate passively. With computer conferencing, trainees must participate.

Networks

Networks provide several desktop platforms to interface with a single source of information. Network technology includes the Internet, intranets, local-area networks (LAN), and wide-area networks (WAN). A study shows that more than 60 percent of businesses had computers attached to a LAN. In 1996 a survey was conducted that indicates approximately 60 percent of computer-based training (CBT) providers said they deliver or will deliver training via the Internet, satellite links, local-area networks, or wide-area networks. This percentage is even greater for organizations with more than 5,000 employees.[18]

Companies utilizing networks to deliver training cut costs. Development of training via network technology does not require complex authoring software. Word processing software in combination with the Internet allows users not only to have immediate access to training information but also to create training.

Multimedia

Interactive multimedia is a cost-effective and efficient way to deliver training. It is computer-based training with two important components. First, the CBT programming allows trainees to obtain information they want when they want it. Programming also allows information to be obtained in the format specified by the trainee. The second feature is the audio and video component. Because of the amount of memory audio and video require, most multimedia programs are on CD-ROMs. These CD-ROMs can be mailed or given to employees who travel but need training while on the road.[19]

Multimedia replacement of traditional instructor-led training shows potential for cost savings. An example of this application comes from First Union National Bank, a large bank on the East Coast of the United States. First Union is faced with the daunting task of training 10,000 new tellers each year. Using a multimedia program to replace previously instructor-led training, First Union converted a two-week stand-up program to a 24-hour technology-based program. Although the program cost $1.2 million, not counting internal costs, the return on investment was quite favorable as First Union saved more than $700 for each of the 10,000 tellers trained.[20]

The good news is that First Union could easily calculate the return on investment using a standard ROI process and formula that is used by most major training organizations.[21] In addition to reducing training time, multimedia can also save costs in the long term. The important point is technology offers a tremendous payoff if it is carefully selected and the application is appropriate.

Electronic Performance Support Systems (EPSS)

One of the most useful trends in technology is the growing acceptance, application, and interest in electronic performance support systems (EPSS). EPSS is a rapidly changing process and sometimes difficult to define. Early in its application, EPSS was defined as the use of technology to provide on-demand access to integrated information, guidance, advice, assistance, training, and tools to enable high-level job performance with minimum support from other people.[22] Shifting from its earlier development, EPSS now has a goal to improve outcomes in measured changes in performance instead of having a goal of providing information and access to information.

As the evidence in the beginning of this chapter emphasizes, EPSS has improved in its application and use. Dozens of articles are written about the subject each year, and conferences are dedicated to EPSS technology. Hundreds of companies are implementing EPSS with success. It is more than a passing fad. A well-designed EPSS application delivers what expert systems were supposed to deliver but never really did. An EPSS is more than an electronic page turner or multimedia document. It incorporates decision-making support of expert systems. With the information accessibility of electronic text-retrieval systems and the individualized instructional capabilities of computer-based training, a well-designed EPSS works and provides the intended outcome. It simplifies tasks and empowers employees to perform work competently and productively.[23]

EPSS is a way of making software applications work for employees. It is a way of turning software applications into transparent tools that help people do their jobs better. In this environment, the hope is that employees may need little or no formal software training. The benefits are attractive and attainable as some corporations are already demonstrating.[24] A more current definition of EPSS from a systems viewpoint is that it is the electronic infrastructure that captures, stores, and distributes individual and corporate knowledge assets through an organization, enabling individuals to achieve acquired levels of performance in the fastest time with minimum support. This definition is broader than prior definitions; thus an EPSS encompasses all the software needed to support the work of individuals, not just one or two specific software applications. The EPSS integrates knowledge assets into the interface of the software tools rather than separating them as add-on components. For example, company policy information may be presented as a dialogue-box message rather than in a separate online document. EPSS examines the complete cycle, including the capture process as well as the distribution process, and it includes the management of non-electronic, as well as electronic, assets.

In short, EPSS encompasses the use of technology and information components to deliver on-the-job performance. It holds a lot of promise and is making a lot of headway.

Trend Consequences

Impact

The positive impact of utilizing technology for training is substantial. For example:

- With the flexibility to add participants at no additional cost, more people can be trained at a lower cost per participant.
- The quality of instruction increases because of utilization of expertise outside the training facility.
- Trainees learn at their own pace.
- Facilities and resource costs drop because fewer classrooms, instructors, and instruction supplies are required.
- Training becomes decentralized, allowing it to occur any place or time.
- Technology is always available to deliver training, and participants can count on consistent learning opportunities.

Although the benefits certainly outweigh the costs, certain barriers are tied to the use of technology. One is monitoring and evaluating performance. Technology in training provides managers with more information about employee performance than ever before. Managers can keep up with progress in training, time required for employees to complete training, frequency, and types of technology utilized. In many cases, employees feel threatened if management mishandles data received about employee performance via technology. Electronic monitoring of performance is a significant issue being debated in U.S. House and Senate subcommittees. The Privacy for Consumers and Workers Act would limit the way employees' performance is monitored. Under the act, employers would be required to inform employees about how the information is used.[26] Monitoring would be restricted to work-related issues (such as training), and statistics received from the monitoring activity could not be the sole criterion of performance evaluation. Management would have to inform employees when monitoring is taking place and could not conduct random monitoring without employee knowledge.

A second issue regarding the actual cost of the technology is that significant expenditures will be needed in the short term although in the long term the benefits should outweigh the costs. When resources are scarce, it may be difficult to invest properly in the technology needed to reap the long-term benefits. This could be a stumbling block, particularly for smaller organizations or a very decentralized training and development function.

A third issue involves selecting the proper technology mix with the tremendous explosion of technology variations in software and hardware. With the variety of technology combinations available, it becomes difficult to decide what is appropriate for the organization. Increasing numbers of choices often lead to complex issues that could surpass the capabilities of some of the decision makers in the training function. When this lack of decision-making capability is coupled with the training and development staff's lack of expertise with the use of technology, the results can be chaos or, in some cases, indecision. Even worse, a significant purchase of the wrong processes in systems and technology can be disastrous for future investments. This issue builds a case for the need of appropriate evaluation processes to accurately assess the implementation.

A final, and often the most significant, barrier to technology application is the resistance of the staff. Although many staff members are proponents of technology and often serve as technology champions, others may resist new applications, preferring to stick with what they know best and what gives them the greatest level of comfort. In addition, technology replaces staff in many applications. Few staff members want to design a technology implementation that will ultimately eliminate their jobs. Therefore, much communication, careful planning, and implementation—including clear plans of what to do with displaced employees—may be required. This open communication can remove some of the resistance. Although certain jobs may be eliminated or radically changed, others will be created. At the heart of technology implementation is the encouragement of staff members to develop new skills. Staff resistance, if not planned for properly, can spell disaster for the implementation of technology.

This trend will require close attention and analysis before deciding how to continue to address it in the future. The decision to do nothing may be appropriate but is not recommended in most situations.

Key Questions

In deciding whether or not to pursue the use of technology in the training and development function, several key questions should be asked:

Key Questions

1. To what extent is this trend developing in my organization?
2. How important is this trend to me?
3. How much progress has been made introducing technology to my organization?
4. How much effort will be involved in developing new technology?
5. What resources will be required to implement new technology?
6. Which new technology alternatives are best for our situation?
7. Do we have the expertise to select, utilize, and maintain new technology?
8. What are the dangers of implementing new technology?
9. Is senior management asking for new technology?
10. What barriers will prevent the implementation of new technology?
11. What will happen if I do nothing?

Outlook

From all the evidence, the outlook for this trend is for continued improvement. By any forecast, technology applications will multiply dramatically, and the development in software, hardware and configurations of systems will dramatically increase. One challenge is for the training and development function to deal with this issue in a reasonable way. Many issues are involved in working with technology, and these will not only continue but will be intensified in the future. Table 15-4 shows some of the key challenges facing training and HRD executives, based on the results of a survey conducted by the ASTD.[27] Respondents were asked to rank each challenge on a scale of 1 (lowest) to 10 (highest). As this table illustrates, some significant issues must be addressed as the technology continues to evolve.

Table 15-4
Learning Technologies: Future Challenges
(Number of Respondents = 93)

Rank	Challenges	Mean Rating (Average)	Percent of Time Ranked in Top 3
1	Keeping pace with the rate of change	5.92	54.3
2	Assessing the effectiveness of new learning technologies	5.55	39.6
3	Knowing when and where to apply new learning technologies	5.54	41.8
4	Integrating existing technologies with new learning technologies	5.49	35.2
5	Getting top-management buy-in	5.02	45.2
6	Delivering existing courses/training using new learning technologies	4.49	18.7
7	Developing new courses/training for new learning technologies	4.41	22.8
8	Encouraging employees to use new learning technologies	4.30	23.9
9	Finding HRD professionals knowledgeable about new learning technologies	3.76	18.5
10	Other	3.42	29.2

Source: National HRD Executive Survey. *Alexandria, Va.: American Society for Training and Development, 2nd Qtr. 1997.*

One challenge involves assessing the effectiveness of applications of technology. Figure 15-1 shows suggested activities needed to evaluate learning technology. As illustrated in the figure, the first step, planning for evaluation, is a key step and somewhat different than evaluation planning for traditional training.[28] The second step in evaluation is developing the test for the product. Tests should evaluate content, difficulty, clarity in presentation, and effectiveness. The third step occurs during deployment, after the training product has been used. The participant has the opportunity to provide feedback regarding the product. The performance of the trainee is measured against the learning objectives established at the outset of training. Also, the business measures that reflect the outcome are clearly linked to the business objectives measured. This, in effect, places the accountability for new technology in the context of improving the business—a measure

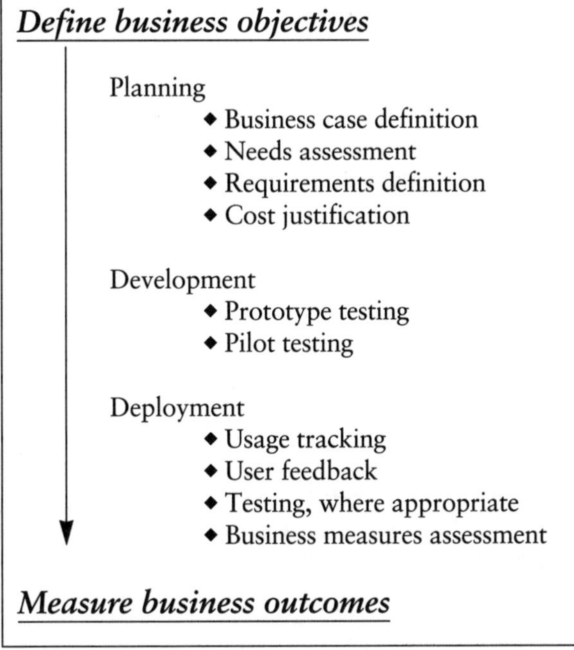

Figure 15-1. *Evaluation Activities for Technology-driven Training.* (Source: Touger, Hallie E. "Impact of Technology on Training Evaluation," in *Evaluating Corporate Training: Models and Issues.* S. M. Brown and C. Sidner (Eds.), Norwall, Mass.: Kluner Academic Press, p. 288.)

that senior executives can understand. Too often the evaluation of technology has been limited to the performance of the technology mix components. The focus almost always has been on the time it saves, sometimes with incorrect and insufficient assumptions. What is needed, and what will be demanded, by the senior management team is more evidence of the actual payoff of technology as it is tied to the training and development and human resource development fields. Fortunately, much progress is now being made as evidenced in the chapter about ROI.[29]

Another critical challenge is the overall approach to the use of technology. Almost every training organization has access to the technology described in this chapter. With the decreasing cost of software and hardware and with the global availability of the Internet at little or no cost, the question is not what is available but how the organization will tackle the issue. Table 15-5 illustrates two different approaches to the use of technology in training and development: conservative versus innovative.[30] As the table clearly illustrates, a conservative approach is a comfort zone of only using completely obvious and proven technology, limiting applications only to those that many others have tested.

A more innovative approach requires stretching and experimenting within each training and development function. The definition of the trend early in this chapter was characterized in this way: Although technology has improved significantly, its application and use in training and development have been limited and slow to develop. This would be a negative twist on an important development. Instead, we chose to examine the actual progress made by training and development departments as they have significantly implemented technology. One point remains obvious and clear: The challenge is to use the technology that is available in the most appropriate and effective way. Often this means moving beyond the conservative approach and trying some new innovative tools and techniques. Otherwise, the training and development function will be pulled along in the technology revolution rather being a driver to enhance performance.

Table 15-5
Two Contrasting Approaches to Technology

Topic	Conservative Approach	Innovative Approach
Main usage of computer power	Imitate the old media, playing back electronic animated talking books	An enabling device used to experience an augmented reality with simulation, modeling, virtual reality (VR) . . .
Views about Internet	A super CD-ROM	The best co-learning environment ever
Main objective	Reduce training costs	Improve performance by empowering learners
Communication: dominant model	One-to-one and one-to-many communication	Many-to-many communication
Main function	Exchanging information	Sharing experiences with VR, distributed simulations, and conferencing sharing information with workshop technology
External support	Full-color leaflets updated in real time; automatic distribution of information to selected targets; online registration forms	Experiential presentation of the organization and of its activities
Conferencing	Tele-tutoring; distributed classrooms	Encourage formal, as well as informal, communication
Newsgroups	Drop in to collect information	Share expertise; influence developments
Training support produced	Electronic books; tools for trainers	Experiential environments; tools for learners
Favored authoring tool	Multimedia and animation editors for electronic books	Activity authoring tools: simulation, distributed simulation, virtual reality, artificial intelligence
Virtual reality (VR)	Recreate existing spaces, like a classroom or lab	Create new experiential and socializing spaces
Artificial intelligence	Simulate tutors (ITS)	Use synthetic agents to populate virtual experiential worlds under learner's control; develop novel tools for learners

Source: Ravet, Serge and Layte, Maureen. Technology-Based Training. *Houston, Tex.: Gulf Publishing, 1997.*

References

1. Joch, Alan. "A Builder of Bridges." *Inside Technology Training,* Oct. 1997, pp. 18–21.
2. Caudron, Shari. "Wake Up to New Learning Technologies." *The ASTD Training and Performance Yearbook,* May 1996, pp. 369–376.
3. Cheney, Scott and Jarrett, Lisa L. (Eds.) *Excellence in Practice, Vol. 1.* Alexandria, Va.: American Society of Training and Development, 1997.
4. "Industry Report." *Training,* Oct. 1997, pp. 67–75.
5. Bassi, Laurie J. and Van Buren, Mark E. "The 1998 State of the Industry Report." *Training & Development,* Jan. 1998, pp. 21–49.
6. Bassi, Laurie J., Cheney, Scott, and Van Buren, Mark E. "Training Industry Trends." *Training & Development,* Nov. 1997, pp. 46–59.
7. Masie, Elliott. "How to Position Your Training Department for the Future." *Inside Technology Training,* June 1998.
8. Touger, Hallie E. "Impact of Technology on Training Evaluation," in *Evaluating Corporate Training: Models and Issues.* S. M. Brown and C. Sidner (Eds.), Norwall, Mass.: Kluner Academic Press, p. 285.
9. Touger, p. 286.
10. Ravet, Serge and Layte, Maureen. *Technology-Based Training.* Houston, Tex.: Gulf Publishing, 1997.
11. Joch, Alan. "The University of Houston Launches the Classroom of the Future." *Inside Technology Training,* Mar. 1998, pp. 18–21.
12. Ravet and Layte.
13. Bassi, Cheney, and Van Buren, pp. 46–59.
14. Adams, Nina. "Web Test." *Inside Technology Training,* Mar. 1997, pp. 32–33.
15. Caudron, pp. 369–376.
16. Reynolds, Angus S. "Developing Technology-based Learning Materials," in *Human Resources Management & Development Handbook,* 2nd ed. William R. Tracey (Ed.), New York: Amacom, 1994, p. 1234.
17. Reynolds, pp. 1223–1238.
18. Touger, p. 282.
19. Touger, p. 280.
20. Hall, Brandon. "If You Need a Million Bucks . . . You Gotta Know Your ROI." *Inside Technology Training,* Mar. 1997, pp. 22–27.

21. Phillips, Jack J. *Return on Investment in Training and Performance Improvement Programs.* Houston, Tex.: Gulf Publishing, 1997.

22. Gery, Gloria. *Electronic Performance Support Systems.* Cambridge, Mass.: Ziff Institute, 1991.

23. Ruyle, Kine and Biebel, Mary G. *Industrial Strength EPSS: An Implementation Guide for Managers.* Alexandria, Va.: American Society for Training and Development, 1998.

24. Joch, pp. 18–21.

25. Raybould, Barry. "Performance Support Engineering: An Emerging Development Methodology for Enabling Organizational Learning." *Performance Improvement Quarterly,* Vol. 8, No. 1, 1995.

26. Picard, Michelle. "Working Under the Electronic Thumb." *Training,* Feb. 1994, pp. 47–50.

27. *National HRD Executive Survey.* Alexandria, Va.: American Society for Training and Development, 2nd Qtr. 1997.

28 Touger, p. 288.

29. Phillips, Jack J. "The Return on Investment (ROI) Process: Issues and Trends." *Educational Technology,* July–Aug. 1998, pp. 7–14.

30. Ravet and Layte.

16

GLOBAL TRAINING PROGRAMS

Trend Definition and Validation

Brief Definition of Trend

As multinational firms become truly integrated global organizations, more training and development departments are developing programs for global use. A diversity of global programs is being offered to a wide range of target audiences. More importantly, the programs are adaptable to country or culture and are designed to specifically fit the needs of the local area. Individuals who are familiar with the local cultures, languages, and customs deliver these programs, and this makes human resource development truly an important part of an organization's global strategy.

Case Studies: The McDonald's Hamburger University and Intel Corporation

McDonald's. Hamburger University is a corporate university serving the McDonald's restaurant chain. According to its own calculations, McDonald's conducts more training, counting everything from restaurant-level sessions to Hamburger University courses, than any other organization in America, including the U.S. Army.[1] Worldwide there are about 20,000 McDonald's restaurants in seventy-five countries. This makes Hamburger University one of the most diverse training organizations in the world. One of the key courses at Hamburger University is the Advance Operations Course (AOC). This two-week combination of operations enhancement, equipment management, and interpersonal skills training is designed for restaurant managers. Each year about 4,000 individuals from around the world go through the AOC at Hamburger University. To accommodate language requirements, simultaneous interpretations are possible in more than twenty different languages. In essence, the desired language of the participant is the one used at Hamburger University. All course material is translated into the desired language and is available to students upon arrival. As they work in teams, McDonald's makes every effort to group people with common languages together yet also to build on the diverse backgrounds. This allows this important course, which is a cornerstone of the training programs at Hamburger University, to be successful as it fits the needs, cultures, and customs of the participants. Because more than half of the Hamburger University students come from outside the United States, language is only one issue. Customs, cultural differences, and learning style are all factors addressed by the design and delivery of the programs.

Intel Corporation. A high-technology firm that produces computer chips and that has worldwide manufacturing and sales offices, Intel is truly a global organization. Intel forms many global partnerships and alliances around the world, creating tremendous challenges and demand for the training and development organization. Intel designed its global training effort around five areas:[2]

- **Intercultural awareness**—Primarily develops cross-cultural sensitivity within supervisors and managers
- **Multicultural integration**—Designed for foreign-born professionals and focuses on communication, skill building, and career development
- **Culture-specific training**—Focuses on working and doing business with people from different cultures
- **Training for international assignments**—Primarily for expatriates who plan to work in another country for a specific period of time
- **Intact team training**—Designed to support business initiatives and builds the necessary synergy and skills among multicultural teams

These different types of training designs depend on whether a group operates out of one country and travels to another, or whether the training is indigenous to the specific culture. Intel is increasingly incorporating intercultural perspectives into team building and training throughout the organization. The company offers training in the local area on a real-time basis, often referred to as just-in-time training. Intel's training managers must be flexible enough to know the best ways to develop and present a specific program virtually in any location at the time it is needed. This represents an incredible challenge and important opportunity.

These two cases illustrate the change in training brought about by the globalization of business. To ensure that training is appropriate, timely, and effective, the complete training and development cycle, from needs assessment to delivery and evaluation, must be adjusted not only for language, but for cultural and learning-style differences as well.

Evidence of Trend

The globalization of training and development has been occurring for some time and the evidence has been building to show the extent of this critical trend. Now, almost every medium- to large-sized organization must deal with multicultural training in some way. Each larger organization must have a global training and development strategy to ensure that the training is delivered appropriately and effectively. The evidence of this trend comes from several sources.

According to the global survey, the extent to which practitioners recognize this trend is impressive. It garnished a rating of 3.72 out of 5 for the level of agreement with the trend's existence (see Appendix 1). The practitioners rated the importance of the trend even higher—4.14 out of a possible 5. Although some organizations are more globally integrated than others, this appears to be a significant trend when all the data are combined.

This trend has been developing for many years and parallels the development of global firms. For example, one of the major publications in the field, *Training & Development,* published by the American Society for Training and Development, has devoted a significant portion of print space to this particular topic. For example, almost two decades ago the journal devoted an entire issue to international training and development. In that issue, most of the articles focused on specific training issues surrounding multicultural training and development and international training and education.[3] More recently, *Training & Development* expended more effort to develop global training, including publishing several books and even covering the topic in its InfoLine series.[4] This particular InfoLine, *How to Globalize Training,* provided detailed instructions about how to develop global training programs while ensuring that the design, development, and delivery of training is consistent with the local needs of the participants.

Globalization of organizations has occurred in every industrialized nation and in most emerging nations. Globalization and the global manager are here to stay.[5] Three important principles emerge with these global firms:

- Things today are not what they were, and things will be different again tomorrow.
- Globalization also requires some revision of old thinking.
- Global managers must learn not only new information but also new ways of thinking, feeling, and behaving.

One important study shows that most international corporations are conducting some form of global training. Cross-culture training was found to be an important tool for successful assignments in foreign countries. Cross-culture training gets high marks for helping people adjust to assignments in other countries and for improving performance in those countries. Coming at a time when many organizations, whether they like it or not, are competing globally, cross-culture training has become a necessity. However, it has not necessarily become part of their specific strategies.[6]

Another study indicates that globalization of business is a new corporate reality generating intense international competition. Because of this, a new workplace has emerged, placing increased emphasis on productivity, performance, and return on investment. New leaders with expanded competencies are being developed to drive these changes and to shape corporate, national, and global economies. A total and complete rethinking, restructuring, and reengineering of education and training is now required to cope with these new realities.[7]

Signs of this emerging age of globalization are all around as investment capital, information, and people travel the world with increasing speed and ease.[8] With globalization, a single marketplace has been created by a combination of factors including global telecommunication, growing free trade among nations, abundant energy sources, and worldwide financial services and resources. As more companies, both small and large, adapt to the demands of global competition, they find that human resource development is the lever for strategic success in the global marketplace. This has important influence on thousands of global professionals working around the world as they develop new competencies to meet the challenges, responsibilities, and requirements of the global business environment.

Finally, a major study involving human resource managers underscores the status of global business and highlights predictions for its future influence. According to the study, an explosive growth of companies doing business across borders has occurred. This requires many organizations to develop an international work force, thereby creating challenges to develop cultural understanding and sensitivity.[9] The role of HRD in this has been significant and will remain at the center of this activity. Human resource development professionals have backgrounds in international businesses, multicultural sensitivity, and multiple languages. The mega-global business alliances, which have begun to develop with some organizations, continue to grow in number.

Clearly the age of globalization has occurred, leaving significant challenges for the HRD field. Training and development departments have developed a variety of strategies and techniques to cope with globalization.

Causes and Drivers

Although there are some obvious drivers for this trend, five major influences created this tremendous growth in global training and development and the need to develop a comprehensive approach for the process.

- The increase in global trade, globalized organizations, and the global marketplace drives many organizations into the international economic arena. Some have to enter whether they want to or not, based on the market demands. Thus, in effect, the market pushes firms into the globalized economy, and as the organization becomes a truly integrated global organization, it must readjust its training and development strategy to meet needs for training and development in international arenas.
- In some situations, significant problems develop when the cultural aspect of training and development is overlooked or ignored. Programs developed with the one-program-fits-all philosophy usually prove disastrous, and the outcome can truly be significant for an organization.[10] From a cultural perspective, one of the best ways to avoid problems is to ensure that programs meet expectations and requirements, considering language, culture, customs, and value systems.
- The adequacy of the training needs assessment process was never more critical than in global settings. The needs of the organization in one culture or country may be completely different from its needs in another. Program needs may be different and often vary significantly. In some countries, the training program may need to be more comprehensive with more time devoted to some very different issues. In others, the training may take less time and be more focused. As training needs assessments and analyses are conducted in local markets, different profiles of needs are revealed, requiring different approaches to training and development in different cultures.
- In most situations, it is more efficient to have training developed and delivered locally, utilizing local professionals, where the process and materials can easily be adapted to local use. The alternative of bringing participants to headquarters or even regional locations can be quite expensive and ineffective. Having

participants attend programs locally saves travel costs, lodging costs, and the cost of lost time for travel. In addition, the cost of maintaining a comprehensive staff at headquarters to develop programs for all cultures may be too expensive. Using regional or local professionals to design, develop, and deliver the programs should provide a cost advantage, thus improving the overall efficiency of the training and development process. The economic issues are particularly critical when considering the tremendous competitive pressures facing these organizations as they operate in a global market.

- Finally, the need for local acceptance of training and development and the need to obtain appropriate buy-in from stakeholders in the local area often drive decisions to tailor the programs to the local culture. A program that reflects a situation vastly different from the local culture or situation would not be accepted and would possibly be completely ignored. Also, to obtain the appropriate support and buy-in from the management group, the program must be realistic and relevant, responding to specific needs locally and reflecting the situation faced by participants.

In summary, several important drivers are causing more organizations to focus on developing global programs. The next section describes some of the processes used to ensure that global programs are developed effectively.

Trend Description

Globalization: What Does It Mean?

Globalization is actually a progressive process through which an organization becomes totally integrated in all of its processes as it develops, manufactures, or produces products and services and delivers them throughout the globe. A global firm actually progresses as illustrated in Figure 16-1.

A firm typically begins as a domestic enterprise and progresses into the fully global organization. The figure also shows the traditional emphasis on training and development for global and international issues. The domestic organization resides within its own country, where it manufactures or supplies products and services. It has no internation-

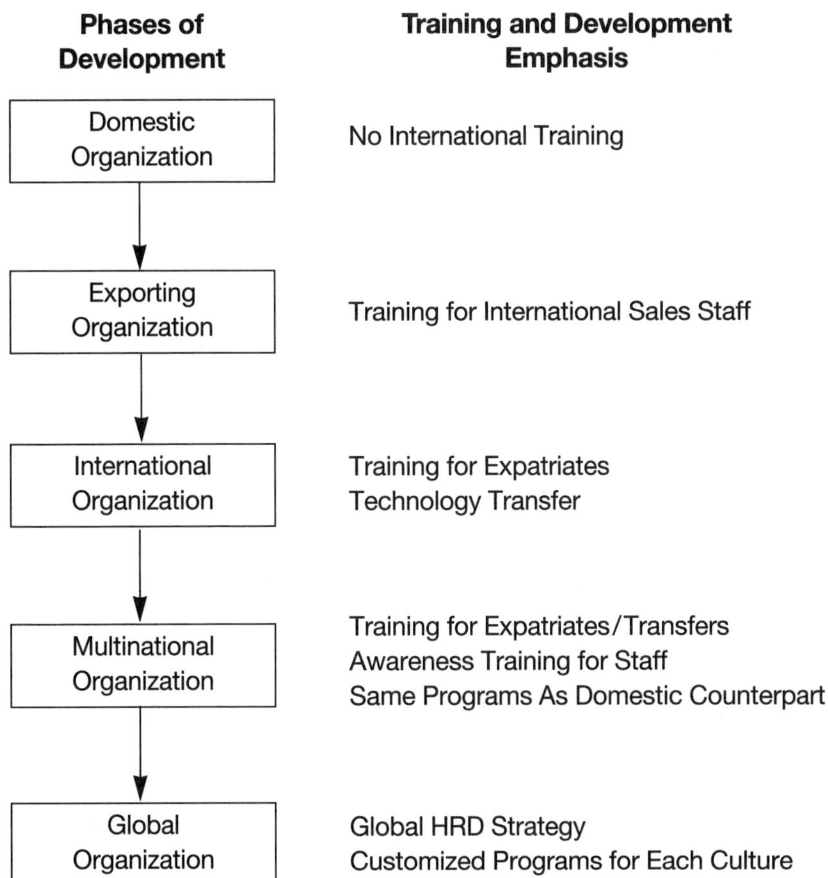

Figure 16-1. *The Evolution of a Global Organization and Training and Development.*

al operations although it will be influenced by the global marketplace through competition, suppliers, technology, and other issues. There is no international training or development in this type of firm.

The exporting organization sells its products and services outside the borders of its own country. It ships the products to or provides the service in another country usually through a manufacturer's representative in that area. The exporting organization typically conducts training and development for the sales support staff members so that they can function effectively in the countries and cultures where the products and services are sold.

The international organization has an international division through which it establishes a sales and distribution network in other countries, including a manufacturing or service facility. The scope of international training and development increases and usually involves training for expatriates who work for limited amounts of times in these organizations. Training for technology transfer is an important effort as the technology and processes of the organization are transferred to foreign operations.

The multinational organization basically replicates the domestic organization in design and operation for each of the countries in which it operates. International training and development programs include training for expatriates and for others who travel to foreign locations. Various types of awareness training programs are also available for staff functions that support the multinational parts of the organizations. The programs offered are the same programs as their domestic counterparts, but usually in the local language.

Finally, the truly global organization will be completely integrated throughout the countries in which it operates. Resources are shared, and processes are integrated. It becomes difficult to distinguish one part of the operation from another. The company sheds its national identity, and sometimes it is even difficult to know where the international headquarters is located. In these situations, a global human resource development strategy often exists to address the various concerns, issues, and problems of each country, taking into consideration languages, cultures, and customs. Instead of using the same programs, the programs are unique to each country and are customized for each setting.

Many organizations have progressed through this evolution to become completely global. For example, IBM, General Electric, McDonald's, Ford, Shell, Sony, Philips, NCR, and Unilever are considered global organizations. They have shed their national identities, are highly adapted to the changes in the environment, and are sensitive to all global trends that may affect the future.[11]

Contrasting Global HRD with Domestic HRD

Another useful approach to examine the training and development practices of the global organization is to distinguish between the components of global human resource development and the components of domestic HRD programs. Marquardt and Engel identified ten factors that differentiate the two categories.[12]

- **Participants**—Can vary depending on the location of the training and organization; this group includes local/host country nationals, expatriates, and third-country nationals
- **Culture**—Varies from one country to another and even within regions of a particular country
- **Administration**—Can vary from one country to another and may involve local administrative issues, government regulations, and accepted practices and policies
- **Learning styles**—Often influenced by educational systems and culture
- **Physical and financial resources**—May dictate the type of facilities used and the equipment and resources available
- **Environment**—Reflects economic, political, and social issues
- **Distance**—Varies with the proximity of participants and training locations
- **Role of trainers**—Can vary significantly because of the differences in cultures and practices
- **Language**—May be the single largest difference and varies from one country to another
- **Designers**—Often work hand in hand with the local instructors

With these significant differences, it is easy to understand why a truly global HRD strategy represents a tremendous operational shift for the organization. These differences also highlight the complexity of the process and underscore the fact that successful domestic HRD may not guarantee successful global HRD.

Global Strategy

To support a global organization, an integrated strategy for human resource development is needed. This moves training and development from the domestic approach to the globalized approach and often involves a complete redesign or reengineering of the training function. One proponent of this integrated global strategy suggests that the following human resource development issues be addressed to develop the strategy.[13]

- Human resource and training functions are linked to the international goals of the global organization.
- Policies and practices are designed to reflect the value of the development of the individual, regardless of where that individual works and lives.
- The competencies for global leaders are identified and measured.
- The strategic planning model is used to align people strategies, business processes, and structure with the company's vision, values, mission, and business practices.
- The issues that represent barriers—such as cultural differences, managing in a multicultural setting, or building culturally diverse teams—should be addressed quickly.

As these issues are addressed, the company establishes a direction that is considered strategic and fully global in its scope and that recognizes the desires, needs, and contributions of each individual.

Training and Development Model

Another important challenge for a global HRD organization is to adjust the traditional training process model to consider the various cultural and language differences along with the customs and practices of the local areas.

A variety of models is available for the design and implementation of global training and development programs. A model can be useful to observe the total training and development process and examine the cultural differences needed at each step to develop programs for global use. Figure 16-2 shows a complete training and development process model that emphasizes results throughout the steps. Because several of the trends reported in this book reflect widespread adoption of more comprehensive evaluation strategies, including return on investment, this model was chosen as a recommended framework for developing global programs. Some organizations might not focus on evaluation to the extent reflected in the model. However, the model provides a proper direction and framework to produce results needed in global settings.

As each step of the model is addressed, the culture, language, learning styles, and practices of the region or country must be taken into consideration. The following text explains each step in detail.

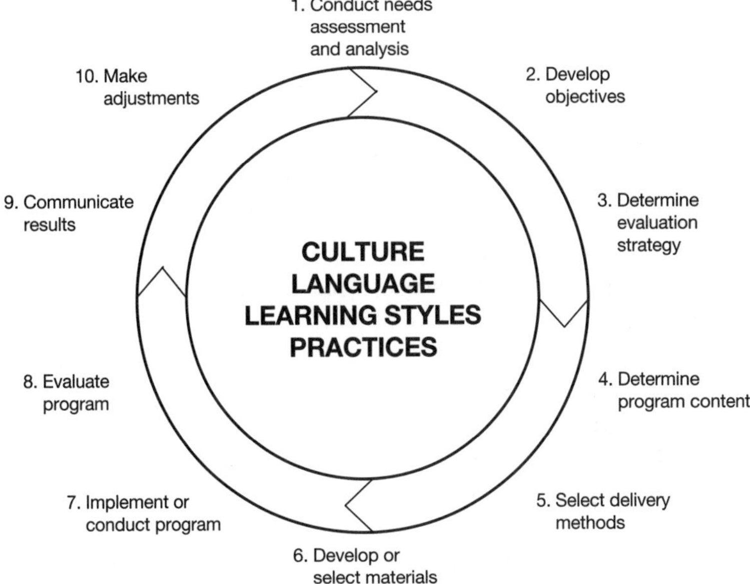

Figure 16-2. *Progress of a Global Firm.*

1. **Conduct a Needs Assessment and Analysis.** Conducting a needs assessment is the first step of any model for program design, development, and delivery. Several events could trigger this step, such as discovering a performance deficiency, fulfilling a request for training from top management, observing a problem, responding to the need to improve productivity, satisfying a government regulation, or addressing a need to improve employee job satisfaction. Regardless of what triggers the program, some type of needs assessment should be conducted to determine specific deficiencies in knowledge, skills, or attitudes. The fact that a training need exists in one country or culture does not necessarily mean that it exists in another country, even in the same job category.

   Needs assessments are typically conducted by interviewing participants or their managers or by administering surveys and questionnaires. Because of cultural differences, the environment surrounding the performance deficiency should be examined to identify any other circumstances affecting performance. These circumstances may include procedures, systems, leadership, compensation, culture, value systems, and work climate.

Collecting data for needs assessments may pose difficulties in some cultures. Participants may not want to admit to a training deficiency. Out of politeness in some cultures, the participants may agree with the issues or attempt to guess at the desired responses on a questionnaire. In such cases, collecting the necessary data may require additional time and some adjustments in the design of the data collection instruments.

2. **Develop Program Objectives.** The next step is to develop program objectives. This step follows the needs assessment and analysis, and ideally each objective should relate to data that reflects the needs. For example, suppose a program is planned to improve the relationship between supervisors and employees. The objective might include reducing the number of grievances by 20 percent in the next six-month period. A more complete training objective then becomes:

> To prepare supervisors and team leaders with the skills needed to conduct effective counseling discussions and administer the labor contract so that the number of grievances is reduced by 20 percent in the next six-month period.

Program objectives provide direction to course developers and program participants, as well as to senior management, who must determine whether or not the program should be conducted. Program objectives should follow the normal criteria for sound objectives. They should be challenging, precise, timely, achievable, and easily understood. To meet these criteria, all stakeholders must participate in setting objectives. This helps to ensure that the objectives are precisely what management wants and are relevant to the jobs in the organization.

It sometimes helps to consider objectives at different levels, as presented in Chapter 8. For example, specific end-of-course objectives may define what learning should occur (Level 2). On-the-job performance objectives define expected on-the-job changes (Level 3). Finally, business-impact or outcome objectives reflect the impact of the on-the-job application (Level 4). On rare occasions, objectives may be set for the expected return on investment (Level 5). This approach ties objectives to the framework of different levels of evaluation.

Setting objectives can cause problems in certain cultures. Some participants may find objectives threatening, and they may be concerned about forecasting or predicting performance because it may conflict with their religious beliefs. This requires the organization to pay more attention to constructing the objectives and to explaining their purpose and how they are actually used.

3. **Determine Evaluation Strategy.** Before pursuing program development, the evaluation strategy should be determined, consistent with the other trends reported in this book. In most cases, an organization will undertake evaluation to assist in making a decision about the future of a program. In practice, there are other reasons for evaluation, and these reasons will affect the type of data and the data collection method(s) chosen. For example, if evaluation is undertaken to improve the learning process, a questionnaire at the end of the program would be appropriate and sufficient.

   Ideally, performance data are collected both prior to the program and after its completion. Data may exist in a variety of forms and generally reflect the conditions that created the need for training. Typical examples include the number of defects in the past six months, the number of errors in processing claims in the past year, the accident frequency rate for the past quarter, and the average monthly sales cost for the previous year. Baseline data reflect the information that is most important and represents the performance deficiency. In some countries, performance data may be inadequate or not available. In others, data may be plentiful. Establishing baseline data after the needs assessment enables the training and development professional to focus more clearly on the changes the program should deliver.

   Selecting the evaluation method answers the question of how to evaluate, as the method must be appropriate for the type of data, learning environment, participants, and program content. The types of evaluation methods include questionnaires, interviews, focus groups, observations, action planning, and performance monitoring. This step in the process also answers the questions of who, where, and when for the evaluation process. The answers to these key questions are important in planning the evaluation.

Although evaluation has received increasing attention in recent years, it may be an unfamiliar process as a preliminary step in the design and development of a training program. Up-front evaluation planning produces important benefits in addition to the intrinsic benefit of evaluating the program. For example, it provides more specific direction to the developers and more focus on results from participants. Participants may resist these planning efforts because they do not understand the purpose of the evaluation and the planned use for the data. In these situations, additional efforts may be needed to explain the purpose of the evaluation and how the data will be used.

4. **Determine Program Content.** Probably one of the most important steps of this model is to determine the program's content. The content may be determined with the help of subject-matter experts (SMEs) who decide what participants need to know (such as principles, facts, and skills) to meet the program objectives. In this step, it is important to use SMEs from the country where the program will be conducted. Reviewing and revising should continue throughout the design process. Program designers may rely on previous programs or similar programs conducted with other groups. For example, a training session about safety improvement designed by one organization may be adapted for use in another. Program material that is nice to know but unrelated to objectives will probably be excluded. Program development is beyond the scope of this book, but other works provide detail about this topic.[14]

   In some cultures, the structure and sequence of the training could create problems. Some prefer highly structured programs while others prefer flexibility. The specific learning styles of a culture are an important factor in developing the content and the structure of the program. This step may require the most attention. It should be designed around a specific target audience, considering culture, language, learning styles, and practices.

5. **Select Delivery Methods.** Selecting delivery methods to meet the program's objectives is a major step for global programs. Common methods of training delivery include:

   - Presentation-discussion
   - Conferences

- Case studies
- Role-plays/skill practices
- Computer-based instruction
- Simulations and games
- On-the-job training
- Team teaching/training
- Demonstration
- Field trips

The effectiveness of these methods varies in different cultures. Lectures are generally considered among the least effective, but some countries prefer them. The methods that require extensive participant interaction are considered the most effective in some cultural settings, such as in the United States. However, they may be ineffective in other settings, such as Indonesia, where participants are reluctant to become involved in group discussions. The selection of a method (or methods) depends on such factors as:

- Effectiveness in the culture
- Acceptability of the method
- Budget
- Available resources
- Program objectives
- Time frame
- Ability of participants to adjust
- Ability of instructors to teach
- Location of training

In global settings, presentation methods can exert considerable influence on the outcome of the program. Just as businesses and individuals are becoming more reliant on cutting-edge technology, savvy training managers are integrating new media and methods into programs. The culture of the participants may influence the role of the facilitator because, in some cultures, the facilitator is more of an authority figure. The role of discussion can be also a distinguishing issue; some cultures prefer much discussion while others tend to ignore or avoid serious discussions.

6. **Develop or Select Materials.** Another crucial step to the process is to develop or select the materials to use in a program. This

includes workbooks, handouts, case studies, instructor guides, and videos. The materials not only should be produced and developed in the local language but also should reflect the particular cultural differences of the target audience. A literal translation of material used in one country may not work in another. It may need to be completely rewritten and presented in a different way to provide the same message or meaning.

There should be much caution taken in this particular step as the materials become visible and reflect the quality and content of the program. Translation is a critical part of this process. The quality and clarity of the materials are also important issues. In general, a generous number of handouts should be provided because they are highly regarded in some cultures.

7. **Implement or Conduct Program.** After the program is developed, a pilot test may be appropriate. A well-planned pilot program can make the months of analysis, interviews, and program development pay off, especially for global programs. Taking appropriate steps before, during, and after the pilot provides an opportunity to analyze the program's strengths and weaknesses and to improve the chances of a flawless, fail-safe program. A fail-safe approach involves choosing the test audience carefully, establishing ground rules, developing group cohesiveness, and watching for warning signals as the program is delivered.

   Implementing or conducting the actual program is an integral part of the training and development process. This is the most visible step in the process, next to the actual materials. The facilitator should convey the appropriate message and meaning, reflecting not only the language but also learning styles, culture, and practices. Ideally, the facilitator should be from the same culture as the participants although that is not possible in every situation. The delivery issue often causes the most problems because of its high visibility and its ultimate effect on the outcome of the training. The delivery often reflects the appropriateness of the program and influences the acceptability and buy-in of the training.
8. **Evaluate the Program.** Evaluation is a logical and critical step. A system to accomplish data collection must be implemented at the appropriate time, and the predetermined schedule for data col-

lection must be closely followed. Data analysis sometimes presents a difficult challenge. This step also involves the analysis and the interpretation of the data. Responses to questionnaires should be tabulated and prepared for presentation. Variances are analyzed. In the past, some programs omitted this step. However, as the trends in this book indicate, more emphasis is being placed on evaluation.

Collecting evaluation data can present problems in global settings. Data collection issues in evaluation are similar to those in needs assessment. In some cultures, participants may not want to provide data, and they may be reluctant to criticize the process. They may choose not to respond at all rather than provide negative data. Some of these problems can be overcome with explanations and by matching the type of evaluation methods, processes, and data to the setting. Above all, participants should clearly understand who will see the data and how the data will be used. If possible, they should receive copies of the data analysis and conclusions.

9. **Communicate Program Results.** Communicating the results of the program is sometimes an overlooked step. Although perhaps several target audiences should receive evaluation information, four groups are imperative. One important group is the training and development staff, who needs this information to improve the program. Senior management is another important group because key decision makers determine the future of the program. A fundamental purpose of evaluation is to provide the basis for sound decisions. Should funding continue for this effort? Was the program worthwhile? Answers to these questions should be communicated to the management group. The third group is the participants, who need to know about the success of the program and compare their performance with that of others. This feedback can alter their efforts in future programs. In some cultures, this feedback may be unnecessary, as the participants may not be interested in outcomes. A fourth group is participants' immediate managers, who must make adjustments when participants attend programs. These managers are usually interested in their subordinates' success.

The internal practices in each region or country, combined with local cultures, may dictate how much evaluation data is communicated and to which particular groups. The four groups outlined above are considered essential because of their attachment to the training and development cycle. Others may be added as appropriate for different cultures.

10. **Make Program Adjustments.** Changes in the program may be necessary, based on the analysis of the information collected. If the program did not produce results or if something went wrong, adjustments to or cancellation of the program may be in order. If the evaluation indicates that parts of the program are ineffective, those parts must be redesigned or improved.

    Unacceptable results should be examined to determine the cause of failure. Some common reasons for failure include improper content, inappropriate delivery, inadequate reinforcement on the job, and lack of motivation of the participants. Every part of the program should be examined for potential improvement.

    When the results of the program are disappointing because of mismatches or lack of alignment with global issues, such as culture, language, learning styles and practices, specific actions need to be taken as quickly as possible. The value of the evaluation data rests with the actions that are taken with the data. If program adjustments are not made when they are needed, then the usefulness of the evaluation data is seriously diminished. Thus, appropriate actions must be taken as a result of the evaluation after the appropriate analysis takes place and appropriate conclusions are drawn. This requires that various individuals involved in the process have the necessary data and are charged with making those adjustments.

Applying the Model

Although this ten-step model appears extensive, it addresses the critical issues and the designs of training and development programs intended for global use. The key areas where cultural differences often cause the greatest problems are the program analysis and the design and delivery of a program. In addition, the administration and environment can also influence the overall success of this process. Table 16-1 presents a checklist for a global training program design. It serves as a quick reference to key cultural issues as a program is designed and implemented in a global setting.

Table 16-1
Checklist for Global Training Program

Trainers need to acculturate various program components before implementing them in other cultures. Use the following checklist to guide you along the acculturation process. Once you answer "yes" to a question, also ask yourself, "How?" This will help you double-check your responses for completeness and accuracy.

1. ❑ Has the organization developed its internal global and cultural mind-sets?
2. ❑ Have political and economic systems, geographic distance, availability of resources, and government regulations been considered in the handling of such things as recruitment and selection of trainers, logistics, facilities, and finance?
3. ❑ Has the effect of cultural and social customs been considered in determining venue, schedule, meals, and other administrative aspects of the training program?
4. ❑ Has the needs assessment been adjusted to be effective in "face-saving" cultures, as well as in more direct cultures?
5. ❑ Were differences between more deterministic, past-oriented cultures and freedom- and future-oriented cultures addressed when setting the training programs' objectives?
6. ❑ Have the materials been developed, adapted, and translated in a manner that is clear to and appropriate for the target culture?
7. ❑ Has the curriculum been designed to incorporate the learning style of participants—for example, by rote rather than through experiential learning—in the target culture?
8. ❑ Are the program's situations, examples, and case studies realistic and appropriate for the target culture?
9. ❑ Have the facilitators been prepared for the target culture and participants' role expectations?
10. ❑ Have the styles and values of facilitators from various cultures been integrated?

(table continued on page 340)

Table 16-1 (continued) Checklist for Global Training Program

11. ❑ Have learning methodologies been adjusted for participants from cultures that do not use certain ways of instruction—for example, experiential vs. didactic, or learner-centered vs. teacher-centered?
12. ❑ Has the technology of delivery been selected to fit the setting?
13. ❑ Have the cultural values regarding age, gender, status, and ethnicity been taken into consideration before forming groups or teams?
14. ❑ Will objective evaluative data be collected from cultural groups that are "indirect" or uncomfortable critiquing superiors?
15. ❑ Is there a mechanism in place to provide feedback from the evaluation data?

Adapted from: A job aid in Marquardt, Michael J. How to Globalize Your Training. *InfoLine Series, Issue 9505. Alexandria, Va.: American Society for Training and Development, May 1995.*

Developing Global Trainers

To meet the requirements of designing, developing, and delivering global training consistent with the global HRD strategy, trainers need a new or extended set of competencies in addition to technical expertise and competency with the training and development process. One study identifies twelve personal attributes for global trainers.[15] These are as follows:

- Tolerance for ambiguity
- Cognitive and behavioral flexibility
- Personal self-awareness and a strong self-identity
- Cultural self-awareness
- Patience
- Enthusiasm and commitment
- Interpersonal sensitivity and relationships
- Tolerances for differences
- Openness for new experiences and people
- Empathy
- A sense of humility
- A sense of humor

Although these appear overly comprehensive, they provide a global framework for the type of individual who may succeed in this particular role. Selecting and developing the appropriate staff members will not be easy because they may not be available in every country where the programs will be conducted.

The stakes for moving to a global organization are high, and the training and development function plays an important role in the process. The most qualified individuals must be assigned to global training responsibilities. In addition, the appropriate processes must be followed to ensure that the programs are efficient, effective, and relevant to the target audience.

Trend Consequences

Impact

Many of the influences for this trend are often out of the control of the training and development function. The decision for an organization to continue through the evolution chain of globalization may be beyond the influence and responsibilities of the training and development function. Consequently, the challenge is for the training and development function to adapt to the extent of globalization practiced by the organization. Global training design and delivery requires a significant paradigm shift, which the training and development staff may resist. The ten key differences in domestic human resource development and global HRD outlined in this chapter underscore the shift that must take place as global programs are developed and implemented. Global programs are not just extensions of current programs; instead they may represent completely different programs, designed for an environment that is often more complex, confusing, and challenging.

As a result of this, the most capable and competent staff must be assigned to global HRD roles. During the transition, some individuals who desire to participate may have insufficient levels of the competencies that are desired or necessary to succeed in the field. Others who are competent may not want the assignments because of the travel, time pressures, and unique challenges.

Because of the resources needed for this process, budgets may expand, although costs may be allocated to global operations. It is more expensive to develop some types of global programs than to develop the same programs in a domestic setting. The increasing globalization of firms will add to the HRD budget and could possibly drain resources needed for other projects within the training and development department.

Finally, the risk of failure with global programs is quite high. And when a failure occurs, it is often high profile. The design, development, and administration of global programs requires closer adherence to the appropriate training and development process than any other type of program. Ineffective, inappropriate, or disconnected programs will be quickly noticed and communicated throughout the organization. Because stakes are high, some training and development professionals will resist this effort.

Key Questions

Before continuing to expand into a more globalized HRD strategy, several key questions should be asked.

Key Questions

1. To what extent do I agree with this trend in my organization?
2. How important is this trend to my organization and me?
3. What progress has been made to develop a global strategy for my organization?
4. What is the reaction of the staff concerning global HRD?
5. What resources are required to continue to develop and implement a global HRD strategy?
6. What resistance or barriers will be encountered as a global HRD strategy is developed?
7. What happens if I do nothing?
8. What are management's expectations and concerns about a global HRD strategy?

Outlook

From all indications it appears that this trend will continue as the global economy develops. The rate of development appears to be accelerating, requiring additional efforts to develop a global HRD strategy for many organizations. Because of the influences driving it, this trend is here to stay. On a positive note, an effective global HRD strategy helps the training and development function increase its value and demonstrate the value in a variety of ways. The importance of the training and development function is often more visible when there is a global HRD strategy.

A successful global HRD strategy also builds important relationships in various countries that are essential for building the business. It represents an exciting challenge that not only adds value but also offers much satisfaction to the training and development staff.

References

1. Schaaf, Dick. "Inside Hamburger University." *Training,* Dec. 1994, pp. 18–24.
2. Odenwald, Sylvia. "A Guide for Global Training." *Training & Development,* July 1993, pp. 23–31.
3. Nadler, Len. "HRD and the Spaceship Earth." *Training & Development,* Oct. 1983, p. 18.
4. Marquardt, Michael J. *How to Globalize Your Training.* InfoLine Series, Issue 9505. Alexandria, Va.: American Society for Training and Development, May 1995.
5. Rhinesmith, Stephen H. *A Manager's Guide To Globalization,* 2nd ed., Chicago: Business One Irwin, 1997.
6. Odenwald, Sylvia. *Global Training: How to Design a Training Program for the Multinational Corporation.* Chicago: Business One Irwin, 1993.
7. Shandler, Donald. *Reengineering the Training Function: How to Align Training with the New Corporate Agenda.* Delray Beach, Fla.: St. Lucie Press, 1996.
8. Marquardt, Michael J. and Engel, Dean W. *Global Human Resource Development.* Englewood Cliffs, N.J.: Prentice Hall, 1993.

9. Kemske, Floyd. "HR's Role Will Change. The Question Is How. HR 2008: A Forecast Based on Our Exclusive Study." *Workforce,* Jan. 1998, p. 50.

10. Odenwald, Sylvia B. *Global Solutions for Teams: Moving from Collision to Collaboration.* Chicago: Business One Irwin, 1996.

11. Rhinesmith, Stephen H. "Training for Global Operation," in *ASTD Training and Development Handbook,* 4th ed., Robert Craig (Ed.) New York: McGraw-Hill, 1996.

12. Marquardt and Engel.

13. Shandler.

14. Ford, Donald J. (Ed.) and Phillips, Jack J. (Series Ed.) *In Action: Designing Training Programs.* Alexandria, Va.: American Society for Training and Development, 1996.

15. Odenwald, *Global Training: How to Design a Training Program for the Multinational Corporation.*

17

OUTSOURCING

Trend Definition and Validation

Brief Definition of Trend

As reengineering and downsizing become a way of life, the training and development (T&D) department is a target for reductions and outsourcing. Parts or all of the function are being outsourced at an amazing pace with several factors driving the actions. This is partially because management does not always believe training and development contributes directly to the bottom line. Still T&D costs continue to escalate. Some executives perceive they can control training costs, quality, and effectiveness by using expertise from outside sources. Outsourcing can involve any type of program, activity, service, or function. At the extreme, outsourcing may include the management of the entire training function, including needs assessment, design and development, delivery, and evaluation.

Case Study: DuPont

DuPont is one of the most cited examples of outsourcing. In 1993, DuPont initiated a tremendous reengineering process with the goal to be a global company by utilizing its employees. Costs were expected to be reduced by $1 billion. All divisions of the organization were under scrutiny, including the training and education function. At the beginning of the reengineering process, training offered open-enrollment programs to all employees. Although training offered many programs, it had no real proof of the courses' impact on the performance of the participants or the business. DuPont's training and education department focused on measuring the number of employees participating in programs rather than measuring the business impact of the program.

To meet the needs of the new organizational structure, the training department had to change its mode of operation. Changes included:

- Moving from a corporate staff function to a value-adding business
- Moving from building competencies to addressing business issues
- Moving from a fixed-cost organization to a variable-cost service provider

The training department turned to outsourcing and selected an external training supplier to combine its resources with the best of the training staff at DuPont. This new organization, the Forum Learning Alliance, was staffed by the Forum Corporation, one of the leaders in the outsourcing industry. By enlisting the services of the external training supplier, DuPont's training and education function retained knowledge and expertise of the existing DuPont employees, offered new training capabilities, and operated as a value-adding, variable-cost provider of training services.[1]

Evidence of Trend

Outsourcing continues to be a major topic of interest among training and development managers and executives. When questioned about the visibility of outsourcing in the global trends survey, practitioners rated it 4.49 out of 5 in terms of agreement with the existence of the trend (see Appendix 1). They ranked the importance of the outsourcing trend at 4.21 out of 5 possible points.

Outsourcing receives its share of coverage in publications. Books have been developed on the topic. Major magazines and journals routinely devote space to it. A special supplement of the July 1998 issue of *Training & Development* addresses the issue of outsourcing in detail. Research reported in this issue indicates that organizations spent more on outsourcing from 1996 to 1997 than from 1995 to 1996.[2] This implies that organizations are finding business cases to allow external training suppliers to manage certain aspects, if not all, of the training function. This focus on outsourcing provides clear indication that the trend is significant and will continue on its current path.

Data Quest Worldwide conducted a survey revealing that two thirds of the survey respondents use training suppliers to develop programs. More than 40 percent use training suppliers for assistance in conducting needs assessments. Another major survey indicates that more than 90 percent of the organizations surveyed outsource at least one activity.

On a macro level, outsourcing is growing in all areas. A survey conducted by Outsourcing Institute indicates that more than one half of the organizations responding increased their outsourcing in 1996, with almost $100 billion spent on outsourcing services. The expectation is that by the year 2001 more than $318 billion will be spent annually on outsourcing.[3]

A survey of 1,750 human resource executives determined which human resource services were most likely to be outsourced. Results show that 46 percent of the respondents identified training delivery and 40 percent identified training program development as services suitable for outsourcing.[4]

The results of the July 1997 National HRD Executive Survey indicate that one of the most significant trends in HRD during the next three years will be a shift from providing training to providing performance improvement.[5] This integration between training and performance improvement implies the need for outsourcing. With the focus on performance improvement, organizations will keep many of the results-based programs as in-house training while outsourcing the more general training programs, such as computer training or interpersonal skills training, to more effectively utilize resources.

The outsourcing trend is so significant that conferences about the issue are being held. A typical outsourcing conference is the 1998 conference in San Diego, California, conducted by Linkage Inc. At this conference, representatives of organizations such as Hewlett-Packard, Coors, Knight Ridder, and NCR presented their practices, processes, and philosophies of outsourcing.[6]

Companies consider the development of employees' skills, knowledge, and abilities invaluable and critical to the success of an organization. However, in most situations companies do not see the bottom-line value of training; therefore, training is a prime target for outsourcing. A study conducted by the Manufacturer's Alliance found that HRD functions are more likely than any other function to be outsourced and training is now cited as the area in which outsourcing will increase.[7]

Causes and Drivers

Research on organizations reveals many reasons why training is being outsourced. The drivers vary depending on the organization and the services to be outsourced. The most common are related to efficiency and expertise. The American Society for Training and Development asked the Benchmarking Forum members to indicate the level of importance they place on various factors when deciding whether they should outsource training, learning, and performance improvement initiatives.[8] The five most important factors include the following:

- Increasing operational efficiency of the training function
- Offsetting reduction in training staff
- Accessing external, state-of-the art expertise
- Reducing operating costs
- Increasing the impact of training

Other reasons involve saving time, increasing flexibility, and focusing on more strategic initiatives.[9]

As organizations grow and develop, inefficiencies sometimes creep into operational practices. The organization develops into a bureaucracy; processes become inefficient or ineffective; and extra procedures and policies often add layers of control over what should be a simple process. Inefficiency exists in many large learning institutes, training and development departments, and corporate universities.

Consequently, outsourcing is a way to achieve a process, deliver a program, or provide a service in a more efficient manner. This brings about the following question: Is there another organization that can provide this service more efficiently—either faster, more accurately, or perhaps with lower costs? Sometimes the answer is "yes." This issue drives many outsourcing decisions.

As organizations continue to downsize, they often mandate cuts in different functions of the business. Sometimes the training and development function is asked to reduce its overall number of employees, yet services of those employees are still in demand. The only way to logically meet these two demands of head-count reduction and increased customer service is to outsource.

Expertise is often needed for a particular function. Staff reductions sometimes eliminate the expertise needed to take care of a particular issue, process, or procedure or to provide a particular program. Thus, outsourcing provides an excellent opportunity to fill a need for expertise in a particular area.

Outsourcing is used as a way to access world-class or best-practice capabilities that may not be available internally. Outsourcing to a firm with an excellent reputation in a particular area, such as conducting programs on project management, provides needed expertise without having to develop it internally and without its associated costs and time commitments. The desire to have the best process available, yet without the expense of added staff to achieve it, steers an organization toward outsourcing.

Coupled closely with the inefficiencies of a training and development organization are the escalating operating costs. Outsourcing sometimes provides a more cost-effective approach to delivering a particular service. Consider the cost, for example, of evaluating programs using the standard reaction questionnaires. If an organization wanted to process its own reaction questionnaires, develop a report, and distribute it to appropriate individuals, this might involve:

- Purchasing the appropriate scanning equipment
- Employing someone to program the software for the organization's specific needs
- Employing someone who is capable of maintaining the equipment
- Processing the forms as they are developed

In some situations, the cost-effective alternative is to seek outside services and outsource the Level 1 evaluation entirely, paying a fixed fee per questionnaire for processing and reporting of the results.

Sometimes training and development programs do not have as much effect as they should, or T&D does not deliver its services in a timely manner. Consequently, an outsource alternative may be the best approach to improve the effectiveness of the process, as well as the ultimate results of the programs.

Many organizations are trying to move back to the basics and develop core competencies around the most important processes and programs. Some training and development services may not represent areas in which T&D has expertise. An area of service may be unrelated to the organization's core values, mission, or strategic objectives. These non-core issues can often be outsourced with little damage or harm to the organization. This frees up staff time to focus on those projects, services, and products that provide more value and are more closely related to the company's strategic objectives and direction.

The need to be flexible and meet critical deadlines drives some organizations to the outsourcing option. The staff may not have the capability, and cannot obtain it in time, to deliver the needed service or product. Sometimes a project is so large that it cannot be delivered in the desired time frame. These flexibility and timing issues are critical and may justify an organization seeking external assistance to manage at least a portion of the work that needs to be done to meet project deadlines or major objectives.

A final driver in the process is a need for objectivity and independence. Some processes involved in the training and development function require an independent viewpoint separate from that of the training and development staff and sometimes independent of the entire organization. For example, the evaluation function should perhaps be a candidate for outsourcing to maintain the objectivity of the assessment. If internal staff members are charged with the task of evaluating the success of programs developed and implemented by their colleagues, the question of objectivity and independence may enter into the final analysis. To provide the complete objectivity needed, outsourcing can be a viable alternative for certain parts of the process, if not for the entire measurement and evaluation function. The same argument applies to the needs assessment and, in some cases, even design and development. Independence is clearly important and may be an appropriate influence for outsourcing.

These outsourcing drivers have a tremendous influence on the way training and development functions operate. They are causing a complete re-examination of the processes and procedures to design, develop, and deliver learning solutions. Many organizations are concluding that outsourcing is a viable alternative and is being explored at an alarming pace.

Trend Description

Outsourcing is the use of external contractors to provide training and performance improvement programs to support an organization's strategic objectives. Through outsourcing, organizations have a variety of choices. Organizations can outsource entire training functions or specific training programs. Although not a new phenomenon, outsourcing has changed during the past three decades as shown in Table 17-1.[10] In the 1970s, outsourcing was driven by the motivation to extend resource capabilities by leveraging internal expertise. In the 1980s, the driver was financial, while in the 1990s, it more directly aligns with strategic objectives.

Table 17-1
Training Sourcing Time Line

	Internal sourcing 1970s	Subcontracting 1980s	Comprehensive sourcing 1990s
Motivation	Leverage internal expertise	Financial	Strategic objectives
Vendors	Few	More	Outsourcing training management companies
Vendor measures	—	Contract fulfillment	Customer success based on performance metrics

Adapted from: Maul, June Paradise and Krauss, Joel D. "Outsourcing in Training and Education." The Training and Development Handbook. *Alexandria, Va.: American Society for Training and Development, 1995, p. 1010.*

Organizations see tremendous value in outsourcing. However, they should consider several issues and concerns when deciding whether or not to outsource.[11] These issues include: (1) selecting the appropriate contractor, (2) deciding which part of the training function to outsource, (3) managing the outsourcing initiative, and (4) measuring and evaluating the outsourcing program. Figure 17-1 lists some key questions identified by the ASTD Benchmarking Forum as important to consider when deciding whether or not to outsource.[12]

Contractor Selection

One of the top issues in outsourcing is selecting the best contractor for the job. The organization is more likely to receive quality, efficiency, and effectiveness if it selects the appropriate training supplier. Three practices can help with the process of contractor selection:

- **Clearly communicate strategic initiatives and goals of the organization.** Clear communication of organizational goals allows the prospective vendor to respond with a targeted proposal closely aligned with the organization's needs.
- **Be methodical in the selection process.** Take care that the vendor understands the organization's needs and objectives. Be sure a long-term relationship with the vendor is possible.
- **Clearly define the criteria by which you will evaluate outsourcing vendors.** Such criteria may include quality, cost, customer service, stability of the organization, experience, industry expertise, and cultural fit.

If the objective in outsourcing is to save money for the company, the organization should also be aware that paying too much attention to costs may bring about an oversight of other important criteria. If this occurs, the cost of doing business with the vendor could actually be much greater than originally estimated. Rather than focus on bottom-line savings of using a training supplier, the organization should compare the cost savings with its current method of doing business.[13]

The quality and capabilities of the vendor should align with those of the client organization. The vendor should be dedicated to both short-term and long-term quality and should possess systems necessary to provide committed service. The vendor should also be able to

		PRIMARY QUESTIONS
1.	❑	Is there a mandate to outsource?
2.	❑	Does the proprietary nature of the training schedule preclude outsourcing?
		STAFFING AND RESOURCES
3.	❑	Are internal support systems currently required for the activity?
4.	❑	Do you have the requirements to provide a wide variety of products and services, or do you have a standard narrow set?
5.	❑	What capabilities do you have in-house? What is your skill mix?
6.	❑	What is the frequency of required updates and maintenance?
7.	❑	Is a stable supplier available?
		AUDIENCE
8.	❑	What is your target audience?
9.	❑	What is the geographic dispersion of your audience?
10.	❑	Do you have peaks and valleys in your needs?
11.	❑	When is this required? What is the time period to prepare? Is there time to reskill?
		COSTS AND VALUE
12.	❑	What are the true systems costs of maintaining the activity internally? Of outsourcing?
13.	❑	What are the cost constraints?
14.	❑	What is the payback period?
15.	❑	What is the global value-add from this initiative, and can it be realized by outsourcing?
		STRATEGIC FOCUS
16.	❑	How does the culture of your company affect this decision?
17.	❑	Does it make sense from a total systems perspective? What would be the true impact on systems if an external supplier was used?
18.	❑	Can outsourcing affect your ability to maintain control of the strategic issues of your business?
19.	❑	What is the role of changing technology?

Figure 17-1. *Questions to Ask When Considering Outsourcing.* (Adapted from: Salopek, Jennifer J. "Outsourcing, Insourcing, and In-Between Sourcing." *Training & Development,* July 1998, p. 53.)

grow with technological advances to ensure that the organization continues to receive cutting-edge service.

The vendor should have a genuine commitment to customer service. It should have a clear understanding of the client organization's needs and be able to respond to those needs. The vendor's stability and experience are factors in determining the longevity of the vendor/client relationship. The vendor should have a healthy financial background, have excellent management, and be in the business of outsourcing for the long term. Experience in outsourcing should be closely reviewed; however, a newer company may provide better, more current services. The vendor should also have a clear understanding of the industry and the business of the client organization. That understanding will help the vendor respond more directly to the client's needs.

The final two criteria for selecting a training supplier are shared values and cultural fit. A training vendor should be compatible with the client organization in terms of decision-making abilities, commitment to service, and methods of conducting business.[14] Although these criteria provide a good place to start when assessing potential vendors, many of them are also easily falsified, such as costs, experience, and expertise. An organization should obtain good references when selecting a training vendor.

Following is a list of questions to consider when evaluating prospective training vendors.[15]

- **Can the vendor accurately establish a need for a training program?** The vendor should be able to verify a disparity between actual and desired performance and judge if the disparity is caused by a lack of knowledge or skill.
- **Does the vendor clearly articulate how the objectives of the training will be derived?** Objectives are key in measuring the results of a training program, and the vendor should be able to explain how the objectives will be developed. If the vendor is unable to explain, either the program will lack clear objectives or the vendor will establish objectives without the input of the client organization.
- **Can the vendor develop the training program within a realistic time frame?** A prospective vendor is likely to propose the same time frame proposed by the client in order to satisfy requirements to get the job. In reviewing the proposal, the client organization must consider the internal workings of the organization. For

instance, the availability of resources involved in the project will impact the time it will take to develop a program. The vendor will not know this information unless it has conducted a thorough investigation of the client's function.

- **Does the vendor provide steps by which the trainee can take the new skills back to the workplace?** Although the training vendor cannot influence the environment in which a program participant works, it can offer steps that will enhance the probability of success for participants once they return to work. The training vendor's proposal should ensure that supervisors of the training participants will:

    - Know what the training participant can do after training that he or she could not do prior to training
    - Provide the tools and opportunities for employees to apply what they learn in the training program
    - Provide the participant with positive feedback as a reinforcement of desired performance

- **Is there a simple yet credible method of evaluation for the training program?** The training vendor's proposal should address concerns regarding:

    - Participant reaction to the training program
    - Knowledge gained from the training program
    - Ability to demonstrate acquisition of job-related skills
    - Impact the program made toward the strategic objectives of the organization
    - The return the organization gained from the dollars invested in the program

The contractual relationship between the client organization and the outsourcing vendor should represent winning opportunities for both parties. The contract should include incentives for incremental value-add. For instance, if an unscheduled program is needed because of an unforeseen event and the training vendor is expected to respond immediately, an incentive tied to expediency of program development and delivery will help the organization meet its objectives, as well as reward the vendor financially.

The outsourcing contract should also outline the method by which the vendor, programs, and outsourcing initiative will be evaluated. Understanding the complete evaluation process will help ensure that the vendor develops programs in alignment with corporate strategy. It will also assist the vendor in responding in a manner acceptable to the organization.

Choosing the Functions to Outsource

Every function in the training and development department may not need to be outsourced. The first step in determining which functions to outsource is to assess the importance and the costs of each training activity. The impact on the customer, as well as departmental staff, should also be considered, and for this reason, each activity should be reviewed based on its strategic impact, as well as its operational impact. A balance between costs, impact, and strategic importance should determine which activities are most appropriate for outsourcing. Activities that are common targets for outsourcing include:[16]

- **Administration**—The behind-the-scenes support that makes the programs take place
- **Analysis**—Determining the performance gaps and assessing the value of a program
- **Design**—Determining the specifications of the program to be developed
- **Development**—Creating the training program
- **Implementation**—Conducting the program with the targeted audience
- **Application support**—Facilitating on-the-job transfer of learning
- **Evaluation**—Measuring the performance results of the program

More insight about how to identify the function to outsource is included in the Preventing Outsourcing section, later in this chapter.

Managing Outsourcing

Ideally, the training vendor and the client will develop an integrated partnership. In doing so, the two bring together goals and strategies.

Total integration of the partnership occurs when the training vendor and the client work as one organization. However, several challenges exist in managing the outsourcing function.

As with any new program, the success of the outsourcing strategy depends on support from internal clients and the management team. To enlist client and management support, a presentation should be made to senior management, illustrating the plan, explaining the process, and reviewing the benefits. Although the presentation cannot be fully detailed until the organization selects an outsourcing vendor, it will build awareness and clarify the approach.

To establish a successful relationship with the training vendor, the organization should thoroughly communicate its needs. This includes explaining the organization's capabilities, mission, and corporate culture.

One concern of training and development departments is the issue of maintaining the right amount of control of the outsourcing venture. A successful relationship between the client organization and the vendor includes clear definitions of roles and responsibilities. By defining responsibilities and continually communicating, both parties will be assured the other is following through with its commitment. The key for the client organization is to allow the training vendor to do its job without feeling threatened, yet at the same time, promote the understanding that the vendor must meet a certain level of service.

Building a personal relationship with the training vendor will deter conflict. Because it is possible to go overboard building this relationship, keeping an arm's length distance will make conflict and problems less likely.[17]

Measuring Outsourcing

The purpose of outsourcing is to meet strategic objectives. To ensure an outsourcing initiative is improving business results, a measurement process must be in place. Measuring the outsourcing results requires accuracy and efficiency in performance evaluation of the training supplier. Outsourcing measures should also include consideration of the level of relationship between vendor and organization. Three types of relationships can exist between training vendors and organizations: a customer/supplier relationship, a client/consultant relationship, and a partnership.

- **Customer/supplier relationship.** In this relationship, the supplier must meet stated requirements. Of the three relationships, this is the most limited. Results of the measurement are concrete; neither party has much incentive to investigate underlying problems and issues.
- **Client/consultant relationship.** In this situation, the consultant or contractor adds to the stated requirements of the client by understanding the needs behind those requirements, which makes this relationship highly collaborative. The consultant focuses on the needs of the client.
- **Partnership relationship.** Here, the client and vendor work to accomplish common business strategies. When measuring this relationship, the evaluation includes not just delivery of service but also how the client and consultant contribute to service development. Partners are evaluated by their contribution to the other partner's bottom line.

Once the client-vendor relationship is defined, a system should be put into place to measure the success of outsourcing. The system to measure performance should first include clarification of the purpose for outsourcing. Dialogue between the client and vendor ensures that the purpose of the outsourcing program aligns with how both the client and vendor expect to realize value from the relationship.

Next, specific performance indicators should be defined. Key performance indicators (KPIs) clarify what the client and vendor think are important gains from the relationship. Once the KPIs are established, the metrics must be determined. Both short-term and long-term measures should be developed. In addition, a balance of types of measures should be included, representing financial processes and customer satisfaction. Using the measures, performance objectives should be established and clearly defined in the contractual agreement. However, dialogue should occur between the two parties to ensure clear understanding.

The final step is designing a measurement system to link the KPIs, metrics, and performance objectives. The more precise the system, the more useful it will be in managing the outsourcing.[18]

Preventing Outsourcing

Because this trend may negatively impact the training and development staff, it often generates more fear than any other trend in this book. Consequently, it is important not only to examine how to adjust to the trend but also to explore what can be done to prevent the outsourcing process from occurring in the first place. Of course, this assumes that outsourcing may not be the most viable alternative. The vast majority of outsourcing cases are initiated or driven by others outside the training and development function. Training and development professionals rarely approach the senior management team with a plan to outsource part or all of the function. Usually, pressure from senior executives leads to the ultimate outsourcing decision. Sometimes, the decision is based on faulty information about the training function. The key question that must be addressed is: *What would prevent senior management from taking this initiative or even raising the issue of outsourcing as a viable alternative?*

Answering this question involves a review of many aspects of the training and development function, including a review of why senior management may request outsourcing. Eight factors can usually influence an executive's decision to pursue this course of action. They are listed below, from most important to least important:

- **Lack of results:** As reported in previous trends, the training and development function does not always produce the results expected by senior managers. Fortunately, two important trends, the application of systematic evaluation and calculating the actual return on investment, are helping to turn this situation around. However, there are far too few examples where a training and development function has presented measurable results to the senior managers in terms they understand—preferably in ROI. Although ROI does not have to be developed for every program, executives must understand that the training process adds value. Armed with this information, they will not take steps to eliminate or outsource it; instead they will help to make it even more effective. Consequently, any attempt to communicate training and development results effectively to the senior management team may be the single most important action to prevent outsourcing. Executives would find it difficult to severely curtail or outsource a process they consider to be vital to the organization's strategic and operational goals.

- **Lack of linkage to business needs.** Too often, learning programs are designed, developed, and delivered with little or no connection to business needs. Although they may teach nice-to-know or useful skills, they are not connected to the operational and strategic direction of the organization. Consequently, executives tend to eliminate the programs or push them outside so they can be provided more efficiently. Some organizations overcame this situation by insisting that every new program or initiative have application and business-impact objectives directly linked to the operational and strategic goals of the organization. If a program does not meet this requirement, the program is not pursued. In these organizations, the training and development manager asks this question: How can we ask the senior management team to support a process if we cannot show the expected behavior change and the impact it will have in our business units?
- **Lack of relevance.** Too often programs are designed, developed, and delivered in a vacuum and are not perceived as relevant to present needs. Sometimes a program focuses on yesterday's skill requirements or on processes irrelevant in today's work environment. Although participants may enjoy participating in this type of program, it may not relate to any issues in the work unit.
- **Excessive costs.** As described in Chapter 10, training and development is expensive. The fully loaded costs of designing, developing, and delivering a program represents a tremendous expense. Expensive programs leave many executives wondering if the programs are really worth the cost or if they can be implemented for less. Excessive costs often drive executives to search for less expensive alternatives—primarily through outsourcing. Controlling costs and providing cost comparisons should minimize criticisms and prevent outsourcing from becoming a way to reduce cost. Benchmarking can be an important service by comparing costs with those of other respected or admired organizations.
- **Lack of adequate service.** Sometimes training and development staff members do not respond to clients appropriately, or they

take too long to provide a product or service. Then when the product or service is provided, its quality may not meet the client's expectations. Also, other customer service issues do not get addressed as effectively as they should. This lack of expected service levels can influence executives to seek an alternative to the internal staff. Outsourcing is a viable alternative. As some executives have said, "If I were your real customer, you would not treat me this way." With outsourcing, the company truly becomes a customer.

- **Lack of expertise.** As discussed earlier, the training and development staff might not have the expertise to tackle a particular issue, and the senior executives may know this. In other cases the expertise should be there, but for a variety of reasons, the training staff may not have the desired level of competence. When these situations occur, executives may request that the program or service be outsourced to those who know how to do it best.
- **Lack of productive relationships.** As discussed in Chapter 14, the training and development function often does not develop an appropriate productive relationship with the senior team. With little or no effort to build a partnership relationship, the senior team often knows little about the training and development function and team. When executives know little about the staff and the product or service, it makes their decision to pursue outsourcing easier.
- **Overall image.** Finally, the overall image of the training and development function can cause the outsourcing issue to be raised. If the department has a negative image, some executives may want to replace the group with a more professional group. For example, in some organizations, training and development staff members are considered individuals who are unprofessional, are out of touch, are incapable of delivering needed services, and lack knowledge about the business. When this is the case, it is an easy decision for senior management to recommend outsourcing.

When not properly addressed, these issues cause executives to pursue outsourcing or, in some cases, reduce their commitment to training and development. An outsourcing mandate can be avoided if these issues are effectively handled and the process works as it should.

Trend Consequences

Impact

Outsourcing will have a significant impact on training and development organizations because outsourcing presents real opportunities and challenges. External expertise can serve as a rich resource in developing, implementing, and evaluating training programs. The training and development department can transform itself into a network of organizations by partnering with outsourcing vendors.

No other trend in this book will meet with such resistance as will the threat of outsourcing. Immediately, the staff will see the possibility of job loss and will resist any attempts to contribute to a productive outsourcing decision. Much of the anxiety can be avoided if enough attention is devoted to the sensitive issues. When addressing legitimate outsourcing issues, it helps to remain open and honest with the staff and to explain the various alternatives and possibilities. If job loss is an immediate possibility, the various options need to be explored in terms of the fate of the staff. Early discussions often reduce resistance and create a much smoother process. Operating in a cloud of secrecy often makes the decisions more difficult and the transition rocky. Taking extra steps to develop several viable alternatives often eliminates much of the resistance. Communication, involvement, and action will make the process work.

Although the thought of outsourcing creates fear among the training staff, it can serve the company well from a strategic viewpoint. After the appropriate vendor is selected, the benefits of outsourcing should outweigh the costs. The training and development function can benefit in several ways through outsourcing. One benefit is the freedom to utilize additional resources without increasing payroll expenditures. Another advantage is the ability to bring new skills and capabilities into the organization. For example, experts in learning technologies are often outsourced rather than hired as permanent staff. Finally, bringing outsiders into an organization will generate new ideas and innovative ways of achieving objectives. Using vendors to implement programs frees the staff to focus more time on strategic initiatives.

Alternatives to Outsourcing

Because of the tremendous growth of outsourcing activity in the United States and Canada, organizations have explored a number of ways in which they can enjoy outsourcing benefits without actually deciding to outsource. Three processes have accomplished some of the same benefits: (1) insourcing, (2) shared services, and (3) developing alliances.

Insourcing. This concept brings an external supplier into the organization to provide the training and development processes, services, or products. In essence, it is an external resource that is available internally—and is usually on the payroll of the external organization. This creates a hybrid organization that brings the training supplier into close alignment with the client organization. Insourcing allows the client organization to contract training and development services, yet the training supplier is physically located within the organization structure. This provides the organization with a full-time partner to ensure that proper training opportunities are available on an as-needed basis.

Shared services. In this arrangement, several organizations with similar needs share services and pool resources. A centralized group of resources provides products and services to the entire organization. Training is one such service. Training analysis, development, delivery, and evaluation are provided through this centralized organization. Generally only those training programs requested by clients are offered through the shared services organization. Training is no longer offered on a broad basis but instead is offered as needed.

This alternative to outsourcing eliminates the process of selecting appropriate vendors. However, it does increase the training function's accountability in providing quality programs and meeting client needs.

Developing alliances. Another alternative is to explore strategic alliances with other organizations that share similar interests. For example, one firm with a strength in a specific product may develop an alliance with another firm that needs that product. The alliance partner also usually has a strength that is needed by the first firm. In essence, the alliance allows the organizations to build on strengths and share services. An example of this would be a large engineering and contracting company providing project management training—its strength—to one of its key customers, a large paper company. In exchange, the paper company provides management and leadership training—its strength—to the contracting firm. Each firm avoids outsourcing these programs and services by partnering in a strategic alliance.

Assuming that outsourcing is not the best alternative, these three approaches provide some creative alternatives to the outsourcing dilemma. In some cases, outsourcing is not the best approach, and an alternative may work quite well toward resolving the concerns that led to the initial discussions of outsourcing.

Key Questions

Before pursuing outsourcing, the following questions must be considered:

Key Questions

1. To what extent is the outsourcing process developing in my organization?
2. How important is this trend?
3. How much progress has been made in implementing outsourcing in my organization?
4. What are the specific drivers within my organization?
5. Is the training and development staff prepared for outsourcing?
6. What should be done to prepare the staff?
7. How much encouragement/pressure am I receiving now to implement outsourcing?
8. What barriers exist for implementing outsourcing?
9. What happens if I do nothing?
10. To what extent does management support this process?

Outlook

Outsourcing has evolved considerably in the United States and Canada but still has a long way to go to meet the demands of the marketplace. The trend has moved to Europe and is now gaining serious consideration in Australia and Southeast Asia. Organizations are reevaluating their outsourcing objectives and, in the next decade, will be outsourcing most functions that are in the support category, rather than revenue-generating functions. In other words, companies will focus on core business initiatives, allowing outside vendors to support them with non-core initiatives. Many training suppliers will not be able to keep up with the demand. Therefore, large organizations will respond by considering alternatives such as building alliances, developing shared services, and insourcing.

References

1. Van Adelsberg, David and Trolley, Edward A. "Strategic Insourcing: Getting the Most from the Best." *Training & Development,* July 1998, p. 58.
2. Salopek, Jennifer J. "Outsourcing, Insourcing, and In-Between Sourcing." *Training & Development,* July 1998, pp. 51–56.
3. Bassi, Laurie J., Cheney, Scott, and Van Buren, Mark E. "Training Industry Trends." *Training & Development,* Nov. 1997, p. 52.
4. Harkins, Philip J., Brown, Stephen M., and Sullivan, Russell. *Outsourcing and Human Resources.* Lexington, Mass.: LER Press, 1996, pp. 21–23.
5. *National HRD Executive Survey.* Alexandria, Va.: American Society for Training and Development, 3rd Qtr. 1997.
6. Linkage Inc. *The Outsourcing, Insourcing, and Shared Services Conference: Conference Proceedings.* Mar. 1998.
7. Bassi, Cheney, and Van Buren, p. 52.
8. Salopek, pp. 51–56.
9. Harkins, Brown, and Sullivan, p. 26.
10. Maul, June Paradise and Krauss, Joel D. "Outsourcing in Training and Education." *The Training and Development Handbook.* Alexandria Va.: American Society for Training and Development, 1995, p. 1010.
11. Maul and Krauss, p. 1011.
12. Salopek, p. 53.

13. Maul and Krauss, p. 1025.
14. Harkins, Brown, and Sullivan, p. 106.
15. Leibler, Seth N. and Parkman, Ann W. "Outsourcing: How to Make the Right Decisions." *Corporate University Review,* July/Aug. 1997, p. 46.
16. Salopek, p. 53.
17. Harkins, Brown, and Sullivan, p. 134.
18. Anderson, Merrill C. "A Primer in Measuring Outsourcing Results." *National Productivity Review,* Winter 1997, pp. 33–41.

18

WORKING WITH THE TRENDS

The Need for Action

The chapters in this book describe sixteen important trends that are evolving in the training and development process. Each trend represents a critical area of change that can have a tremendous impact on the training and HRD function. Few organizations have made significant progress in all sixteen areas. Although some leading-edge firms have made progress with every trend, there is still room for improvement. The challenge is to identify the areas for improvement and implementation.

As described in Chapter 1, the rationale for examining trends is to take action, if needed. The appropriate action may come in the form of a complete restructuring, reengineering, or repositioning of the training and development function. In other situations, specific steps may be needed for only a few trends. Continuous improvement is necessary for training and development to add value and become an integral part of an organization. This chapter briefly outlines the steps to implement the necessary changes.

Steps Toward Change

The First Step: Assessing Current Status

Figure 18-1 shows the practitioner survey, altered to report the progress made with each trend. Please take a few minutes to complete this survey. For each trend identified in this book, indicate the progress made within the context of what is important in your organization. The responses are summarized using the ratings with each description. Any item rated Unimportant or Somewhat Important is not considered further, at least on a formal, planned basis. For those items you rated Important (3), Very Important (4), and Critically Important (5), you should take specific actions. Those items rated Critically Important deserve the most attention, and you should address these first. A rating of less than 3 for progress in any trend is considered unacceptable, and much progress is needed in that area. A rating of 3 on progress (Moderate Progress) indicates that improvement has been made in an area but there is much to be done and immediate action is needed. A rating of 4 on progress (Much Progress) indicates that significant improvement has been made on a trend and minor adjustments are needed. A rating of 5 (Very Much Progress) indicates that much improvement has been made and usually reflects leading-edge practices. The same analysis is used with items rated in the Very Important and Important categories.

The Second Step: Setting Goals

To capture those items where improvement is needed, a goal-setting process is needed as reflected in Figure 18-2. On this chart, list each trend requiring action. Next to the trend, check either Important (3), Very Important (4), or Critically Important (5), based on your answers to the survey in Figure 18-1. List the terms marked Critically Important first, followed by those marked Very Important. List those marked Important last.

Global Trends in Human Resource Development Progress Survey

Instructions:
Each of the following issues was identified as a trend in training and development and HRD. Please read each issue and indicate the level of progress your training and development department has made with this issue. Also, to the right of that response, indicate the relative importance of the trend to your training and development department. The following scales are used:

Extent of Progress with the Trend		**Level of Importance of the Trend**	
5	Very Much Progress	5	Critically Important
4	Much Progress	4	Very Important
3	Moderate Progress	3	Important
2	Some Progress	2	Somewhat Important
1	No Progress	1	Unimportant

Global Training Trends	**Extent of Progress**	**Level of Importance**
1. Training is linked to the strategic direction of the organization.		
2. Needs assessment and analysis are receiving more emphasis.		
3. Training is shifting to a performance improvement role.		
4. Corporate universities continue to gain acceptance.		
5. Training delivery is changing rapidly.		
6. The responsibility of training is shared among several groups.		
7. Systematic evaluation processes measure the success of training.		
8. Measuring the return on investment in training is growing in use.		
9. Training costs are monitored more accurately to manage resources and demonstrate accountability.		

(figure continued on page 370)

Figure 18-1. *Progress Survey.*

Global Trends in Human Resource Development Progress Survey

Global Training Trends	Extent of Progress	Level of Importance
10. Training and development functions are converting to a profit center concept.		
11. Training and development budgets are increasing.		
12. The learning organization concept is being adopted.		
13. Training staff and line management are forming partnerships to achieve common goals.		
14. The application of technology to training is developing rapidly.		
15. More training is designed for global use.		
16. More training is outsourced to contractors.		

Figure 18-1. *Progress Survey (continued).*

This is a personal assessment tool, and for this reason, it is difficult to compare your own ratings of progress and importance to those of other organizations or to known data. Essentially, if an organization does not perceive a trend to be important, it drops out of the analysis. Thus, the assessment of importance could greatly affect actions or lack of actions. Nevertheless, this process can serve as a useful planning, progress-reporting, and communicating tool in the future. You can also develop a similar analysis to reflect the relative urgency of action in addition to the extent of progress.

Now, list specific objectives for each trend in the ample space provided on the right side of the goal-setting form. Figure 18-3 illustrates how the goal-setting tool is used. For example, if the profit center is an important trend to you and action is required, your first objective may be to establish fees and charges for all products and services and to have them accepted by the various stakeholders. A second objective may be to prorate the cost for certain types of programs to the departments where the participants are actually employed. Your third objective may be to reach an agreement on the timing and schedule for the profit center implementation. A fourth objective may be to charge fees for specific programs. This analysis allows the training and development department to plan specific steps around objectives.

The Third Step: Action Planning

You can accomplish further detailed planning with the action-planning form, illustrated as Figure 18-4. This approach uses the successful action-planning process that is often used to implement change in an organization. Use a separate action-planning form for each objective. The form lists a particular trend, the objective, and the action steps needed to achieve it. You can also indicate other pertinent information surrounding responsibility, progress, and resources.

Reproduce these forms and use them with each trend's corresponding objectives. They become the framework for detailed planning to transform your training and development department from its current state to the desired future state, focusing on the trends you consider important to your organization. In essence, this process positions your training and development function where it needs to be.

When determining the importance of a trend, it may help to gain additional input from other groups, even beyond the training and development staff. Even though the training and development staff may perceive a trend to be unimportant, such as a profit center, senior executives may consider it critical to the future of the department. To ensure you have secured adequate input about the importance of each trend, you may want to obtain additional input from senior staff members using the original survey (see Appendix 1). By changing the instructions and providing additional explanation, you can easily adapt the original survey for managers to determine their progress with, and opinion of the importance of, each trend. After integrating the data with a composite score, you may ignore those trends not making the Importance cut discussed in the Assessing Current Status section during planning. This helps ensure that the senior leadership team has appropriate input as you develop specific plans.

(text continued on page 376)

Working with Trends: Goal Setting

Trend—Start with Critically Important	Level of Importance 5, 4, 3	Objectives	
1.	❑ ❑ ❑	1.	3.
		2.	4.
2.	❑ ❑ ❑	1.	3.
		2.	4.
3.	❑ ❑ ❑	1.	3.
		2.	4.
4.	❑ ❑ ❑	1.	3.
		2.	4.
5.	❑ ❑ ❑	1.	3.
		2.	4.
6.	❑ ❑ ❑	1.	3.
		2.	4.
7.	❑ ❑ ❑	1.	3.
		2.	4.
8.	❑ ❑ ❑	1.	3.
		2.	4.

Figure 18-2. *Goal-Setting Form.*

Working with Trends: Goal Setting (continued)

Trend— Start with Critically Important	Level of Importance 5, 4, 3	Objectives	
9.	❑ ❑ ❑	1.	3.
		2.	4.
10.	❑ ❑ ❑	1.	3.
		2.	4.
11.	❑ ❑ ❑	1.	3.
		2.	4.
12.	❑ ❑ ❑	1.	3.
		2.	4.
13.	❑ ❑ ❑	1.	3.
		2.	4.
14.	❑ ❑ ❑	1.	3.
		2.	4.
15.	❑ ❑ ❑	1.	3.
		2.	4.
16.	❑ ❑ ❑	1.	3.
		2.	4.

Figure 18-2. *Goal-Setting Form (continued).*

Working with Trends: Goal Setting

Trend—Start with Critically Important	Level of Importance 5, 4, 3	Objectives	
1. *Profit centers*	☑ ❑ ❑	1. *Establish fees and charges for all products and services.*	3. *Reach an agreement on the timing and schedule for profit center administration.*
		2. *Prorate the cost for certain types of programs.*	4. *Charge fees for specific programs.*
2.	❑ ❑ ❑	1.	3.
		2.	4.
3.	❑ ❑ ❑	1.	3.
		2.	4.
4.	❑ ❑ ❑	1.	3.
		2.	4.
5.	❑ ❑ ❑	1.	3.
		2.	4.
6.	❑ ❑ ❑	1.	3.
		2.	4.
7.	❑ ❑ ❑	1.	3.
		2.	4.
8.	❑ ❑ ❑	1.	3.
		2.	4.

Figure 18-3. *Example of How to Use the Goal-Setting Form.*

Working with Trends: Action Plan for Implementation

Name: ______ Dept./Section: ______ Follow-Up Date: ______

Trend: ______ Objective: ______

Action Steps	Completion Date	Responsibility	Progress	Date
1.				
2.				
3.				
4.				
5.				

Resources: ______

Communication Issues: ______

Figure 18-4. Action Plan for Trend Implementation.

(text continued from page 371)

The Fourth Step: Reassessing Status

Working with trends is a continuous process of change. As time progresses, the relative importance of a trend may change, as well as the progress made. In some siutations, the trend may develop even faster than anticipated. Thus, it is helpful to revisit the status and re-plan specific strategy for the department. An annual review should be appropriate. In some cases, a six-month review may be desired if significant changes are planned.

Conclusion

Globally, today's organizations are undergoing significant change as they struggle for improvement and, in some cases, survival. Success often hinges on their ability to adjust to external forces and changes. Playing a critical role in guiding organizations through the change process are the training and human resource development professionals. The research for this book identified sixteen critical trends common from one organization to another. These trends have a tremendous impact on training and development, and collectively they reflect the key issues confronting the success of the training and development profession.

Some of the trends represent welcomed opportunities for the training and development manager. Others represent problems and challenges that must be addressed quickly. Success will be realized if sufficient attention is focused on the trend and effective and productive actions are taken to adjust to the trend. Whether a trend is welcomed or represents a challenge, this book functions as a survival guide and handbook for continuous improvement.

Appendix 1

TOP 16 GLOBAL HRD TRENDS: SURVEY RESULTS

Instructions Provided to the Participants:

Each of the following issues has been identified as a trend in training and development. Please read each issue and provide your level of agreement with this issue as a trend in training and development. Also, to the right of that response, indicate the relative importance of the trend to your training and development department.

The following scales are used:

Level of Agreement with the Trend		Level of Importance of the Trend	
5	Strongly Agree	5	Critically Important
4	Agree	4	Very Important
3	Neither Agree nor Disagree	3	Important
2	Disagree	2	Somewhat Important
1	Strongly Disagree	1	Unimportant

Top Sixteen Global HRD Trends	Level of Agreement	Agreement Rank	Level of Importance	Importance Rank
1. Training is linked to the strategic direction of the organization.	3.96	10	4.48	6
2. Needs assessment and analysis are receiving more emphasis.	3.76	15	4.64	4
3. Training is shifting to a performance improvement role.	4.25	6	4.37	9
4. Corporate universities continue to gain acceptance.	3.89	13	4.01	16
5. Training delivery is changing rapidly.	4.26	5	4.39	8
6. The responsibility of training is shared among several groups.	4.14	7	4.28	11
7. Systematic evaluation processes measure the success of training.	4.57	2	4.69	3
8. Measuring the return on investment in training is growing in use.	4.02	9	4.71	2
9. Training costs are monitored more accurately and are used in a variety of ways to manage resources and demonstrate accountability.	3.92	12	4.83	1
10. Training and development functions are converting to a profit center concept.	3.80	14	4.11	14
11. Training and development budgets are increasing.	4.32	4	4.07	15
12. The learning organization concept is being adopted.	4.09	8	4.47	7
13. Training staff and line management are forming partnerships to achieve common goals.	3.95	11	4.57	5
14. The application of technology to training is developing rapidly.	4.68	1	4.32	10
15. More training is designed for global use.	3.72	16	4.14	13
16. More training is outsourced to contractors.	4.49	3	4.21	12

Survey Administration

Target audience: The planned survey audience included those individuals who have a leadership role in training and development, education and training, learning, performance improvement, and human resource development. In some situations, facilitators, designers, developers, and evaluation specialists responded.

Settings: Surveys were administered at conferences and workshops that convened to discuss current issues in training and development. The audience was captive, and the responses were anonymous. Participants understood the purpose of the survey along with the need for accurate assessment of both the existence of the trend and its importance.

Geographical dispersion: Questionnaires were administered in several different countries and, in some cases, different regions of the country. For example, in the United States, the questionnaires were administered in all major regions—East Coast, West Coast, Southeast, and Midwest. Most respondents were from large cities. As of September 1998, the following countries were represented: the United States, Canada, Belgium, Italy, England, Germany, South Africa, Venezuela, Mexico, Jamaica, Hong Kong, Malaysia, Singapore, Indonesia, Australia, and New Zealand.

Although the majority of participants were from the country where the survey was administered, attendees at the conferences and workshops came from virtually every country. No attempt was made to identify the specific individuals because the survey was anonymous.

Timing: The surveys were conducted between 1995 and 1998.

Responses: The responses received, by year, are as follows:

Year	Number of Respondents
1995	395
1996	568
1997	636
1998	150
Total	**1,750**

Planned analysis: As the data base continues to grow, analyses will be performed in a variety of ways. First, a longitudinal analysis will be conducted to see if trends change over time in terms of relative importance and the level of agreement with the trend. Second, when the sample is larger, geographical differences for the various countries will be analyzed to see if major differences emerge between settings. To improve the instrument and to add, redefine, or separate trends in the future, input and feedback will continue to be collected.

Appendix 2

SECOND 16 GLOBAL HRD TRENDS: SURVEY RESULTS

Instructions Provided to Participants:

Each of the following issues has been identified as a trend in training and development. Please read each issue and provide your level of agreement with this issue as a trend in training and development. Also, to the right of that response, indicate the relative importance of the trend to your training and development department.

The following scales are used:

Level of Agreement with the Trend		Level of Importance of the Trend	
5	Strongly Agree	5	Critically Important
4	Agree	4	Very Important
3	Neither Agree nor Disagree	3	Important
2	Disagree	2	Somewhat Important
1	Strongly Disagree	1	Unimportant

Second Sixteen Global HRD Trends	Level of Agreement	Agreement Rank	Level of Importance	Importance Rank
1. Training is a critical element in major change processes.	3.92	10	3.29	10
2. Government is more involved in the training and development process.	3.07	15	2.81	16
3. Training is being managed in a proactive way.	3.46	14	3.34	9
4. Measuring intellectual capital is an important issue.	4.85	1	3.97	1
5. Just-in-time training is growing in use.	4.01	8	3.24	11
6. The role and importance of training are increasing.	4.22	7	3.81	5
7. More training and development managers have a business or operations management background.	3.94	9	3.15	13
8. On-the-job training is more structured and formalized.	4.28	6	3.49	8
9. Transfer of learning is an important issue.	4.57	3	3.92	3
10. Training and development functions are developing alliances with other organizations.	3.62	13	3.19	12
11. Training and development is more client-focused.	3.75	12	3.70	6
12. The delivery of training is more decentralized.	4.31	5	3.63	7
13. The training and development function is becoming separated from the human resource function.	2.85	16	2.93	15
14. Training and development staff members have formal preparation in the field.	4.38	4	3.12	14
15. Knowledge management is becoming an important responsibility.	4.65	2	3.83	4
16. Key managers are taking more active roles in the training and development process.	3.88	11	3.94	2

HRD Trends Worldwide—The Second Sixteen

The following trends represent the next sixteen most important trends. The first sixteen presented in this book have importance rankings of at least 4 out of 5. The next sixteen have rankings that range in importance from 3.97 to 2.8.[1] Each trend is briefly described below. (Note: These trends are listed in the same order in which they appeared on the survey.)

Linkage with change programs

The training and development function is becoming a critical element in major change programs. From the beginning it has played an important role, usually supporting the process and providing the training to ensure that employees learn the necessary skills. In recent years its role has evolved to the point that the training and development function is the principal coordinating entity for major change programs. In some cases, change programs are initiated by the training and development leadership in response to defined needs. Still, in other situations, the training and development function is charged with the unique responsibility of measuring the success of these programs and reporting the results to a variety of target audiences, including senior management. This places training and development in a pivotal role to manage change.

Government involvement

Government is more involved in training and development, and the extent of involvement is increasing rapidly. Although the government has attempted to play a productive role in training and development in all countries the results have been mixed. However, both federal and local governments clearly see the need to have a capable, skilled work force. Some see that economic advantages even hinge on the capability of the work force. Consequently, many government initiatives have been implemented in different countries. Some have succeeded in Europe and Asia, but others have been dismal failures. Still, government agencies are attempting to build these critical skills using a variety of approaches.

Proactive approach

Gone are the days when training reacted exclusively to requests. Training is being managed proactively now. For years, the training function waited for training requests and pursued them vigorously. Today it is taking the initiative as it examines problems, issues and concerns, identifies training and non-training needs, and offers solutions. A proactive approach requires the training department to examine current problems and anticipate future events to ensure that training is contributing significantly to the organization.

Intellectual capital

With the tremendous increase in the number of knowledge employees and the importance of having a skilled, stable work force, measuring intellectual capital is becoming an important issue. As organizations attempt to measure, monitor, and manage intellectual capital, the training and development function is usually saddled with this important responsibility. For some firms, the intellectual capital is its greatest asset, particularly in high-tech, computer, and information industries. To survive and maintain a competitive advantage, these firms must discover ways to maintain and enhance the intellectual capital base. The training function, along with key staff and operating specialists, is developing ways to measure and monitor the process, as well as measuring the success of initiatives aimed at improving intellectual capital.

Just-in-time training

Growing in use in all types of organizations, just-in-time training is helping training and development departments meet important challenges in training delivery. The concept of just-in-time processes has existed for many years, and now training clients demand it. This requires that the training and development staff anticipates needs and delivers training precisely when it is needed to the appropriate group. This trend has a tremendous impact on delivery mechanisms, technology use, programs, design and development, and external contractor usage.

Importance of training

The role and importance of training are increasing. More executives are realizing the critical need for training and performance improvement and are using these processes appropriately. The training and development function is expanding its role and providing key operating executives with the level of service desired. Consequently, more success stories are available, underscoring the critical role of training in meeting strategic objectives, meeting operational challenges, and inspiring breakthrough innovation.

Training and development managers as business managers

More training and development managers have a business or operations management background. They are business managers first and training specialists second. They understand the operational and financial segments of the business. These new leaders understand how to develop a budget, maintain control of the function, motivate a team, and ensure that training is producing the appropriate value. They manage the function as a business enterprise, and some operate it as a profit center. Today's training manager will likely have significant experience in areas outside training and development and will leverage expertise and knowledge to gain the necessary support from key operating managers.

Structured OJT

Recognizing that most of an employee's training and development will occur at the work setting, training and development functions are exploring ways to ensure that on-the-job training (OJT) is more structured and formalized. Instead of allowing on-the-job training to unfold informally, these firms recognize that having an organized approach with specific objectives, appropriate guidelines, and thorough preparation will ensure that the largest component of training and development—on-the-job training—is effective and efficient.

Transfer of learning

Because a high percentage of the skills and knowledge acquired in learning activities is not utilized on the job, transfer of learning is an important issue with the training and development function. Innovative organizations are adapting a variety of models, approaches, and frameworks to ensure that training and development is utilized as planned and anticipated. Transfer of learning often involves specific actions taken prior to, during, and after a formal learning activity. It includes actions from a variety of groups including participants, managers of participants, the training and development staff, and the senior management group.

Alliances

Training and development managers are developing alliances with other organizations to accomplish important objectives, deliver new products and services, and provide the necessary expertise. Often developed with complementary organizations, these alliances may involve non-competing firms, universities, colleges, industries, and trade associations. Sometimes an alliance allows a training and development function to overcome a weakness or provide a product or service that could not be provided otherwise.

Client focus

Recognizing the importance of client input and client relationships, the training and development function has focused more attention on the needs and desires of the client. In the traditional approach, products and services were developed, and the client had to choose which product or service to use. Today the process begins with the client in a comprehensive assessment of performance issues and needs and ends when the results are communicated to the client group. The client is involved in all stages of the process, and the concern for the client input and satisfaction is critical.

Decentralized delivery

The delivery of training and development is becoming more decentralized. To provide appropriate customer service, the learning process must be close to the customer with much of the delivery at or near the participant's location. While the overall design and development, including technology selection, are usually centralized, the remainder is decentralized, with local input, coordination, facilitation, follow-up, and evaluation.

Training removed from human resources

The training and development function is being separated from the human resources function. Traditionally, the training function has been one of the key sub-functions of the human resource department. Today more firms are separating training and development from human resources and having it report to an operating executive or, in some cases, the chief executive officer. This shift allows the training and development function to receive more input and support from the top executives while simultaneously initiating important change free of the limiting structure of a traditional human resource function.

Formal preparation

More training and development staff members have formal preparation for their assignments. A variety of programs is available to develop critical skills needed in the learning, training and development, human resource development, and performance improvement fields. Degree programs, certificate programs, seminars, short courses, and self-study programs are available to build these important skills. In some countries, master's degree and Ph.D. programs are available with majors in human resource development, education and training, learning, and instructional design. Training and development has become a professional discipline with theories and core skill requirements.

Knowledge management

For many training and development organizations, knowledge management is becoming an important responsibility. This trend parallels the issue of measuring intellectual capital. Because of the increased number of knowledge employees, organizations are concerned about techniques and methods to manage knowledge. The focus of this responsibility is on acquiring, maintaining, and monitoring knowledge. In some cases, an individual will have the responsibility for knowledge management with a title of chief knowledge officer.

Key manager involvement

Recognizing that they have a tremendous influence on the outcome and success of training, key managers are becoming more involved in the formal learning process. In some cases, these managers take a substantial role in the initiation, coordination, development, delivery, and evaluation of training and development. In effect, this pushes much of the responsibility for training to the line organization where, some will argue, that it rightfully belongs. These key managers are often in the line organization where they have the responsibility to develop and distribute products and services. They understand this new or increased responsibility for learning and take an active role, sometimes dedicating a certain number of part-time and full-time days to the process.

Summary

These additional sixteen trends show another major part of the evolving and changing role of the training and development function. Consequently, they represent important challenges for the training and development field. The staff must be aware of the trends and take the necessary steps to make the most of the changing environment.

INDEX

O

P